Modern Islamic Political Thought

Modern Middle East Series
Sponsored by the Center for Middle Eastern Studies
The University of Texas at Austin

Modern Islamic Political Thought

Hamid Enayat

UNIVERSITY OF TEXAS PRESS, AUSTIN

International Standard Book Number 0-292-75069-2 (cloth); 0-292-75070-6 (paper)
Library of Congress Catalog Card Number 81-70314

Printed in Hong Kong

First Edition, 1982

To Anna, Hādī and Āmeneh

Contents

Preface

This book describes and interprets the major political ideas among Muslims in the twentieth century, particularly those expressed by the Egyptians and Iranians – but also a few writers and thinkers in Pakistan, India, Lebanon, Syria and Iraq. It is a book concerned mainly with ideas: history and sociology have been called to aid only on those occasions when they help to illuminate the background of thoughts. But what needs more emphasis is that it is a book concerned not so much with ideas set forth by Muslims, as with those which are Islamic – that is to say, are articulated in the recognised terms and categories of Islamic jurisprudence, theology and related disciplines, however much they may sound 'unorthodox' or unconventional. This naturally leaves out a great many Muslim intellectuals who may deserve serious study in other perspectives, but it arises from the conviction that in any effort to understand, let alone criticise, Muslim contributions to the political debates of our time, the procedure by which a thinker has arrived at an idea should be given as much weight as the idea itself. It is not enough to extol a writer for his brave new ideas without first ascertaining the extent to which his credal, epistemological and methodological premises have ensured the continuity of Islamic thought. Otherwise, one is apt to allow fascination with novelty to keep oneself from differentiating what is germane from what is extraneous to Islamic culture. The question of any ulterior or hidden motive that these authors may have harboured has been kept out of the analysis, not only because a thorough examination of them threatens to turn a history of ideas into *histoire événementielle*, but also because ideas seem to have a life of their own: people, especially those of the generations subsequent to the authors', often tend to perceive ideas with little or no regard for the authors' insidious designs, unless they are endowed with a capacity for mordant cynicism.

The book starts with an introduction outlining the way in which the traditional heritage has impinged on the development of modern thoughts, or can make them cogent and appealing to religious-minded audiences. This is followed by a study of the political differences between the two main schools or sects in Islam – Shīʿīsm and Sunnīsm, and especially on the two-fold process of conflict and concord between them. The main intention is to show that the relationship between the two has been slowly changing in recent times, at least in the realm of political doctrines, from confrontation to cross-sectarian fertilisation. This approach later re-emerges at several other points of the book, with more examples of the implicit or explicit convergence between the two. The remaining chapters are devoted to two basic themes and their ramifications: the concept of the Islamic State from the time it was revived after the abolition of the Caliphate in Turkey in the 'twenties till the late 'seventies, and the Muslim response to the challenge of the alien, modern ideologies of nationalism, democracy and socialism.

Contemporary Islamic political thought cannot be properly appreciated without a knowledge of that set of doctrinal reformulations and reinterpretations which has now come to be known as Islamic modernism. Since a fair number of books have been published in various European languages on this once-promising movement, discussion of it in the present study has been kept to the minimum – with the exception of Shīʿī modernism, which, having been neglected until recently, is treated in some detail in the concluding chapter. Instead, there has been some concentration on the lesser known but equally or potentially important authors.

The amount of political writing and pamphleteering within strictly Islamic framework, and even in the few countries mentioned above, is still staggering, and a student looking for broad trends and patterns has no option but to take some individual writers as representatives of whole schools of thought. This inevitably opens the arena for critics who might point to other writers and publications presenting different standpoints in order to disprove or question some of the conclusions reached in this book. But such criticisms, however unfair they might be, will be welcome in so far as they bring to light still more facets of the mental efforts of Muslims in their strivings for freedom and progress.

Hamid Enayat

Acknowledgements

I am indebted to a number of my colleagues and friends who read the draft of this book and made useful comments for its improvement. Albert Hourani and John Gurney read the whole of the draft, and spent considerable time discussing its content with me. I particularly benefited from stimulating conversations with Professor Madelung, and my compatriot, Husayn Mudarresī Ṭabāṭabā'ī, who commented on the Introduction, and the chapters on Shī'ism. Michael Cook and Roger Owen made helpful criticisms respectively on Sunnī–Shī'ī polemics and the chapter on 'Nationalism, Democracy and Socialism'. So did Nikki Keddie on the section dealing with Constitutionalism in Chapter 5. However, responsibility for any controversial opinions or inaccuracies in the text is entirely mine. Mrs Angela Turnbull, of Macmillan Press editorial staff, gave me valuable help in making the transliterations and the dates consistent.

I must thank the Tahereh Research Centre for Contemporary Iranian History for their support from October 1979 to March 1980, when I was working on this book. I am also grateful to the staffs of the Libraries of the Middle East Centre of St Antony's College, Oxford, the Oriental Room of the Bodleian Library, and the School of Oriental and African Studies, University of London, for their patient and unfailing services.

* * *

The original idea of this book would never have been conceived were it not for my friendship with the late Murtaḍā Muṭahharī, Professor of Islamic Philosophy at Tehran University, a most original and creative thinker, a dedicated Muslim, and a humanist.

On the System of Transcription, Dates, etc.

For the sake of consistency, Arabic and Persian words have been transliterated both according to the same system, except that the vowel of the Arabic definite article has been given the value 'u' in Persian names and words (hence Faḍlullāh instead of Faḍl Allāh), and the consonantal *vāv* has been rendered as 'v' for Persian and 'w' for Arabic words. The main consideration throughout has been to convey exact phonetic structure. Some inconsistencies have, however, inevitably occurred either because of the necessity of observing the common usage, or in quotations, or owing to the different systems of transliterating Turkish words.

Most years before the sixteenth century have been given according to both the lunar Islamic calendar and the Christian calendar, separated by a stroke. The years after that have been given in the text only according to the Christian calendar.

Translations of the Qur'ānic verses are from J. M. Rodwell, *The Koran* (London, 1861), unless they are paraphrased.

H.E.

Introduction: the relevance of the past

Political thought has been the most active area of Muslim intellectual life over the last two centuries. This can be explained primarily by the ongoing struggle of various Muslim peoples in this period for their domestic freedoms and independence from Western powers – a struggle which has not yet reached its avowed goals, and, therefore, ensures the continual politicisation of the Muslim mind in the future. A further stimulant may be found in the conjunction of substantial economic, strategic and political interests on the part of the outside world in the heartland of the 'abode of Islam', resulting in the Western obsession with the 'energy-crisis' syndrome. Neither of these explanations can, however, be enough to understand the primacy of politics in modern Islam without considering a more fundamental issue: the inherent link between Islam as a comprehensive scheme for ordering human life, and politics as an indispensable instrument to secure universal compliance with that scheme. The authoritarian connotation of this link is a point most frequently seized upon by the Western critics of Islam. But – as we shall try to show in this book – Muslims do not have a unified and monolithic perception of their faith, any more than the followers of other great religions. However much the orthodox dislike it, different groups of Muslims interpret the Qur'ānic injunctions and the Prophetic sayings differently – each according to its historical background, and the realities encircling it – and not always in terms conducive to a dictatorial conduct of individual and social affairs.

Another misconception about the fusion of religion and politics in Islamic culture is to think that in historical reality too all political attitudes and institutions among Muslims have had religious sanctions, or have conformed to religious norms. Often the reverse was true: the majority of Muslims, for the greater part of their history, lived under regimes which had only the most tenuous link with those norms, and observed the *Sharī'ah* only to the extent that it legitimised their power in the eyes of the faithful.

With these points in mind, there can be little doubt that the Muslim consciousness has a certain leaning towards politics which stems directly from the spirit of Islamic precepts. But it is a leaning which is often hidden behind an air of submissiveness, or political apathy, or both. If the essence of politics is the art of living and working with others, then four of the five 'pillars' of Islam (prayer, fasting, alms-giving, pilgrimage, the excluded fifth being testimony to the unity of God and messengership of Muḥammad) are perfectly suited to promoting *esprit de corps* and group solidarity among its followers (*jihād* or holy war, which is considered by some Muslims to be the sixth, has even greater potential for producing the same effect). If, according to another viewpoint, the hallmark of politics is struggle for power, there can hardly be a more political world-vision: always conceiving of human nature in terms of both its physical and spiritual needs, Islam is never content with the mere exposition of its ideals, but constantly seeks the means to implement them – and power is an essential means towards this end. The Qur'ān challenges believers to follow the example of the Prophet Muḥammad, whom it describes as the 'noble paradigm' (*uswah ḥasanah*, 33:21). Since Muḥammad's principal achievement was to lay the foundations of a state based on Islamic teachings, the Muslims have a duty to follow his example in this respect as well.

There is a simpler reason for the concern with politics as the art of government: the accomplishment of a number of the 'collective duties' of Muslims of which the most important are 'enjoining the good and forbidding the evil' (*al-amr bi'l-ma'rūf wa'n-nahy 'an al-munkar*) and the defence of the Muslim territory possible only in a state which is, if not totally committed to Islam, then at least sympathetic to its goals. By this token, a Muslim who lives under a regime devoted, or even favourable, to Islam should actively work for its survival; conversely, one who lives under a regime hostile to Islam should struggle for its overthrow whenever the opportunity presents itself. Finally, if the dispute as to *who should rule?* and *why should we obey the rulers?* is the hub of politics, no conscious Muslim can study his history even in the most casual fashion without feeling the urge to ask these questions, and discuss them with his co-religionists. The impulse to do so would be much more powerful when Muslims are subjugated, as large numbers of them have been during the last four centuries, by alien rulers, or those associated with them.

These are all merely the theoretical or potential elements of the politicisation of the Muslim mind – the doctrinal antecedents which should logically predispose a Muslim to be a political creature of the most assertive type. But the actualisation of these elements plainly depends on a favourable environment, of which the most essential feature is the availability of the freedoms of speech, assembly and action. That is why, despite what we have said so far, political thought as an independent and distinct branch of intellectual activity is a fairly recent addition to Islamic culture. Most Muslims have lived, and still live, under regimes which deny them those essential freedoms. Sociologists would dismiss this reasoning as secondary, arguing that the absence of these freedoms is less important than the absence of the social and political conditions which should precede or accompany the emergence of any democratic system in its broadest sense – such as the development of commerce and industry, and the rise of an autonomous bourgeoisie. This objection raises a host of issues which are not always related to the doctrinal foundations of Islam. Since we are concerned in the present study with ideas, we have to leave these issues aside, although some will be discussed in our chapter on 'Nationalism, Democracy and Socialism'.[1]

Apart from political and social factors, there has also been a methodological reason for the absence of independent political thought in Islamic history. Traditionally, Muslims rarely studied politics in isolation from related disciplines. Problems such as the nature of the state, the varieties of government, the qualifications of rulers, the limitations on their power and the rights of the ruled were discussed as part of the comprehensive treatises on jurisprudence and theology – all securely within the unassailable walls of the *Sharī'ah*. It was only under the trauma of European military, political, economic and cultural encroachments since the end of the eighteenth century that Muslim élites started to write separate works on specifically political topics. One remarkable feature of such works from the viewpoint of the cultural interaction between Islam and the West in modern history is the language in which they were written. So long as Westernisation had not alienated large segments of the new educated groups from their traditional heritage, most reformers expressed their ideas in the language of Islamic sciences – using stereotyped legal phrases, citing Qur'ānic verses and Prophetic sayings, with only occasional quotations from foreign sources. But as time went on, with Westernised intellectuals supplanting traditional leaders at most levels of the educational system, and the growing tendency of the literate classes to hold all that was old responsible for Muslim backwardness, the cultural unity of the élites was shattered. While the majority of the literate and the learned remained loyal to Islamic ideals and values, a small but increasingly influential group had come to praise Western culture and civilisation as being superior to everything else humanity had created, and that in a phraseology largely unknown to most Muslims – whether literate or illiterate. The breakdown of the cultural integration of traditional society was thus reflected in a linguistic rift, which has been one of the chief obstacles to a coherent, sustained and fruitful debate among Muslims of all classes and ages over their social and political problems. One of the remarkable changes in the Muslim mentality since the Second World War has been a growing trend in the opposite direction – namely an awareness that no political idea, however valid and vital for the freedom and prosperity of Muslims, can mobilise them in a successful movement to cure their ills, unless it is shown to conform in both form and substance to the dictates of their religious consciousness.

This book deals with the ideas of those Muslim writers who have been mindful of the necessity of this conformity, and in whose formation the legacy of Islamic culture, particularly the tradition of political thinking as a subsidiary element of the *Sharī'ah*, has played the largest part. A brief survey of the basic strands of that tradition is therefore essential for the understanding of the main issues in modern Islamic political thought.

* * *

The fact that political thought among Muslims in the past was always subsumed under some other discipline in the spectrum of classical Islamic sciences did not by itself restrict its scope, or impoverish its content. Indeed, a student of political ideas will find Muslim history in its first six or seven centuries a fascinating mosaic of competing schools, each with a different perception of the foundations of state authority and the limits of individual obedience to the rulers. Immediately after the Prophet's death dispute broke out at the Saqīfah assembly over the choice of his successor. It was, on the face of it, a dispute over personalities, but underlying it were the same fundamental themes that have preoccupied lively political minds the world over, and at all times. From wrangling over personalities, it was a short step to doctrinal and theoretical altercations. These may now be summarised, but only in so far as they can clarify our later discussions; what will be of interest to us is not so much the original or the real form of such altercations, but the way in which they are interpreted by Muslim writers today, and this is often a function of not only their sectarian and ideological bias but the political needs of their societies as well.

One group of Muslims, which proved to be a minority, believed that the Prophet had in fact designated his successor, and that was his son-in-law and cousin, 'Alī. According to them, the designation had taken place during the Prophet's journey from his last pilgrimage to Mecca, on the eighteenth day of the month of *Dhu'l-ḥijjah*, in the eleventh year of his Hijrah (632), at a place called the Ghadīr (pool) of Khumm, where he made a fateful proclamation which has been reported in different versions, the most popular being: 'He for whom I was the master, should hence have 'Alī as his master.' This group came to be known as the *Shī'ah* (literally, followers) of 'Alī. Another party close to them held that the succession should go to the Prophet's uncle, 'Abbās, on the grounds that if being a relative of the Prophet was to count as the decisive qualification, 'Abbās, being senior to 'Alī, had a greater right by virtue of the Qur'ānic verse which requires that among 'those who are akin' some must be prior to others (8:75). The Shī'ī case, however, went far beyond the personal qualities of 'Alī. It asserted that it was inconceivable given God's justice and benevolence (*luṭf*) towards human beings that he should have left the issue of the leadership (*imāmah, Imāmate*) undecided. The same rational considerations which necessitate the sending of His emissaries and prophets also require that in their absence faultless leaders should be appointed for the custodianship (*wilāyah*) of their followers. Furthermore, the logical corollary to the acceptance of the Prophet Muḥammad's teachings was the commitment to their implementation. Only a sound and thorough knowledge (*'ilm*) of the true meaning of the Qur'ān and the Prophetic Tradition could help the young Muslim community in this direction. That knowledge was available to those who were near and dear to the Prophet – especially 'Alī, and, through him, to his eleven male descendants: this at least was the position of the Shī'īsm of the Twelver school (*ithnā 'asharī*), whose political views will be discussed in this book.

The Shī'īs also argued – mainly in response to the criticisms of those who defended the principle of the electiveness of the successors to the Prophet – that the problem of the leadership of the community was too vital to be left to the deliberations of ordinary individuals who might choose the wrong person for the position, thereby countering the purpose of the divine revelation. Only God is aware of the presence of the qualities of knowledge and infallibility and impeccability (*'iṣmah*) in individuals, and can therefore secure the triumph of his revelations by making these individuals known through his emissaries. It is here that the issue of personalities enters into the debate, because the Shī'īs maintain that only those individuals who were closely associated with, or related to, the Prophet could have possessed such qualities, and these were none other than 'Alī and his male descendants.[2] This part of the Shī'ī argument complemented another thesis which is perhaps the most important element in Shī'ī political theory – namely the absolute and irrevocable necessity of justice as a condition of rulership, in accordance with the Qur'ānic injunction: '"My covenant,", said God, "embraceth not the evil-doers" [*aẓ-ẓālimīn*]' (2:124). A sequel to the Shī'ī case for the Imāmate is the justification of the place of the 'Ulamā' or *mujtahids* in the Muslim community after the disappearance of the Imāms. The word '*Ulamā*' is the plural of '*ālim*, meaning a scholar, or more specifically, religious scholar; *mujtahid* literally means a person who exerts his mental faculties, but is applied to an '*ālim* qualified to derive legal norms from the sources of the law. If the Imāms are charged with the duty of guiding the Muslims after the end of the 'cycle of revelation', that is, after the death of the last of God's emissaries, the 'Ulamā' and *mujtahids* are charged with the duty of guiding the Muslims after the end of the 'cycle of Imāmate', that is, after the disappearance of the Imām – the difference being, of course, that the 'Ulamā' do not partake of the quality of '*iṣmah*, or other extraordinary attributes of the Imāms.

Another group, which formed the majority of Muslims, took the view that the Prophet had deliberately left the question of his succession open, leaving it to the community to decide who would be the most competent person to assume its leadership. These Muslims came to be known as the Sunnīs, or the followers of *Sunnah* (tradition), an appellation which may be taken to symbolise their adherence to principles rather than personalities. Certainly they must have been helped in their conviction by the fact that the Prophet had left no son. Many of them do not deny the authenticity of the Ghadīr story, but contest the construction that the Shī'īs put on it, particularly their understanding of the term *master* (*mawlā*) in the Prophet's proclamation. The Sunnīs instead stand for the right of the Muslim community to choose the Prophet's successor in political leadership rather than the pre-emptive title of any particular individual to it. Typical of this stand is the stress laid on a saying attributed to the Prophet, to the effect that his followers are more knowledgeable or better informed (*a'lam*) in their worldly affairs than him – presumably after his death.

Whatever the true intentions of the Prophet, it was the Sunnī view that prevailed at the Saqīfah assembly. Its proceedings, as reported by Ṭabarī (d. 311/923) and other early Muslim historians, raise some doubts about the spontaneity of its decision. But the fact of the matter is that an animated, and at times stormy, debate *did* take place, and that the assembly finally *did* elect a successor. Abū Bakr, the man chosen and given the title of '*Khalīfah* (Caliph, successor) of God's messenger' was also a distinguished member of the community and a close companion of the Prophet. He was older than other contenders for the Caliphate, had been chosen by the Prophet to accompany him on his migration from Mecca to Medina, an event of such importance as to deserve a mention in the Qur'ān (9:40), gave the Prophet his daughter 'Ā'ishah in marriage and acted as his chief adviser. All this means that in justifying the Saqīfah affair, and the continuation of the basic feature of its procedure, that is, the consensus (*ijmā*') of the élite, or the 'people who loose and bind' (*ahl al-ḥall wa'l-'aqd*) in the election of Abū Bakr, as well as his three immediate successors ('Umar, 'Uthmān and 'Alī, who, together with Abū Bakr, are known as the Rightly-Guided Caliphs (*Khulafā' rashidūn*), the Sunnīs also have to introduce a good deal of personalised politics into the controversy. Besides *ijmā'*, the election of the Caliphs consisted also of *bay'ah*, literally clasping of hands, but meaning the taking of the oath of allegiance to the Caliph by his electors, and '*ahd*, or the covenant whereby the Caliph undertook, in the face of the Muslim community, to rule in accordance with the provisions of the *Sharī'ah*, and the community promised to obey him. So whereas the key political terms for the Shī'īs were *imāmah, wilāyah* and *'iṣmah*, those for the Sunnīs were *Khilāfah, ijmā'* and *bay'ah*. Overlappings were, of course, inevitable: the Sunnīs used the title Imām for the Caliph, especially whenever they referred to his spiritual functions; and the Shī'īs accepted the validity of *ijmā'*, provided that it included the opinion of 'the infallible one' (*ma'ṣūm*).[3]

The third major political trend in early Islam was a rejection of both the Sunnī and Shī'ī positions, and its followers came to be appropriately known as the *Khawārij* (plural of *Khārijī*, meaning an outsider or seceder). It came into existence twenty-five years after the death of the Prophet as a result of the first great schism in Islamic history, when a group of Muslims revolted against the Caliph 'Alī because he had agreed to refer his dispute with the rebel Mu'āwiyah to arbitration. Apparently seeing the dispute as a clear-cut conflict between right and wrong, they emphatically argued that in such matters there could be no arbitration or judgement (*ḥukm*) except by God. This opinion, for which the Khawārij could find literal warrant in the Qur'ān, typified their strict adherence to the letter of the Book. Later on, upon gaining control over some Muslim territories, they modified their idealism – as most revolutionary groups do once they are in power. Allied to their uncompromising attachment to the Qur'ān was a democratic temper insisting on the right of all Muslims, irrespective of their tribal, racial and class distinctions, to elect or depose, or to be elected as, rulers. This set them against the Sunnīs, who for the most part confined the Caliphate to the Meccan aristocracy (Quraysh), and the Shī'īs, who restricted it to one branch of it, the House of the Prophet (Banū Hāshim). When all this is added to the Khārijī exaltation of action as a criterion of faith, and their use of violence against their opponents, the full import of their radicalism, and the conscious or unconscious affinity that some fundamentalist groups in modern history have had with them, becomes apparent. The Muslim Brothers in Egypt have sometimes been accused of being Khawārij. They have always denied the charge, and even spoken of the 'errors' of the Khawārij, but have nevertheless praised their 'rectitude', and their 'struggle in the path of God'.[4] So although the Khawārij never transcended their status as an extremist minority detested by both the Sunnīs and Shī'īs, and have today vanished except in isolated groups in Algeria, Tunisia, Oman and East Africa, they played an important, albeit indirect, part in the development of Islamic political thought by acting for a while as the incorruptible conscience of the Muslims, forcing them to keep in sight the absolute and the ideal, as opposed to the relative and the actual, in their efforts to construct an Islamic society.

These were the three principal political trends in the first four decades of Islamic history, although they do not by any means exhaust all the divisions and the variations within them – for instance, those in terms of class differences, or the rivalries between the *Muhājirūn* (the Meccans who *migrated* with the Prophet to Medina) and the *Anṣār* (his *helpers* or allies of Medina). But such alignments have little or no bearing on what we are going to study in this book. The same largely holds true for the period from the end of the era of Rightly-Guided Caliphs up to the fourth/tenth century. There are, however, one or two features of the intellectual history of the period which are relevant to our study because it was in this period that the first stirrings of philosophical thought enlivened the Muslim mind, confronting it with questions about the limits of Man's freedom within the Islamic scheme of things – questions which are very much at the heart of the modern Islamic critique of traditionalism. They were often raised by inquisitive souls who were perhaps unaware of the political implications of what they asked, or if they were, philosophy for them was a convenient disguise to conceal their conventional ideas so as to avoid provoking both the wrath of the rulers and the terrifying reaction of the bigoted public.

Foremost among the thinkers who aroused the Muslim appetite for speculative investigation were the Mu'tazilah, who flourished in the second/eighth century, and are often associated with the first attempts at reconciling reason and revelation in Islam. Now few of the Muslim modernists in our time would admit that they have been inspired by the pioneering work of the Mu'tazilah, especially in giving a rationalist interpretation of Islam; on the contrary, many of them deprecate the Mu'tazilah either for their intellectual excesses, or their neglect of 'non-conceptual' dimensions of the religious experience – meaning intuition and mysticism.[5] But the similarities between some of the substantive positions of the two groups are so striking that one can hardly escape the conclusion that many of the modernists must have been secretly delighted to find such early precedents for their innovative ideas. Like the Mu'tazilah, the majority of the modernists emphasise the high place of reason in their scale of values, and try to show the perfect compatibility of 'true Islam' with the findings of a mind free from the scourge of ignorance, prejudice and superstition. Like the Mu'tazilah, the modernists think that Islam upholds the principle of free will (*ikhtīyār*), as opposed to that of predestinarianism (*jabr*), since it has been obvious to both groups that Muslims will never desist from meekly enduring injustice unless they become first convinced of their capability to determine their destiny. A favourite theme in the rare philosophical writings of the modernists is commenting on the Qur'ānic verse: 'Verily God will not change (the condition of) a folk, till they change what is in themselves' (13 : 11). Nowadays, belief in free will is not obviously regarded as a heresy, but in the second/eighth century, apart from the Khawārij and the Shī'īs, the only other major group of Muslims who were prosecuted for their unorthodox ideas were the advocates of *ikhtīyār*, a notion which soon acquired the same significance in Islamic history as the concept of liberty in Western political thought.

Attitudes towards the West provide another parallel: the Mu'tazilah saw no harm in adopting rationalism and logic to sharpen the tools of dialectic theology in order to defend Islam against Christianity, Manichaeism and other alien creeds; the modernists overtly or covertly apply categories of thought derived from Western philosophy, political theory and science to enrich their own reformistic or revolutionary propositions – apart from urging Muslims to emulate the West in its technological and scientific achievements while condemning its moral and spiritual depravity. Another similarity, which may be accidental, but nevertheless deserves attention, is the prominence afforded by both groups to the doctrine of *tawḥīd*, the unity of God. The Mu'tazilah did this to vindicate the oneness of God against not only its non-Muslim detractors, but also against those Muslims who, through a literal interpretation of the Qur'ān, threatened to erect God's attributes into independent hypostases, which made nonsense of His unity. The modernists reiterate the meaning of *tawḥīd* to denounce devotion to anything other than God, and this includes not only the apotheosis of 'perfect man' as suggested by Ṣūfī teachings, but also servile obedience to the tyrants and *ṭāghūts* ('satans', or illegitimate rulers): the result in both cases, however, is to turn the meaning of *tawḥīd* from a mere theological formula into a comprehensive system of faith and political action.

Another instance of the catalytic role of intellectualism in the politics of early Islam can be noticed in the movement of *Al-Ikhwān aṣ-Ṣafā'* (the Brethren of Purity') who probably lived in the third or fourth/ninth or tenth centuries. Their *Rasā'il* (Epistles) constitute the first known Islamic encyclopedia, an impressive compendium of the sciences of their time. The Ikhwān appear to have espoused the Ismā'īlī school of Shī'īsm, which was at that time more radical than the Twelver school in challenging the orthodox regimes, and their agitations convulsed the lands of the 'Abbāsīd Caliphate until the Mongol invasion in the seventh/thirteenth century. It may be true, as has been suggested by some scholars, that the Ikhwān's central teaching had no direct relevance to politics, being essentially concerned with matters such as the transmigration of souls or the doctrine of emanation. But the circumstances in which the *Rasā'il* were composed, as well as some of their contents, tell a different story. The fact that their authors undertook such a momentous enterprise in secrecy and anonymity, evidently to protect themselves against both obscurantist rulers and ignorant masses, should in itself be of great political significance. More to the point, there are extensive passages in the *Rasā'il* which indicate that their authors took a serious interest in the social conditions of the Muslims, and endeavoured to identify some of the causes of their moral bankruptcy and enslavement by despotic systems of government. They did this chiefly through the expedient of allegory which has always been the favourite literary style of élitist–esoteric movements in Islam, whether revolutionary or conservative. Their political theses do not seem to be different, in essence, from those of Shī'īsm, especially in their emphasis on the functions of the Imāms, and their attacks on "unjust temporal rulers". One theme which unfailingly runs through their entire work is the necessity of knowledge and consciousness as the pre-condition of worldly and other-worldly salvation. But instead of leaving this enlightened teaching to wither into a sterile lesson in public morality, the Ikhwān made their tracts a strong proof of their dedication to the dissemination of knowledge among the people – knowledge not only in the customary sense in such texts, that is, understanding religion, but the combination of the 'sciences and wisdoms' in their time. What is more, they valued only that kind of knowledge which could be conducive to action, which they conceived as an effort for both the spiritual and material amelioration of the individual and society. Combined with their belief in free will, and the inevitability of change and movement in all natural and social phenomena, the *Rasā'il* contained the outlines of an indictment of Muslim beliefs and practices in the third and fourth centuries, plus a thinly veiled call for a watertight programme of doctrinal re-education and revolutionary struggle.[6] All this makes the Ikhwān irresistibly appealing to all those Muslim intellectuals today who find their co-religionists in the same state of moral drift and social stagnation as that prevailing in the third or fourth century. This statement is meant not to overstate the importance of the *Rasā'il* as such, but rather to underline the relevance of its genre, and of literary symbolism in general as a vehicle of political expression. Modern Arab, Persian and Turkish literary works, as those of medieval times, contain innumerable applications of the same style, on a scale which is rarely matched by the legacy of those cultures in which freedom of expression has enjoyed a longer and more secure tradition.

However successful the Sunnī rulers were in suppressing the movements of Shī'ism, the Khawārij, the Mu'tazilah and Al-Ikhwān aṣ-Ṣafā', they could not for long ensure the immobility of the political institutions which constituted the targets of such oppositions. Gradual but far-reaching changes in political reality worked against their conservatism. The linchpin of all political institutions, the Caliphate, soon fell victim to the process of the disintegration of the 'Abbāsid state. The rise of the rival Caliphates in Cordova (Spain) and Cairo, and of autonomous Persian and Turkish dynasties, together with the causes intrinsic to all empires held together by a mixture of naked force and unifying myths, deprived the Caliphate in Baghdad of real power, and turned it into a hollow shell of pontifical honours, performing the ceremonial act of endorsing the transfer of powers into the hands of less dignified figures. The formulation of the theory of the Caliphate dates back to this period – a further proof of the rule that it is the decline of an institution that prompts deliberation on its structure. So far as the Sunnī thinking on the Caliphate enjoyed any continuity and sequence, one can detect in it a pronounced sense of realism, an eagerness to adjust theory to practice. Three names stand out in the history of Sunnī realism: Abu'l-Ḥasan al-Māwardī (d. 450/1058), Abū Ḥāmid Muḥammad Ghazālī (d. 505/1111), and Badr ad-Dīn Ibn Jamā'ah (d. 732/1332).

Māwardī defined and justified the necessity of the Caliphate at a time when the ascendancy of the Sunnī Ghaznavīds had put an end to the humiliations suffered by its occupants under the pro-Shī'ī Buyids, and had created a favourable atmosphere for affirming its authority. But in fact nothing had changed: it was the Ghaznavīd and later the Saljūq dynasties which wielded the real power. Ostensibly, Māwardī defended the supremacy and indivisibility of the Caliphate; but since in elaborating the qualifications, methods of investiture and duties of the Caliphs, he relied not only on the precepts of the *Sharī'ah*, but also on historical precedents as crystallised in the *ijmā'* (consensus) of the community, his work amounted to an implicit admission that political authority can be as valid as religious norms. More significantly, by envisaging the seizure of executive power by local rulers as one of the conditions under which the Caliphate is forfeited – something that his predecessors had not dared to recognise in, for instance, the Buyid domination over the Caliphs – Māwardī opened the way to the later legalisation of the transfer of power to persons other than Caliphs.[7]

The next step in this direction was taken by Ghazālī, in whose time conditions had deteriorated even further: the Caliphate 'was no longer regarded as conferring authority, but merely as legitimating rights acquired by force'. Betraying a concern for expediency uncharacteristic of the self-examining intellectual that he was, Ghazālī declared that: 'We consider that the function of the caliphate is contractually assumed by that person of the 'Abbāsid house who is charged with it, and that the function of government in the various lands is carried out by means of sultans, who owe allegiance to the caliphate. Government in these days is a consequence solely of military power, and whosoever he may be to whom the possessor of military power gives his allegiance, that person is the caliph.'[8] With the overthrow of the 'Abbāsīd Caliphate by the Mongols in 1258, even casuistical pretensions were set aside. Although a nominal Caliphate was after a while established in Cairo to confer legitimacy on the Mamlūk dynasty, this was not allowed in Sunnī jurisprudence to conceal the truth about the political system. The recognition of this last phase in the evolution of the classical Caliphate was the main achievement of Ibn Jamā'ah, who declared military power pure and simple as constituting the essence of rulership.[9]

So much readiness to revise political thought in the light of changing circumstances may be explained by the fact that all the three theoreticians mentioned here were high functionaries at one time or another in the administration of the 'Abbāsīds, Saljūqs and Mamlūks. But it would be a mistake in any such analysis to ignore the special nature of the Sunnī Caliphate which, in contrast to the Shī'ī Imāmate, is relieved of all metaphysical sanctions. This has made it more liable to realistic redefinitions at its turning-points in history. Undoubtedly, generalisations about Sunnī realism can be as inaccurate as those concerning Shī'ī idealism: both sects have in varying degrees permitted their followers in different periods to accommodate with anomalies in the political system, whenever faced with unscrupulous rulers. In the historical practice of both, therefore, open rebellion against injustice has been an exception rather than a norm. Dominique Sourdel has tried to show how, contrary to Corbin's portrayal of Shī'īsm as a purely religious movement insulated almost completely against all external vicissitudes, the character of this sect has in fact undergone changes which 'can only be explained in terms of the social and political circumstances of the moment'. He illustrates his thesis by examining the content of a treatise by Shaykh Mufīd, the mentor of a long line of Shī'ī jurisconsults, minimising the differences between the Shī'īs and other Muslims on various theological and political points in response to the relaxed political atmosphere largely made possible by the tolerant attitude of the Buyids.[10] Likewise, the widely held notion among both non-Shīʿī Muslims and Western scholars that Shīʿīsm has always been opposed to all temporal rulers as usurpers of the Imām's power smacks of a cliché when one notes that in sources as old as the works of Shaykh Ṭūsī (d. 461/1068) and Ibn Idrīs (d. 598/1202) Muslims are recommended, if not instructed, to pay allegiance to a type of ruler who is called 'righteous, just ruler' (*as-sulṭān al-ḥaqq al-ʿādil*), who is evidently not the same person as the Imām.[11] Nevertheless, important differences separate the political theory of the Shīʿīs from that of the Sunnīs, which will be discussed in Chapter 1. All that needs to be mentioned here is that, compared with their Shīʿī counterparts, the Sunnī exponents of the theory of the Caliphate between the fifth/eleventh and eighth/fourteenth centuries – not to mention the present period – displayed much greater flexibility in adapting their ideas to political realities.

This flexibility eventually reached a point at which the supreme value in politics appeared to be, not justice but security – a state of mind which set a high premium on the ability to rule and maintain 'law and order', rather than on piety. Writing at a time when the Mongol invaders threatened his homeland, Syria, the great Ḥanbalī jurisconsult and theologian Ibn Taymiyyah (d. 728/1328) gave a vivid expression to this viewpoint:

> It is obvious that the [affairs of the] people cannot be in a sound state except with rulers, and even if somebody from among unjust kings becomes ruler, this would be better than there being none. As it is said: 'Sixty years with an unjust ruler are better than one night without a ruler'. And it is related of [the fourth Caliph] 'Alī, May God Be Satisfied With Him, to have said that: 'The people have no option but to have a rulership [*imārah*], whether pious or sinful'. People asked him: 'We understand the pious, but why bother for the sinful?' He said: '[Because,] thanks to it, highways are kept secure, canonical penalties are applied, holy war is fought against the enemy, and spoils are collected'[12]

Acknowledging the necessity of strong government to repulse foreign aggressors is one thing; justifying tyranny in the name of religion is another. The price of medieval flexibility was to sanctify the latter position, which soon became the ruling political doctrine among the majority of Muslims of all sects. There followed a long period of stagnation in political thought, as indeed in most forms of intellectual activity, which ended only with the abolition of the Ottoman Caliphate in the second decade of the present century. It was centred around the belief in the unquestionable duty of Muslims to obey their rulers, and the inherent sinfulness of any rebellion against the established order. The question as to why this rigidity pervaded the Muslim mind has been a moot point among educated Muslims since the end of the nineteenth century. The answers have unfortunately often been coloured by ethnic, racial and denominational prejudices, with each group accusing others of having been responsible for the decline of the Islamic civilisation in general. As we noted at the beginning, there have also been intellectuals who, under the influence of European writers of Marxian or non-Marxian persuasion, have believed in a direct causal relationship between the very principles of Islam and the social and political plight of the Muslims. Recent Western stereotypes emphasising some of the exclusive features of the Eastern peoples, such as 'oriental despotism', and theories of geo-political determinism, have also been bandied about. But perhaps the real explanation lies in the fact that stagnation is the inescapable lot of any system of thought which is wedded to the state, and is thereby constantly exposed to the danger of becoming an ideological tool of vested interests – especially those which are determined to impose their own understanding of it as the indivisible creed of whole societies. This danger existed right from the earliest years of Islamic history – from the time when, with the end of the era of the Rightly-Guided Caliphs, the prestige of the rulers rested no longer on the successorship to the Prophet, but largely on sheer force. And, as has always been the case in history, sheer force was every now and again in need of doctrinal legitimation. The rulers could not fulfil this need without striking at the roots of independent thinking. Whether it was the Umayyad Caliphs, who ordered the execution of the advocates of free will: or, conversely, the Caliph Ma'mūn (198–218/813–33), who patronised the Mu'tazilī supporters of free will, and instituted a *miḥnah* (inquisition) against their opponents; or the Caliph Mutawakkil (232–247/847–61), who again reversed the trend in favour of orthodoxy; or Ghazālī, who declared war on all esoteric sects; or the founder of the Ṣafavīd state, Shāh Ismā'īl (907–30/1502–24), who visited the most brutal punishments on those who refused to vilify Abū Bakr and 'Umar, the result was always the same: the retreat of critical thought before the encircling rigidity of the official dogma. Whenever the state flagged in ideological zeal, the venality of the 'Ulamā' filled the vacuum.

But perhaps in saying all this we are missing an aspect of traditional political thought among Muslims which offers a completely different picture of the relationship between the rulers and the ruled. It is a picture contained in the type of literature which has come to be known in Persian as *andarz-nāmih* ('Book of Advice') and in Arabic *naṣīḥat 'al-mulūk* ('Counsel for Kings'), written by such geniuses as Ghazālī and Khājah Naṣīr Ṭūsī, and statesmen like Niẓām ul-Mulk, and developing a theory of kingship clearly influenced by the pre-Islamic Iranian notions of government, though dressed in an appropriately Islamic garb. One can find examples of it even in the works of those same jurists who defended tyranny as the lesser of two evils when the alternative was anarchy. Here the emphasis is on justice as an indefeasible precondition of rulership, on the dire consequences of injustice, and on service to the cause of religion and welfare of the people as the only legitimating factor of occasional acts of despotism. When a politically minded Muslim who is eagerly seeking to discover the causes of the present backwardness of his people reads such pieces of literature and compares them with what he also reads of the crimes of the past dynasties, the only impression he is likely to form is that of acute cynicism. Where were those just rulers to be found? To what use were all those perorations on justice put? Did they not merely serve to pacify their readers and perpetuate tyranny? If periods of tyranny, as some apologists of Muslim history might claim, were exceptional and short-lived, why did the Muslims fail to prosper? Why did political thought stagnate among them? Scholarly attempts at evading these questions, or treating them as anything other than rhetorical, can only produce greater cynicism in those who ask them. Within this perspective, all discussions on justice in classical Persian or Arab literature are relevant to current Muslim political thinking only in the negative sense – by being used as evidence that only radical solutions, and not just such pious invocations of Qur'ānic verses or Prophetic sayings, can wipe out injustice.

* * *

At the end of his outline of the ideas of Māwardī and his successors, H. A. R. Gibb warns us against overestimating the influence of these founding figures in the history of Sunnī political thought by reminding us that 'in the Sunnī community there was no one universally accepted doctrine of the caliphate'. The very basis of Sunnī thought, he goes on to say, 'excludes the acceptance of any one theory as definitive and final. What it does lay down is a principle: that the caliphate is that form of government which safeguards the ordinances of the Sharia and sees that they are put into practice. So long as that principle is applied, there may be infinite diversity in the manner of its application.' Gibb is referring here to what in the jurisprudential theory has come to be known as *ikhtilāf,* or legitimate divergency of opinions in the secondary matters of the religion. He finds his survey as furnishing a 'striking example of . . . the truth, that Muslim thought refuses to be bound by the outward formulae'.[13] The fact, however, remains as we shall see in Chapter 3, that when the issue of the Caliphate was revived after its abolition by the Turks in 1924, most of those who took part in the controversy had to rely on the expositions of Māwardī, Ghazālī and other early masters. The Egyptian 'Alī 'Abd ar-Rāziq, the most renowned of a few who dared to break out of this circle, was consequently accused of heresy.[14] So much loyalty to the past could be excused in the name of cultural continuity; but the modernists saw it rightly as the sign of a static mind.

As will be explained in subsequent chapters, one of the urgent tasks of Islamic modernists has been to demolish what they see as the presumed theological and canonical foundations of this stagnation, and by derivation, of Muslim submissiveness and quietism. To do this, they have had to conduct a twofold campaign: on the one hand, to bring out all the progressive tenets of Islam to prove that it is in essence a religion of freedom, justice and prosperity for Mankind; on the other, to subject the attitudes, values and modes of thought of the Muslims to a searching reassessment which ends up by stigmatising the whole of Islamic history, except the period of the Rightly-Guided Caliphs (11–40/632–61), as a departure from the teachings of the Qur'ān and the Prophet. Historical criticism has thus proved to be an integral part of political revisionism. Although a number of Muslim authors have risen to this challenge, pre-occupation with politics has on the whole prevented the more thoughtful Muslims from enriching their political observations with philosophical insight. The achievements of the great philosophers of the past, such as Fārābī, Ibn Sīnā and Ibn Bājjah, and much less those of such unorthodox Shī'ī thinkers as Suhrawardī and Ṣadr ud-Dīn Shīrāzī, could not be of much use, because of their unhistorical and abstract character, as well as the fact that the Hellenistic or Iranian influences in them have been blamed as one of the sources of corrupt beliefs among Muslims. Consequently, although over the last half-century there have been renowned philosophers or teachers of Islamic philosophy such as Ibrāhīm Madkūr and 'Abd ar-Raḥmān Badawī in Egypt, or Muḥammad Ḥusayn Ṭabāṭabā'I and Sayyid Jalāl Āshtīyānī in Iran, keeping alive the best scholastic traditions of the past, and there have also been numberless political writers loyal to the *Sharī'ah*, there has nevertheless been little effort in either camp to graft its own discipline or interests on to the other's in a common intellectual exercise.

Another concern of the modernists has been to offset the effects of the conservative realism of the earlier 'Ulamā' – if by realism is meant a willingness to forgo the demands of high principles in order to adjust to ephemeral conditions. This kind of changeability with the times is offensive to many Sunnī Muslims, who are convinced that the Islamic ideals of social justice are and should be applicable in all circumstances, however much the verdict of hard facts may be to the contrary. Their indignation is echoed in the work of writers like 'Abd al-'Azīz al-Badrī who, himself a victim of official displeasure because of his fundamentalist convictions, has produced a different version of the behaviour of the 'Ulamā' towards the rulers in the formative period of Islamic jurisprudence. He describes how the founders of the four main legal schools or rites of Sunnīsm – Abū Ḥanīfah, Mālik, Shāfi'ī and Ibn Ḥanbal – as well as the compilers of the Prophetic sayings (*ḥadīth*) such as Bukhārī, all endured hardship and imprisonment rather than submit to the irreligious demands of the rulers.[15] His account is largely accurate, but this does not disprove the realism of a Māwardī or an Ibn Jamā'ah: it does not diminish the overall impression of adaptability to the changing political scene gained from important Sunnī treatises on government between the demise of the Buyids and the consolidation of the Mongol power. It is interesting to note that the traditional realism is now being increasingly discarded in Sunnī political literature. The converse of all realism is idealism. But the new idealism of Sunnī writers should be distinguished from the fashionable romanticisation of the lives of the Prophet Muḥammad and other heroes of early Islam, which tries paradoxically to depict them as part of present *realities*.

The question of the relationship of the authority of the Caliphs to the power of the *sulṭāns, amīrs, maliks* and other categories of temporal rulers can be noteworthy for modern Muslim political writers mainly as an index to the changes of the political thought in the past. There have, however, been three other issues from traditional debates which are of a more practical concern to these writers: (a) the right to elect rulers, (b) the method of election, and (c) the right to revolt against injustice. To the extent that these issues are still vital for the Muslims, the history of Islamic political thought is still relevant. These issues have usually been discussed in the context of the theories of Islamic democracy, generating a vast literature around the concepts of *bay'ah* (contract of allegiance to the Caliph), *shūrā* (consultation) *ijmā'* (consensus), and *ahl al-ḥall wa'l-'aqd* (the elective body), which mostly relate to the first two issues, and examples of which can be culled from the practices of the Rightly-Guided Caliphs. The third issue (the right to revolt) has understandably proved more intractable, since for the reasons already mentioned it was often overshadowed by the consideration of 'avoiding disorder' (*ittiqā' al-fitnah*). However much the modernists quote from classical texts to demonstrate its solid basis in the legal right of the community to dismiss a sinful ruler, there is no known example of this right having ever been exercised in the past with the consensus of the 'Ulamā'. This lacuna has reinforced a latent tendency in modern works which is ironically as unhistorical as the abstractions of the philosophers, since in its zeal to reach the democratic essence of Islam it bypasses the awkward testimony of history, which shows the majority of Muslims often condoning despotic regimes. Another tendency arising from the same historical crux about democracy has been to play down the importance of political institutions in favour of the economic infrastructure of the Islamic state. This has given rise to the different schools of 'Islamic socialism', with a completely different set of symbols and idioms: here the stress is on the examples of the second Caliph, 'Umar (13–23/634–44), the fourth Caliph, 'Alī (35–40/656–61), some members of his family, especially his wife Fāṭimah and his son Ḥusayn; and Abū Dharr al-Ghifārī, the most outspoken 'anti-capitalist' companion of the Prophet. More important than the personal examples are the principles of equality, public ownership of lands, and restrictions on private ownership, all purportedly drawn from the Qur'ān and the Prophetic Tradition. Again history can be pertinent only in so far as it produces rare instances of peasant revolts against landowning exploiters.

To sum up, the revival of the Sunnī – and, as we shall later see, Shī'ī – political thought in our age has been focused on four basic themes:

breaking the spell of the sanctity of *status quo*; rejecting the corrupting realism of medieval writers; historical criticism; and salvaging the democratic and socialistic elements of the past. The roots of this revival have been numerous, some socio-political, others psychological and moral, all inextricable from one another. These will be surveyed in Chapters 2 to 4. Before that, we have to study briefly the development of the internal dynamism of Islam, as represented in the dialogue between its two major sects, Sunnīsm and Shī'īsm, since it is a development which has had far more momentous consequences in the evolution, and convergence, of both, than has so far been appreciated.

1 Shīʿīsm and Sunnīsm: conflict and concord

I The spirit of Shīʿīsm

The Sunnī-Shīʿī divergences have been studied in a variety of ways. There are scholars like James Darmsteter and Henri Corbin who have implicitly or explicitly viewed them in terms of the encounter between Iranian and Arab cultures: the former has singled out the Shīʿī doctrine of Mahdism as an Islamic adaptation of the pre-Islamic Iranian belief in the Divine Grace (*farrih-i īzadī*),[1] and the latter's *En Islam iranien* is a monumental testimony to the close affinity between the Iranian penchant for the esoteric and the mystical, and the philosophical foundations of Shīʿīsm.[2] At the other end of the spectrum, Montgomery Watt has called attention to the social factors in the genesis of Shīʿīsm by reminding us that early Shīʿīs came mostly from south Arabian tribes among whom the traditions of kingdoms 'with a semi-divine king' were particularly strong. So, as an ideology congenial to their pre-Islamic beliefs, Shīʿīsm remedied the social and psychological problems involved in their transition from nomadism to integration in the military caste of the Islamic empire.[3] Louis Massignon has stressed the relationship between Shīʿīsm and, not south Arabian tribes, but the political aspirations of middle-class artisans.[4] A more forceful version of this sociological treatment can be found, predictably, in the works of Marxist historians. Thus Petrushevskii explains the success of the Zaydī sect in the areas lying south to the Caspian Sea by reference to the peasant rebellion against the Sunnī landed aristocracy, and attributes the popularity of Mahdist ideas to their harmony with 'the hopes of artisans, peasants and the poorest strata of desert-dwellers for a social evolution'.[5]

But such theorising, however useful it might be in throwing light on Shīʿīsm as a social protest against Sunnīsm, does not detract from the importance of analysing the doctrinal differences between the two sects. Such analysis would not only widen our understanding of an important aspect of Muslim intellectual history, but would also show the extent to which each school has affected the political thinking of the other, and how—and this is what the present author contends—the differences between the two have been reduced in the process.

These differences can be studied in one of two ways: first, by identifying those characteristics of Shīʿīsm which explicitly differentiate it from

Sunnīsm, and, secondly, by surveying some of the crucial arguments in the deliberate polemics between them. This is what we intend to do in this section and the next section. Meanwhile, since what we have designated in Chapter 5 as Shī'ī modernism consists partly in a reinterpretation of some of the traditional characteristics of Shī'īsm, and partly in a shift in emphasis on the main differences with Sunnīs, our comments here can also serve as an introduction to that chapter. One point, however, needs to be emphasised at the outset. George Makdisi has rightly noted in another context, discussing the Ḥanbalī school, that it is wrong to characterise any particular school or sect in Islam as belonging totally to the right or left of the political spectrum, or as having espoused solidly rationalistic or traditionalist positions: opposing trends have always existed at one and the same time within each and every Muslim school.[6] The same remark applies to Sunnīsm and Shī'īsm; any generalisation about either of them can be proved to be false by producing a contrary, however untypical, piece of evidence. Nevertheless, the concept of 'broad features' is valid in any effort to understand their political implications, but one which cannot possibly be formulated without some prejudice to the nuances and diversities within each school.

* * *

The distinguishing features of Shī'īsm in relation to Sunnīsm should be sought not only in its fundamental principles, but perhaps more importantly in its ethos, in the tone of historically developed attitudes which have informed and infused the Shī'ī stance on the controversial issues of Islamic history, society and dogma. The actual disagreements between the Sunnīs and Shī'īs in certain details of theology and legal practices have not been as important as this ethos, or in the words of the modern Shī'ī scholar S. Husain M. Jafri, 'as the "spirit" working behind these rather minor divergences'.[7] In trying to understand this ethos, one has to deal with 'Historical Shī'īsm', namely, a Shī'īsm which has taken shape in the actual, living experience of specific groups of Muslims, through attitudes which stemmed sometimes clearly from Shī'ī tenets, and sometimes from individual interpretations and a slowly emerging consensus, without necessarily being recognised as fundamental principles in the Shī'ī sources.

Considered in this light, perhaps the most outstanding feature of Shī'īsm is an attitude of mind which refuses to admit that majority opinion is necessarily true or right, and – which is its converse – a rationalised defence of the moral excellence of an embattled minority. One can find numerous examples of this attitude in classical Shī'ī sources. An anecdote, for instance, in the *Amālī* of Shaykh Ṭūsī (d. 461/1068), unquestionably the prime founder of Shī'ī jurisprudence, typifies it vividly: Kumayl Ibn Zīyād an-Nakha'ī, a close disciple of the first Imām, 'Alī, relates:

I was with the Prince of the Faithful at the Kūfah Mosque. When we finished the last evening prayer, he ['Alī] took me by my hand, until we left the Mosque, until we left Kūfah, and reached the suburb of the town. And all that time he had not uttered a word to me. Then he said: "O Kumayl, the hearts of men are like vessels, the best of them is the most retentive of them. So keep with yourself what you hear from me. The people are of three kinds: the divine scholar, those who seek knowledge and tread the path of salvation, and the rabble [*hamaj ra'ā'*] who follow every crowing creature, never partaking of the light of knowledge, never relying on a solid base."[8]

This anecdote is significant in several respects: first, its adage is attributed to 'Alī, namely the only Imām among the twelve who became ruler of all Muslims. Secondly, the incident reported takes place in the Kūfan period of 'Alī's career when after years of overt or covert opposition to 'usurping' Caliphs, he achieved political power: the reader is thus warned to take 'Alī's censure of popular fickleness not as the fulmination of an impractical, anti-social visionary but as the considered judgement of an experienced statesman. Thirdly, the extreme caution and discretion exercised by 'Alī in making his remark makes the bigotry, ignorance and unreliability of the 'rabble' to appear all the more reprehensible.

In his treatise *al-Īḍāḥ*, to mention another example from a less important but earlier source, the third century jurisconsult and theologian Faḍl Ibn Shādhān Nayshābūrī (d. 290/902) is at pains to discredit the Sunnīs' constant boasting of majority support as evidence of their righteousness, by arguing that the Qur'ān, in an overwhelming number of verses, takes a sinister view of the majority, and only rarely accepts it as a factor of legitimacy; it deprecates the majority for following its whims and conjectures (6:116), lacking knowledge and understanding (7:187; 49:4; 5:103), being polytheists at heart (12:106), ungrateful (7:17; 12:38) and transgressors to one another (38:24). That is why, in the history of the conflict of ideas 'many a small party has triumphed over a large party' (2:249).[9]

The reverse of the same attitude – the inherent virtue of belonging to a militant minority – is illustrated by Sayyid al-Murtaḍā (d. 436/1043), the teacher of Shaykh Ṭūsī. In his *Kitāb al-Intiṣār*, enumerating in minute detail the legal and ritual points of difference between Shī'ism and other Muslim sects, he defiantly insists on the 'isolationist' character of Shī'ism (*ma'nfarad bihi'l-imāmiyyah*) by arguing that the paucity of the following of an idea does not affect its validity, just as the immense popularity of another cannot be proof of its truth.[10] But more relevant to the spirit of present-day Shī'ism is the expression of this defiance in the revolt of the third Imām, Ḥusayn Ibn 'Alī, and his seventy-two companions, in 61/680. The memory of Ḥusayn's martyrdom serves as an everlasting exhortation to the Shī'īs of all times to brave their numerical inferiority in the face of firmly established majorities.

In sustaining both aspects of their cautious attitude towards majority amidst the global Muslim community, the Shī'īs have had to contend with powerful shibboleths. This has been partly due to the collectivist slant of Islamic political doctrines, greatly accentuated in the case of Sunnīsm because of its belief in the sanctity of the consensus (*ijmā'*) of the community. 'My community will never agree in error': the Prophet is thus claimed by the Sunnīs to have conferred on his community the very infallibility that the Shī'īs ascribe to their Imāms. The Shī'īs have tried to prove the Sunnīs' unfitness to qualify as the community envisaged in the Prophet's prediction by pointing to their connivance in the misdeeds of their rulers during the greater part of Islamic history. An outcome of the Shī'īs' refusal to be intimidated, let alone bound, by false 'public opinion' is the restricted permissibility of consensus among them as a source of jurisprudential rules. Whereas the Sunnīs have defined consensus as 'the agreement among the "people who loose and bind"' (namely, the holders of power and position, according to Imām Fakhr ud-Dīn ar-Rāzī), and even as the agreement of the community in general (according to Ghazālī), the Shī'īs hold consensus to be valid only when it includes the opinion of 'the infallible and the impeccable' (*ma'ṣūm*), namely the Imām. This doctrine has not caused the Shī'īs to abandon consensus as an element of their legal system, since they always justify it by invoking the convenient maxim that 'the earth is never empty of the *ma'ṣūm*', which means that whenever a consensus is formed, one has to presume that the community of concurring scholars must have included a *ma'ṣūm* in their midst. But the doctrine has been a perfect safeguard against majority impositions.[11]

The Shī'ī view on majority seems to be primarily a result of its legitimist theory of succession to the Prophet, confining rightful government in the first instance to members of his House. Any political theory so exclusive in its outlook tends to breed exponents who jealously guard its purity from diffuse notions of authority. But as time went on, Shī'ī authors resorted to diverse philosophical, theological and mystical vehicles to elaborate their principal beliefs. By their very nature, these vehicles too were élitist, capable of being developed and appreciated by only tiny literate groups. Significantly, of all these components in the Iranian Shī'ī culture, literature which is alone suitable for popular appreciation has fared the worst, since it has been allocated mainly to recounting the lives of the Imāms, often in stilted and morose style, and aimed merely at eliciting maximum grief over their sufferings.

Further explanation of the same attitude comes from the imperative of survival in hostile environments. Any minority constantly harassed and persecuted inevitably turns inward and, distancing itself increasingly from the majority, gradually develops its own mental habits and attitudes. In this capacity, the Shī'ī attitude towards majority was supplemented by two other idiosyncratic practices: the esoteric style of teaching religious truths, which is mainly cherished by the Ismā'īlī school, and *taqiyyah*, which can temporarily be translated as expedient dissimulation, but will be defined in some detail in Chapter 5. These two practices, which have sometimes further enhanced Shīʿī particularism, can be interrelated and mutually complementary: Corbin has defined *taqiyyah* as 'the discipline of esoterism'. Since we will consider *taqiyyah* later, here a brief discussion on esoterism is in order.

Esoterism is closely interwined with Shīʿī theosophy, which explains the rationale of Shīʿīsm as being merely the awareness and guardianship of the secret truth of Islam. Shīʿīsm came into being to preserve and gradually communicate the essence of Islam. According to one of the most fundamental principles of Shīʿī theosophy, the truth of Islam, like the archetypal reality of all things in the sensible world, can be found only in the *mundus imaginalis*. So the worldly manifestation of Islam merely reflects part of its truth. Its full truth is only known to God, the Prophet and the members of his House. This doctrine has given rise to a set of dual notions, or binary oppositions, across the whole spectrum of Islamic sciences. They start with the Qur'ān, which is considered by the Shīʿīs to contain two aspects: an inner or secret meaning (*bāṭin*), and an outer or apparent meaning (*ẓāhir*). Hence the dichotomy between Shīʿī hermeneutics (*ta'wīl*), or allegorical interpretation of the Qur'ān, reaching for its mystical depths, and the Sunnī literal interpretation (*tafsīr*) which aims at a straightforward clarification of the verses. Then on a higher plane comes the division of the entire corpus of religious teachings into the truth (*ḥaqīqat*), and the Law (*Sharīʿah*). It would be perhaps an over-simplification, though by no means wrong, to say that Shīʿīsm propounds the first items in these pairs (*bāṭin, ta'wīl* and *ḥaqīqat*), while Sunnīsm is mostly associated with their opposites. But the division does represent a sharp breach between those Muslim intellectuals who remain firmly committed to theosophy (*'urafā'*), and those well-versed in juridical sciences and formalistic casuistry (*fuqahā'*). This division was responsible not only for the diverging 'spirits' of Shīʿīsm and Sunnīsm, but also for the occasional rifts inside Shīʿīsm itself as can be observed in the Ṣafavīd period, when in the face of the ascendancy of hidebound jurists Shīʿīsm was forced to hide its truth from itself: now it was the turn of the *'urafā'* to seek shelter in *taqiyyah*. According to Corbin the distinction between *ẓāhir* and *bāṭin*, the apparent and the hidden, and the exoteric and esoteric, forms the philosophical aspect of the Shīʿī case for *Imāmat* as the heart and truth of *nubuwwat* (Prophecy). It is in view of all this that Corbin calls Shīʿīsm 'the sanctuary of Islamic esoterism'.[12]

Esoterism generated an educational philosophy which related accessible knowledge to the moral integrity as well as the cognitive ability of its recipients, with the consequence of requiring the withholding of information from the uninitiated. The Platonic and neo-Platonic ancestry of this philosophy has been much debated, but nowhere is its essence more clearly adumbrated than in the introduction to the *Rasā'il* (Epistles) of the Brethren of Purity (*Al-Ikhwān aṣ-Ṣafā'*) whose Shīʿī, Ismāʿīlī affiliations are now in little doubt. In it, the initiates are warned not to make the Epistles available except to those who are 'free, beneficient, of sound mind, having a sense of purpose, looking for the right path, from among the seekers of knowledge, admirers of letters, and lovers of philosophy, exercising maximum care in preserving, concealing, revealing and communicating these Epistles'. The Ikhwān then go on to justify their advice by explaining the contradictory effects that knowledge can produce, depending on the disposition of the novice: it can both remedy and make sick, revive and destroy. In this respect, knowledge is like food and light: 'Just as a small child', they write, 'needs to be fed gradually, stage by stage, until it reaches adolescence, so that it may not eat something detrimental to its constitution, and just as light is appropriate only to persons with open, healthy and strong eyes, so that a person whose eyes have been shut, or has just emerged from darkness, will be severely dazzled by daylight, in the same way, those who get hold of these Epistles should communicate them only one at a time to those who are in need of them.'[13]

The same reasoning, writ large, is behind the gradual communication of religious truths to Mankind. Although Muḥammad, as the last of the prophets, was the repository of the complete treasure of religious precepts, he revealed only some of them, leaving the rest undeclared, either because of their inapplicability at the time, or because of the inexpediency of disseminating them in that particular period of history. This was necessitated by the 'wisdom of gradualness' (*ḥikmat' at-tadrīj*). Muḥammad, therefore, entrusted the undeclared precepts to his Executors, namely the Imāms, and *through them*, to the *mujtahids*, 'so that they would progressively reveal them at appropriate junctures, according to their wisdom, whether by [inferring] the particular from the universal, or the relative from the absolute, or the concrete from the abstract'.[14]

All that has been said so far in describing the general characteristics of Shī'īsm is seriously questioned by those Shī'ī modernists of the Twelver School who now play down, if not totally reject, all the particularistic, élitist and esoteric accounts of their religion, and instead – as will be shown in the next section and Chapter 5 – try to prove Shī'īsm to be, at least politically, an open and democratic system of beliefs. But traditional attitudes still persist, and continue to shape the Shī'ī world-view. This is clearly apparent from the statement that we just quoted on the 'wisdom of gradualness': it has come from a prominent contemporary Shī'ī scholar, Muḥammad Ḥusayn Kāshif al-Ghiṭā' (d. 1954). He not only enjoyed immense prestige among Twelver Shī'īs of all persuasions, but because of his efforts to bring about a Sunnī–Shī'ī conciliation was respected by many Sunnīs as well. His interpretations of Shī'īsm as a whole eliminates or minimises many of its features which have drawn some of the most bitter vituperatives of Sunnī polemists. And yet his statement not only demonstrates the continuity of the Shī'ī philosophy of education, but has also a typically Shī'ī, historicist connotation.

Revelation is thus described as the process of the growing religious consciousness of Man, as the evolution of his knowledge from the universal to the particular, from the abstract to the concrete, through the agency of the Imāms and the mujtahids. But historicism, which is another salient feature of Shī'ism when compared with Sunnīsm, arises from a more fundamental principle, not directly connected with its educational philosophy: that of Mahdīsm, the conception of history as a trend of events, not so much following a predetermined course (because contrary to orthodox Muslims the majority of Shī'īs believe in human free will), as moving towards a fixed goal, the return of the hidden Imām, the Mahdī, and the Rehabilitation of the universe.

The Shī'īs agree with the Sunnīs that Muslim history since the era of the four Rightly-Guided Caliphs (11–40/632–61) has been for the most part a tale of woe. But whereas for the Sunnīs the course of history since then has been a movement *away* from the ideal state, for the Shī'īs it is a movement *towards* it:

'The incidence of fortune', say the Brethren of Purity, 'among certain peoples and nations, the increase in the power of some rulers, the outbreak of rebellions, the renewal of governorship in the kingdom, and other similar events [are aimed at] the betterment of the conditions of the world, and its elevation towards progress and wholeness. But often the factors of destruction prevail, such as wars, seditions and ravages, resulting in the ruin of the cities, the loss of the fortunes of a people, and the demise of their prosperity, but *ultimately they all conduce to the good.*'[15]

True, the Sunnīs too, in their fighting moments, like the militants of all times, produce rhetoric replete with expressions of faith in the final triumph of their cause – whether it is the fight against the infidels, or struggle for national independence, or confrontation with Israel. But there is nothing in their creed or theology which would make this triumph an inevitable occurrence in the divine scheme of things. Hence their general relectance to indulge in philosophising about history. The few historians who have overcome this reluctance among them have usually come up with cyclical theories, expounding the notion that history consists of alternating patterns of the rise and fall of nations, or even of tedious repetitions of past events. Thus Ibn Khaldūn explains the gradual decline and collapse of powerful dynasties and polities as an inexorable, and almost mechanical, transition from the virtuous ways of the desert life to the corrupting prosperity of urban settlement.[16] And Maqrīzī (d. 841/1437) sees the internecine conflicts between the Umayyads and Hāshimites, and indeed the whole history of the Muslim Caliphate after the death of Muḥammad, as a complete replica of the history of the Israelites.[17]

By contrast, what lends an historicist thrust to the Shī'īs' confidence in the ultimate victory over the 'forces of injustice' is their millenarian anticipation of the Return of the hidden Imām. The Qur'ānic verses usually invoked by Shī'ī commentators as evidence of the doctrine of the

Return, although making no apparent mention of a future Mahdī, promise the sovereignty of the earth to the righteous and the oppressed:

1 'God hath promised to those of you who believe and do the things that are right, that He will cause them to succeed others in the land, as He gave succession to those who were before them, and that He will establish for them that religion which they delight in, and that after their fear He will give them security in exchange. They shall worship Me: nought shall they join me' (24:55).
2 'And we were minded to show favour to those who were brought low in the land, and to make them spiritual chiefs [*Imāms*], and to make them *Pharaoh's** heirs' (28:5).
3 'My servants, the righteous shall inherit the earth' (21:105).
4 'the earth is God's: to such of His servants as He pleaseth doth He give it as a heritage' (7:128).

Sunnī commentators interpret the promise contained in the first verse as addressed to Prophet Muḥammad's followers in his own time, that in the second to the Israelites, and that in the third and fourth to the entire community of the faithful.[18] Shī'ī commentators, however, maintain all of them to be referring to the Mahdī's followers at the end of time; they particularly substantiate their reading on the basis of a saying attributed to Muhammad to the effect that: 'Even if there remains but one single day of the world, God will lengthen that day until He has designated a righteous man from my House to fill it with justice and equity, just as it was filled with injustice and oppression.'[19] This link between the Return and the ultimate, global sovereignty of the righteous and the oppressed makes Shī'ī historicism a *potential* tool of radical activism. But throughout the greater part of Shī'ī history, it never went beyond the potential state, remaining in practice merely a sanctifying tenet for the submissive acceptance of the *status quo*. This is apparent from the semantic structure of the term for the millenarian anticipation of the Return: *intiẓār*, which denotes an essentially submissive expectation of things to come. Hence a tendency grew among the Shī'īs to consider just government in the strict sense as an ideal which is impossible to achieve before the age of the Return. This eventually made the ideal state in Shī'īsm to appear as a regime beyond the reach of ordinary human beings, and pushed it into the realm of meta-history:

'It is well-established by the Tradition,' says Qāḍī Sa'īd Qumī (d. 1103/1691) a theosophist of the Ṣafavīd period,' that the Apostle of God, having been offered the choice between the status of servant and that of kingship, chose to be a Prophet Servant (*'abd nabī*) rather than a Prophet King (*malik nabī*). Thus, there cannot be an exoteric kingship (*salṭanah ẓāhirah*) to succeed him, much less the kind of sovereignty

* Italics indicate addition by the translator (Rodwell).

exercised by the tyrants (*imāmat' al-jabābirah*). Because, when such sovereignty did not belong to the Prophet himself, how could it belong to his successor? So if the Prophet is to have a successor, it is imperative that this succession should be of a religious nature (*khilāfah diniyyah*), guaranteeing to the faithful the best conditions of viaticum and the Return, and that this spiritual kingship (*salṭanah ruḥāniyyah*) should fall on him who is of unshakeable devotion, he of whom it can be said that he is the very soul of the Prophet, just as the Prophet has declared it in the case of 'Alī, Ḥasan and Ḥusayn.'[20]

Statements such as this rendered Shī'ī views of the Prophetic succession, and indeed of politics in general, highly idealistic. Idealism in politics usually means a whole-hearted commitment to lofty social and political goals, irrespective of their practicability or otherwise, and certainly with no concern for the material and spiritual costs of their realisation. But it can also mean conscious attachment to a utopia, and pursuance of aims which are admittedly impossible of achievement within normal circumstances. Although there have been periods in Islamic history when the Shī'īs could be said to have acted as idealists in the first sense by virtue of their resolute struggle to seek redress of specific political and social grievances (such as the Sarbidāriyyah movement in the eighth century in Kirmān, or popular uprisings in Iran in the nineteenth century against foreign concessions), the predominant form of their idealism has been of the second, utopian kind. Idealism of the latter type was not necessarily always a function of political conditions. Qāḍī Sa'īd Qumī made his remark about the unworthiness of 'exoteric kingship' not in the age of the low fortunes of Shī'īsm, but at the height of its political power, in the Ṣafavīd period.

All this does not mean that Shī'īsm never compromised with the powers that be. On the contrary, for the best part of their history, Shī'ī theologians and jurisconsults displayed an impressive ingenuity in devising practical arrangements with the rulers to ensure the safety and survival of their followers. But what distinguishes Shī'ī pragmatism in such cases from its Sunnī counterpart is that these arrangements were often in the nature of *ad hoc* dispensations which never abrogated or diluted the basic Shī'ī doctrinal position that all temporal authority in the absence of the hidden Imām is illegitimate. So to the extent that the Shī'ī insistence on the indivisible legitimacy of the rule of the Imām has remained in force, Sunnīsm can be considered a realistic political ideology because of its greater adaptability to changing circumstances, and its inclusion of modifications and revisions carrying the stamp of the theologians' approval.

Idealism has had a rather paradoxical effect on Shī'ī political behaviour: far from predisposing the Shī'īs to relentless activism, it tended to make them apathetic to prevailing political conditions. This is perhaps because the dividing line between idealism and political apathy can be a very thin one. The belief that all temporal authorities are either illegitimate, or owe their legitimacy to a dubious *modus vivendi*, led the Shī'īs often to avoid all involvement in politics, considering it as a preserve of unscrupulous, ambitious souls. It is somewhat immaterial to argue whether Shī'īsm lost its interest in politics after Ḥusayn's martyrdom, or when the immense spiritual prestige of the sixth Imām, Ja'far aṣ-Ṣādiq, put him beyond the need of temporal power. What is more pertinent is that by the time Shī'īsm was called to guide national life in Iran in the sixteenth century 'its long period of existence mostly as a scholastic relic had made it insensitive to politics'.[21]

Aloofness from politics was heightened by another implication of Shī'ī idealism which maintained the administration of genuine justice to be impossible save with the return of the Imām. This implication is directly linked with the Shī'ī ethical view of Man. Although the Qur'ān does not accept the notion of Original Sin, it contains several verses describing Man as sinful, oppressive and ignorant. Among them, the following verse figures prominently in the Shī'ī theosophical arguments on the necessity of the Imāmate: 'We offered the trusteeship [*al-amānah*] to the heavens, the earth and the mountains; all refused to assume it, and were terrified by it. But Man accepted to take charge of it, because he is wrongful and ignorant' (33:72). It is in the interpretation of this verse that the paradox referred to in the preceding paragraphs becomes more apparent. Interpreting the word *trust* as the esoteric mission of the Imāms or the Friends of God (*walāyah*),[22] the Shī'ī hermeneutics demonstrate the ambiguity and duality of human nature. The dark and wicked side of Man's existence is redeemed by the intervention of 'the Fourteen Impeccables' (*chahārdah ma'ṣūm*: Prophet Muḥammad, his daughter Fāṭimah and the Twelve Imāms). Thus belief in the fallibility of Man, and the doctrine of the infallibility and impeccability of the Imāms are the two sides of the same coin.

The conviction that Man is inherently fallible has been behind the Shī'īs' extreme caution in accepting responsibility for the administration of justice. In all the authoritative sources of Shī'ī jurisprudence, the chapter on adjudication (*kitāb al-qaḍā'*) opens with dire warnings about the enormity of the task of judges, and the almost superhuman qualities demanded of them by religion. 'O Shurayḥ,' 'Alī is reported to have said to his appointed judge, 'you have occupied a seat which nobody would occupy except prophets or their executors, or the wretched. The judge's tongue is between two flames of fire.' According to another *ḥadīth* ascribed to Ḥusayn, 'of every four judges, three are in hellfire'.[23]

From the same conviction arose a sense of humility and self-effacement that today would seem incredible in view of the overweening attitude of militant Shī'īs and their confidence in Man's flawless ability to overcome all social and political imperfections. Indicative of that humility and self-effacement is an invocation to God, still recommended to be recited after the inaugural phrase 'God is Great' (*takbīrat' al-iḥrām*), at the beginning of each prayer: 'O Benefactor, verily has the sinner come to Thee. Verily hast Thou commanded benefactors to forgive sinners. Thou art the Benefactor, and I am the sinner. By the right of Muḥammad and the People of Muḥammad, confer Thy blessing on Muḥammad and the people of Muḥammad, and forgive the evil that you know of me.'[24]

This characterisation of Man as being of a feeble and wrongful disposition, and dependent on the Imāms' guidance to attain his salvation, stands in sharp opposition to that furnished by the Sunnī exegetics. In the latter although the emphasis on the vicious desires of Man is maintained, one notes a marked nuance approximating his glorification. God's appointment of Adam as his viceregent, despite the angels' protest that Man would be prone to evil (Qur'ān, 2:30) certainly underlines Man's capability to act as the agent of the divine will. Likewise, God's command to his angels to bow in reverence to Adam, and his subsequent punishment of Iblīs (Satan) for disobeying him, is further evidence of ennoblement of Man. It is also held by Sunnī commentators to denote Man's superiority to angels in the hierarchy of beings, whereas the Shī'īs, in common with the Philosophers and indeed all the Islamic schools of Iranian and Greek influence, consider the angels as the intermediaries between God and Man, and, therefore, superior to the latter.[25] Even acceptance of God's 'trust' (Qur'ān, 33:72) which, as we saw, is explained by the Shī'īs on grounds of human wrongfulness and ignorance, confirms for the Sunnīs that with 'all his frail and faltering nature', Man is possessed of 'an innate boldness to transcend the actual towards the ideal'.[26] Both Shī'ī pessimism and Sunnī optimism about Man, however, share the recognition that the signs of a true Muslim are the virtues of submission, humble-mindedness, patience, trembling fear and avoidance of ostentation, and one of the great sins that Man can commit in consequence of realisation of his innate nobility is *istikbār*, i.e. 'to consider one'self big', or haughtiness.[27]

Finally, a word on emotionalism, which perhaps more than any other aspect of Shī'īsm has drawn comment from those Western scholars who find popular manifestations to be a more truthful index to the essence of Shī'īsm than the mystical, esoteric literature. Dwight Donaldson's *The Shi'ite Religion* is a well-known example of this approach, seeing in Shī'īsm nothing except a framework for lamentations, self-flagellation and other passionate rituals in memory of the martyred Imāms.[28] For F. Bagley, too, the vital force of Shī'īsm is its emotional quality, particularly when compared with latter-day Sunnīsm. 'The Sunnī modernists,' he says, 'stemming from the School of Muḥammad 'Abduh, seem to lack a comparable emotional vitality. Having rejected Ṣūfīsm because of the discredit brought upon it by the darvish orders and also because of its anti-rational aspect, they sometimes give the impression of having little except a social reformism which is bound to lag behind the demands of purely rational thought and of lay opinion, and a nationalism which is bound to come up against other nationalisms.' Bagley concludes that because of this, 'perhaps the Shī'a emotionalism carries with it a more humanistic message'.[29]

Shī'ī emotionalism manifests itself most vividly in the annual mourning ceremonies for the Imāms, and the day-to-day scenes of the fervent entreaties of the pilgrims at the tombs of the Imāms and their real or presumed descendants. Its avowed justification is a theory of emotions which exalts grief and sorrow as a solvent of the 'smear of sin'. Asceticism and suffering, because of going counter to the appetitive and corporeal faculties of the soul, remove the effects of sins which emanate from Man's hedonistic desires, and thus act as a penance to invoke intercession with God.[30] This is also the argument adduced to explain why the prophets and the Imāms subjected themselves to all manner of adversities while they had the power to overcome their enemies.

But emotionalism is also a corollary to the philosophy of the Imāmate. Any theological system which is as insistent as Shī'īsm on the indispensable patronage of specific divinely designated men (whether called saints, or the Fourteen Impeccables, or Imāms, or Friends of God) for the preservation of the faith and salvation of the individual inevitably promotes the development of a voluminous literature devoted to the 'saga' of these men. Since the most significant aspect of the biographies of the Imāms is the account of their endurance of humiliations, persecutions and martyrdom, the principal genre of the literature of Imāmology has been elegia (*marthīyah*). The pathos of this literature, which is the main reason for its great popularity, has in due course permeated the spirit of Shī'ī culture, further enriching its emotional content.

Every great religion has undergone in its historical development a rift between an entrenched hierarchy, representing the austere and aloof image of the orthodoxy, and the mass appeal of the mystics, saints and pastors who satisfy the cravings for a warm and personal guidance. In Sunnīsm, the Ṣūfī orders which performed the latter function have had a difficult time warding off the charges of heterodoxy. Shī'īsm, as we hinted before, has not been entirely immune against this rift. But since Imāmology has formed an integral part of its theology, this has furnished it with a greater resilience to absorb the sentimental resonances of the popular faith. An example of the difference between Sunnīsm and Shī'īsm on this score is their attitude towards poetry. Although the Ṣunnīs acknowledge the works of Ḥassān Ibn Thābit, Ka'b Ibn Mālik and Umayyat 'Ibn Abi'ṣ-Ṣalt as testimony to the high place of poetry in the early propagation of Islam despite the Qur'ān's denunciation of some poets, only Shī'īsm has admitted poetry and song into popular devotional acts.[31] This is evidenced by the introduction of *ta'zīyah* (passion play) and *rawḍah-khānī* (recitation of the afflictions of the Imāms) in religious ceremonies. The occasional orthodox Shī'ī disapproval of these innovations is by no means comparable in doctrinal depth and moral indignation to the orthodox Sunnī condemnations of, for instance, the dervish dances.

But Shīʿī emotionalism has exercised a much more far-reaching influence on Shīʿī political culture than Ṣūfī tendencies have in Sunnī societies. It has been a most powerful ally for despotism not only by providing convenient outlets for popular feelings of frustration, but also by fostering an attitude of mind which derives greater satisfaction from 'oppressedness' than from defying established authority, and although abhors political injustice, prefers to repel it in the same way that it confronts other unpleasant things in life, whether they are diseases, obnoxious neighbours or insects – by supplications to God and the Imāms.[32]

* * *

It was the combination of the broad features discussed in this chapter – particularism, esoterism, historicism, idealism, a pessimistic conception of human nature, a paradoxical apathy in politics, and emotionalism – that constituted the basic mood of historical Shīʿīsm in contradistinction to Sunnīsm. There is certainly a rational link between these features, so that not only do they all form a coherent whole, but each constituent of the whole – perhaps with the exception of historicism – can be considered as the logical result of the preceding, and the carrier of the following one. This does not mean that there was no tension between them. Tension was indeed inevitable not least because, as we said at the beginning of this chapter, while some of these features have flowed directly from Shīʿī fundamental principles, others were the product of individual interpretation or collective understanding, sometimes at variance with those tenets. Thus particularism often collided with effusive popular rituals, and idealism stood ill at ease with a civic apathy which was in a way its distant, but unwanted progeny. Most important of all, rationalism as an attribute of élitism, enshrined in the principle of *ijtihād* was outraged by all other features when these were carried to immoderate limits. Shīʿī modernism has been aimed as much at resolving such tensions as at adapting Shīʿīsm to altered social and political conditions.

We also noted at the beginning of our discussion that none of these features has been explicitly acknowledged by the Shīʿīs among their fundamental principles. This has been a source of both the strength and weakness of these features: strength, because they have always permeated Shīʿī political attitudes merely as intangible and implicit agents, and have not, therefore, been able to be pinpointed easily whether by Sunnī polemists or indigenous critics; weakness, because when Shīʿī modernists launched their assault on orthodox strongholds, they could not be readily accused of contravening any specific canon of the faith.

II The polemics

Of a completely different kind are the Sunnī–Shīʿī polemics. These are concerned, not with the imponderables of the 'spirits' of the two sects, but with the concrete details of Islamic history, theology, rituals and law. Most of the pivotal issues in the polemics have remained more or less unchanged throughout the ages. Thus the main themes of the Ḥillī – Ibn Taymiyyah exchanges in the eighth/fourteenth century have been reproduced during the last hundred years or so in the Sunnī censures of Shīʿism by Rashīd Riḍā, Aḥmad Amīn and ʿAbd Allāh al-Qaṣīmī, and the Shīʿī responses by ʿAbd al-Ḥusayn Amīnī, Muḥammad Ḥusayn Kāshif al-Ghiṭā', Abu'l Ḥasan al-Khunayzī and Sharaf ad-Dīn al-Mūsawī. But the intellectual level of the arguments, the reasonings of the disputants, and the foci of emphasis have varied considerably from one period to another. The degree of tension has also varied as a function of the sectarian affiliations of the polemists. The most violent Sunnī opposition to Shīʿism has come from the Ḥanbalīs, who nevertheless consider the moderate Twelver Shīʿīs as less blameworthy than the Ismāʿīlīs, or the Bāṭinīs in general. For their part the Shīʿīs, while reciprocating this opposition, have been similarly careful not to antagonise other Sunnī sects and have even sometimes paid compliments to the fair-mindedness of the Shāfiʿīs and Ḥanafīs, for instance in praising the third Shīʿī Imām, Ḥusayn. In recent times, the modernists in both camps have contributed their share to all these variations, either by introducing fresh issues into the controversy, or by efforts towards a reconciliation of the two sects.

In its original form the Sunnī–Shīʿī dispute is not concerned with the fundamentals of religion. Unlike, for instance, the disagreements among the Christians, it does not relate to the nature of God, or the function of his Emissary, or the manner of achieving human salvation. Rather, it involves issues which, as will be shown, are decidedly marginal to these matters, and in any case have no bearing on the basic duties of a Muslim (praying, fasting, pilgrimage, alms-tax, and the holy war). But over time, it has degenerated from a quarrel about the Prophet's successorship into a ritual, theological and legal rift which can, at least obliquely, affect certain basic beliefs and attitudes.

The polemics are clearly of two kinds: those dealing with historical personalities, especially some of the crucial figures in early Islam, and those dealing with concepts and doctrines. The predominance of each of these two sets of themes depends on which side has initiated the debate: the Shīʿīs are usually concerned with personalities, the Sunnīs with concepts and doctrines, without, of course, this precluding a good deal of overlap. The reason for this customary 'division of labour' lies in the original cause of the controversy, which revolved around the few individuals aspiring for the succession to the Prophet. Since in the contest immediately after the Prophet's death, ʿAlī was defeated by his opponents, the initial reaction of his followers, the Shīʿīs, was confined to attacks on the particular misdeeds of the first three Caliphs as a converse vindication of his rightful succession. One could plausibly surmise that the later doctrinal altercations resulted from these early personal attacks. Before explaining this, we must briefly consider the Shīʿī criticisms of the first three Caliphs.

The most serious objection to Abū Bakr is his complicity in convening the Saqīfah assembly which appointed him as the first Caliph. That single act was enough in the Shīʿī eyes to throw grave doubts on his integrity as a just and faithful follower of Muḥammad. But then other wrongful deeds followed: he deprived Fāṭimah of her rightful inheritance from Muḥammad – the famous 'Fadak affair', relating to an oasis in Arabia near Khaybar, inhabited by the Jews who had submitted to Muḥammad after his punitive assault on Khaybar. Abū Bakr refused to deliver Fadak to Fāṭimah, referring her to the words of the Prophet, 'No one shall be my heir; what I leave behind belongs to the poor.' If these acts harmed the rights of the Prophet's family, his other offences damaged the community at large: for instance, his pardoning of his general, Khālid Ibn Walīd, after the latter had murdered a Muslim notable, Mālik Ibn Nuwayrah, under the pretext that Khālid's services were indispensable for the young Islamic state; or his discontinuation of the practice of registering the Prophet's sayings, a measure which was later hardened by ʿUmar, ostensibly to reinforce the authority of the Qur'ān as the unique source of religious precepts.[33]

ʿUmar is taken to task primarily for his conduct in the 'Thursday Calamity': on the day of his death, the Prophet, who was gravely ill, bid his companions to fetch him paper and inkpot to write his will, so that they 'may not err after his death', a clear reference, according to the Shīʿīs, to his intention to designate ʿAlī as his successor. But ʿUmar prevented those present from complying with the Prophet's request, arguing that 'his illness had reached a critical stage, and he has become delirious'. Another instance of his insubordination was that he twice refrained, together with Abū Bakr, from carrying out the Prophet's order to execute Ḥurqūṣ Ibn Zuhayr, whom the Prophet had found to be a renegade despite his pious appearances, and who later became a Khārijī leader. But again like Abū Bakr, ʿUmar is also censured for more fundamental reasons concerned with his legal and ritual innovations. His banning of temporary marriage (*mutʿah*) is held to be in conflict with the Qur'ān; so is his ruling that husbands could divorce their wives by 'triple repudiation', which was intended to discourage divorce, but which the Shīʿīs reject as a misinterpretation of the Qur'ānic verse on the subject. His prohibition of *tamattuʿ* (the act of performing the 'lesser pilgrimage' to Mecca until its completion, and then performing the pilgrimage proper or *Ḥajj* as a separate ceremony) and of the inclusion of the formula 'Hasten to the best act' in the call to the prayer (because of his fear that this might divert people from the duty of waging the holy war against the infidels in a sensitive period) is said to have infringed Prophetic practices. Finally, his appointment of a council of six to designate his successor is denounced both on grounds of its composition (which was weighted in favour of ʿUthmān) and of its aggravating effect on factionalism among the Muslims.[34]

The task of Shī'ī polemists is relatively easier in the case of 'Uthmān since even Sunnī opinion is divided about his Caliphal competence. In Shī'ī estimation, his gravest weakness was nepotism, shown in the appointment of his close relatives as provincial governors. The reverse of this was his oppressive attitude towards the partisans of 'Alī; it was in his time that 'Abd Allāh Ibn Mas'ūd, an outstanding Companion of the Prophet, was killed under torture, and Abū Dharr al-Ghifārī, the first 'socialist' in Muslim history, was sent into exile at Mu'āwiyah's insistence. There was thus widespread discontent against him, and his assassination took place by virtue of the consensus of the community, although 'Alī was not party to it. The Shī'īs also question 'Uthmān's record as a companion of the Prophet: they particularly point to his absence from the Prophet's campaigns at Badr and Uḥud, and from the fateful ceremony known as *Bay'at 'ar-riḍwān* at which the companions reaffirmed their allegiance to him. But like his predecessors, he is also accused of disregarding Qur'ānic injunctions, for instance, by abrogating the dispensation allowing travellers to shorten their prayer.[35]

These criticisms would probably have passed as legitimate historical appraisals had it not been for two subsequent developments. The first was that they took on an increasingly scurrilous tone, and were eventually institutionalised into the practices of *sabb* (vilification) and *rafḍ* (repudiation of the legitimacy) of the first three Caliphs. But the second development was more important: the intrusion of Iranian nationalism into the controversy, particularly in the case of 'Umar, whose Caliphate coincided with the Arab conquest of Iran, and the destruction of Sassanian–Zoroastrian culture. This was enough to assure him a high place in Iranian folk demonology. Shī'ī sources as early as the fourth/tenth century attack 'Umar's discrimination against the Iranian Muslims, and his prohibition of Arab–Iranian intermarriage, which were considered to be all the more loathsome in view of a saying attributed to the eighth Imām, 'Alī Ibn Mūsā ar-Riḍā, confirming that ever since Muḥammad's death the Iranians had been accorded a special status among Muslims.[36] Seven centuries later, the great codifier of Ṣafavīd–Shī'ī jurisprudence, Muḥammad Bāqir Majlisī (d. 1111/1700) added further ethnic spice to the debate by claiming that 'in the matter of faith, the Iranians are superior to the Arabs.' He quoted the sixth Imām, Ja'far aṣ-Ṣādiq, as having said in justification of this superiority that: 'If the Qur'ān had been revealed to the Iranians, the Arabs would not have believed in it. So it was revealed to the Arabs, and the Iranians came to believe in it.'[37] Sometimes, 'Umar's pro-Arab policies were contrasted with 'Alī's equitable treatment of the Arabs and Iranians.[38] Meanwhile, popular, Iranian nationalistic hatred of 'Umar manifested itself in numerous burlesque plays, carnivals and festivities celebrating the anniversary of his assassination (*'umar kushān*) on the twenty-sixth day of the Muslim month of *Dhu'l-ḥijjah*, or as part of the expiation for Ḥusayn's martyrdom on the tenth day of Muḥarram. They started to fall into desuetude only from the beginning of the present century, out of respect for the Sunnī Ottomans, but their traces in some folk practices and colloquial expressions die hard.[39]

There are similar objections levelled against the Prophet's favourite wife, 'Ā'ishah (whose hatred of 'Alī knew no bounds), and many other Companions, such as Ṭalḥah, Zubayr and Mu'āwiyah, although in terms of their implications for the Sunnī–Shī'ī breach, these are not as important as the repudiation of the first three Caliphs.[40] But the real issue behind such polemics goes far beyond mere Shī'ī carping at the members of the Sunnī 'Establishment'. It concerns the choice between the *naṣṣ*, or divine ordinance, and arbitrary, personal discretion. The common denominator in all the criticisms of the first three Caliphs and their followers is the accusation that by exercising their individual judgement, they all violated, ignored or tampered with clear scriptural guidelines or Prophetic practices.[41] This accusation is all the more noteworthy because it involves the only case in which the notion of 'exercising one's judgement' (*ijtihād*) is deprecated by the Shī'īs, who are otherwise its staunch exponents within the bounds of the Qur'ān and the Prophetic Tradition, as a device for the dynamic application of Islamic law to changing circumstances. So if the Shī'īs sometimes denounce the Companions, it is not because the latter exercised their individual judgement, but because they exercised it in violation of the Qur'ān and the Tradition.

To the Shī'īs, the most glaring example of this defiance is, of course, the decision of the Saqīfah assembly, which, in spite of the Prophet's previous designation of 'Alī at the Ghadīr (pool or ditch) of Khumm as his successor, elected Abū Bakr as the Caliph; all other examples are merely mentioned, on the margin of the dispute about the Ghadīr, as additional proof of the disposition of the offending Companions to violate the norms. The implicit reasoning is that if after the Prophet's death, those Companions went ahead with the election of a successor other than 'Alī, this was a misdemeanour on their behalf which fitted the general pattern of their behaviour. This raises another issue which is a corollary to the dispute about the Prophetic succession: were the Prophet's Companions endowed with any particular quality or virtue which placed them over and against the rest of the community, or were they ordinary, fallible mortals? In countering the Shī'ī criticisms of the Companions, Sunnī writers have often tended to assert that they all were men of unimpeachable character, a claim which is not easy to substantiate when one remembers that their number has been put at around twelve thousand. Moreover, the Shī'īs seize upon it as proof of the inconsistency of the Sunnīs, saying that the Sunnīs on the one hand refute the dogma of infallibility (*'iṣmah*) of the Imāms on the grounds that it confers on them superhuman status, but on the other themselves ascribe a similar quality to the Companions.[42]

The polemics are thus gradually transposed from the domain of personages to that of ideas. But to consider the ideological differences further we have to shift our standpoint and look at the Sunnī polemics which, as was noted earlier, are richer in conceptual disputation. The prime source for these is undoubtedly *Minhāj as-sunnat' an-nabawiyyah fī naqd kalām ash-shī'at 'al-qadariyyah* ('The Way of the Prophetic Tradition in the Critique of the Theology of the Qadari Shī'ism') by Ibn Taymiyyah (d. 728/1328). His arguments against Shī'ism have remained influential to this day, and have been forcefully revived in the works of modern Sunnī fundamentalists. His treatise is in reply to *Minhāj as-sunnah fī ma'rifat al-imāmah* ('the Way of the Tradition in Understanding the Imāmate') by Ḥasan Ibn Yūsuf Ibn Muṭahhar Ḥillī, known as the 'Allāmah (d. 726/(1325),[43] whose works gave an unprecedented scope to the practice of *ijtihād*, and made a major contribution to the development of the Shī'ī jurisprudential theory (*uṣūl*).[44] Although mainly concentrating on Ḥillī's exposition of Shī'ism, Ibn Taymiyyah at times directs his attacks against the Ghulāt and the Seveners (Ismā'īlīs), and occasionally lampoons the popular manifestations of Shī'ism – a device which is used in argument by many contemporary Sunnī polemists as well, ignoring the important doctrinal and practical differences between various Shī'ī sects. But Ibn Taymiyyah is at pains to point out that while the Twelver Shī'īs are only misguided Muslims, the Seveners are heretics and hypocrites.[45] His main criticisms of Shī'ism in general can be summarised as follows:

There is nothing in the Qur'ān and the Tradition to support the Shī'ī claim that the Imāmate is one of the 'pillars' of religion. How can it be otherwise when the Imām's disappearance has in practice reduced him to a useless being, unable to serve any of the worldly and other-worldly interests of the Muslims? The hidden Imām has now been absent for more than four hundred years. The anticipation of his return has produced nothing but false hopes, sedition and corrupt practices among certain groups of Muslims. Obeying God and the Prophet is enough to entitle every Muslim to Paradise (Qur'ān, 4:13, 69). By requiring obedience to a hidden Imām whom no one can see, hear or communicate with, Shī'ism imposes a duty on Muslims above their capacity – an impossibility in view of God's justness. The doctrine of the Imāmate thus aims at creating a regime which it is impossible to achieve.[46]

The belief that 'Alī was the rightful successor to the Prophet on the basis of the divine ordinance (*naṣṣ*) carries absurd implications which are particularly damaging to the principle of divine justice. If God really did designate 'Alī as the Prophet's successor, He must also have known in His omniscience that He was thus appointing to the Caliphate a man who was not going to enjoy the total allegiance of the community and whose rule was going to lead to a civil war. If this assumption is true, it then follows that God and the Prophet committed a gross injustice against the Muslims, which is again absurd.[47]

Equally untenable is the doctrine of *'ilm*, in the sense of the special knowledge inherited by 'Alī's descendants from Muḥammad, endowing them with the unique capacity of perceiving the 'branches' or subsidiary rules (*furū'*) of religion. Since at the time of Muḥammad's death, only 'Alī was of an age appropriate for the acquisition of sophisticated religious knowledge from the Prophet (his two sons Ḥasan and Ḥusayn were still minors), 'Alī's descendants could inherit this knowledge only in one of two ways: either by receiving it from their elders, in which case any Muslim, whether Hāshimid or non-Hāshimid, could have received it from the same source; or through revelation, which is impossible because this is a privilege exclusive to the prophets. If it is claimed that 'Alī's descendants obtained this knowledge by diligence and hard work, the answer is that there were many Sunnī Muslims as well who were equally diligent and hard-working, and some of them were in fact more knowledgeable than the 'Alīds (for instance, Mālik, Awzā'ī, Shāfi'ī and Ibn Ḥanbal were more learned than their contemporary Shī'ī Imāms, Mūsā Ibn Ja'far, 'Alī Ibn Mūsā and Muḥammad Ibn 'Alī).[48]

The Shī'īs, continues Ibn Taymiyyah, confuse the issue of the power to rule with that of the competence to rule. If the Sunnīs pay allegiance to their rulers, this does not mean that they deny the competence or virtues of other claimants to rulership, it simply means that those rulers are capable of administering Muslim affairs *by virtue of their power* (*shawkah*), whereas others are not. Nor does this allegiance mean that the rulers should be obeyed absolutely in all matters. Rather, they should be obeyed only in so far as they themselves obey God and the Prophet, and enforce religious tenets. For the Sunnīs, the Amīr (prince), Imām or Caliph is the person who has the power to fulfil the purpose of his leadership, just as a prayer-leader is the man who says prayers for others, and is followed by them, not the man who says a prayer only for himself, but in theory is worthy of being a leader.[49] For this reason, Sunnī realism which recognises the legitimacy of powerful, competent rulers is preferable to Shī'ī idealism which, craving the ascendancy of an inaccessible leader, can only be conducive to anarchy.

Ibn Taymiyyah does not bother to comment on the other aspect of the doctrine of the 'special knowledge' of the Imām, namely his supposed ability to predict future events. But both aspects of the doctrine can only be meaningfully studied within the larger notion of *'iṣmah*, the Imām's infallibility and impeccability, about which Ibn Taymiyyah is inexplicably curt. All he has to say is that the Shī'īs' belief in *'iṣmah* flows from their ignorance or whim, without adducing any reason in support of his assertion.[50] But it is easy enough to infer the Sunnī position on this issue from his other pronouncements, as well as from the arguments of other medieval critics of *'iṣmah*, notably the Shāfi'ī Qāḍī 'Abd al-Jabbār al-Hamadānī (d. 415/1025). To make a convincing case for the *'iṣmah* of the Imāms, the Sunnīs justly remark, is impossible without claiming for them a state higher than that of ordinary men. The only individuals one might consider as holders of such a status are God's emissaries; but even the *'iṣmah* of this category of men is a controversial point, let alone that of

ʿAlī and his descendants. Besides, ʿAbd al-Jabbār argues that if one admits the necessity of the *ʿiṣmah* for the Imāms on the ground that God's benevolence (*luṭf*) towards His creatures will not be complete without the flawless leadership of the Imāms after the Prophet's death, one should on the same grounds admit it for other groups of men. There are other areas of social life which would function ideally only if their agents were immune against error and sin. For instance, the entire structure of the Islamic legal system depends on the truthful testimony of witnesses whether for concluding marriage contracts, or examining accusations of theft or adultery against individuals, and so on. Why not lay down the necessity of *ʿiṣmah* in their case too?[51] The point has been carried to its absurd extremes by a Sunnī polemist of the twelfth century who says that 'for the Shīʿīs even the crow should possess *ʿiṣmah*', otherwise its untimely cawing would cause people to wake up, and say their prayers at the wrong time![52]

In addition to the fundamental principles, Ibn Taymiyyah denounces what he calls the Shīʿī 'follies and superstitions', by which he means certain popular beliefs and practices: for instance, the Shīʿīs' refusal to name their children after the names of the first three Caliphs and their reluctance even to have any dealings with men called by these names; their adulation of certain places as likely sites for the reappearance of the hidden Imām;[53] and their exercise of *taqiyyah* which 'makes them speak with their tongue contrary to what is in their hearts'.[54] In the same class of practices he includes the practices of levelling the graves and hanging down the hands in prayer.[55]

These invectives are not, of course, left unanswered by the Shīʿīs. But it will not serve any useful purpose to carry on examining the exchanges between the two sides in the major polemical works of later periods, since they are all variations on the same themes. Any important difference among them is a matter of style and approach, rather than of substance. Thus, on the Sunnī side, while ʿAbd al-Jabbār's *al-Mughnī* ('Summa') is a work of the highest intellectual standard, blending a rationalist outlook with consummate dialectical skill, Ibn Jawzī's *Talbīs Iblīs* ('The Deception of Satan') is a dreary indictment of heterodox sects in Islam. Similarly, on the Shīʿī side, Ḥillī's scholastic *Minhāj* should be contrasted with ʿAbd al-Jalīl Qazvīnī's *Kitāb an-Naqḍ* ('The Book of Rebuttal'), a spirited treatise aimed at scoring debating points rather than formulating a creed.

While controversy was raging at all these levels, attempts were also made at solving sectarian differences. One such attempt was made by the Kubrawiyyah, a Ṣūfī order of the thirteenth and fourteenth centuries, shortly after the Mongol invasion. It is to M. Molé that we owe the account of the essential teachings of the order in this respect.[56] The founder of the order, Najm ud-Dīn Kubrā, who was killed by the Mongols in 618/1226, and all his disciples were Sunnīs – perhaps with the exception of Saʿd ud-Dīn Ḥamūyah, who is said to have been a Shīʿī. Foreshadowing the grand scheme of some of his disciples for the unity of Muslims of all persuasions is a dream related to Najm ud-Dīn himself, in which the Prophet is portrayed as being flanked on his right by Abū Bakr, 'Umar, Uthmān and 'Alī, and on his left by Ibn 'Abbās and the *Qurrā'*, while behind him are seated the Ṣūfī shaykhs, and the founders of the principal Sunnī rites, such as Abū Ḥanīfah, Mālik, Shāfi'ī.[57]

That Ṣūfism was made the medium for bringing the two sects together was natural enough. With its theoretical aversion to bigotry and prejudice, its exaltation of tolerance and humility as virtues necessitated by the patient quest for the Truth or Right, and its inherent dislike of any doctrinal regimentation, Ṣūfism has always been an ideal framework for such exercises. Moreover, the destruction of the Sunnī Caliphate by the Mongols had created something in the nature of an ideological vacuum which could only work to the benefit of unorthodox movements. This may be one explanation for the Shī'ī infiltration of the Ilkhānīd court, highlighted by Naṣīr ud-Dīn Ṭūsī's ministry under Hūlāgū, and Khudā Bandih Uljaytū's conversion to Shī'īsm. In any case, the absence of an official creed appears to have brought about a favourable psychological atmosphere for the sort of irenic campaign launched by the Kubrawiyyah. The method they employed for their purpose was that favoured by most confessional peacemakers: eclecticism. Thus 'Alā' ud-Dawlah Simnānī, a prominent disciple of Najm ud-Dīn, combined in his teachings benign rebukes to the quarrelling sects, with convenient gleanings from their principles towards the creation of a Sunnī–Shī'ī synthesis. While condemning the Shī'īs' vilification of the Prophet's Companions, he confirmed the authenticity of the Ghadīr story about the Prophet's designation of 'Alī as his successor, and maintained that 'Alī had a greater right to the Prophetic succession than the first three Caliphs because he combined in himself the three qualities of successorship (*khilāfah*), heirdom (*wirāthah*), and Friendship of God (*walāyah*). He likewise expressed deep attachment to other members of the Prophet's 'House'. Another indication of his intermediary position can be noted in his frequent quotations from the *Nahj al-balāghah*, a collection of maxims attributed to 'Alī, not in defence of Shī'ī theses, but to refute Shī'ī extremism.[58]

Adoration of 'Alī and 'Members of the House' has been a shared characteristic of many Ṣūfī orders. What gives it a particular significance in the case of the Kubrawiyyah is its merging with a strong plea for Sunnī–Shī'ī peace. Pro-'Alīd tendencies, however, became more marked in the doctrines of Najm ud-Dīn's followers, 'Alī Hamadānī, Isḥāq Khatlānī and most important of all, Muḥammad Nūrbakhsh, under whom the order veered towards Shī'īsm. By virtue of his supposed descent from the seventh Imām of the Twelver Shī'īs, Mūsā al-Kāẓim, Nūrbakhsh received the title of al-Mahdī, and was proclaimed Caliph by some of his followers. These pretensions alarmed the ruling monarch, the Taymūrid Shāh-rukh, who ordered Nūrbakhsh to be imprisoned on several occasions.[59] In his formal teachings, Nūrbakhsh also tried to strike a balance between Sunnīsm and Shī'īsm. For instance, on the theory of the Imāmate, he differentiated between what he called the 'conditions of the Imām, and his 'attributes'. The conditions are the same *a posteriori* prerequisites mentioned by the Sunnī jurists with reference to the 'Abbāsid Caliphs (masculinity, majority, wisdom, Qurayshī descent, etc.). But the 'attributes' or bases (*arkān*) are evidently those of the Shī'ī Imāms (descent from Fāṭimah, knowledge, piety and generosity).[60] Similarly, his view about the mystic unity of men with God purports to make it less offensive to orthodox taste by interpreting it in metaphorical terms, through the analogy of 'iron in the fire': so long as the iron is in the fire, it can truthfully say, 'I am the fire'. Once it is withdrawn from the fire, it would be lying if it made the same claim.[61] In the same manner, the prophets and Friends of God (*awlīyā*) can assume God's attributes while they are in a state of ecstasy, but this does not mean that they become identical with God. But in spite of the conciliatory tone of many such doctrines, it seems that with the death of Nūrbakhsh in 869/1464, the Kubrawī dream of Muslim unity also ended, perhaps because in his person, the movement had become too closely associated with the messianic connotations of Shī'īsm. Besides, the rise of the Ṣafavīd state, which made Shī'īsm the official creed of Iran in 1502, intensified sectarian recrimination. The systematisation of Shī'ī jurisprudence, theology and philosophy – a gradual, but relentless process which lasted till the very end of the Ṣafavīd period – elevated the Shī'īs' sense of self-confidence and identity to a level unprecedented since Buyid times. Against the background of ideological rigidity, and Iran's wars with the Ottoman state, any suggestion of a Sunnī–Shī'ī dialogue, still more of a conciliation, could be no more than wishful thinking. Relations between the two communities deteriorated so much that the Sunnīs now, contrary to Ibn Taymiyyah's differentiated judgement on the varieties of Shī'īsm quoted earlier, considered the Shī'īs as outright infidels. This is clearly shown by an exchange of letters between the Shī'ī 'Ulamā' of Khurāsān and the Sunnī 'Ulamā' of Transoxiana following the Uzbek invasion of Mashhad at the beginning of Shāh 'Abbās's reign. In reply to the Shī'īs' protest at the encirclement of Mashhad, and the destruction and pillaging of its surrounding fields by the Uzbek 'Abdullāh Khān, and his son 'Abdul Mu'min Khān, the Sunnī 'Ulamā' declared that by their persistent vilification of the first three Caliphs the Shī'īs had forfeited their status as Muslims; it was therefore quite legitimate for the Sunnī rulers to wage war against them, and destroy or confiscate their belongings.[62]

Little wonder, then, that the next significant step towards Sunnī–Shī'ī understanding was taken almost three centuries after the death of Nūrbakhsh, in the interregnum between the Sunnī Afghans' overthrow of the Ṣafavīd regime, and the emergence of the Qājār dynasty at the end of the eighteenth century. This time, the initiative was taken by a Shī'ī monarch, Nādir Shāh, the founder of the short-lived Afshārid state in Iran. Exhaustion from more than a decade of anarchy and bloodshed caused by the Sunnī–Shī'ī strife which accompanied the Afghan invasion of Iran and the destruction of the Ṣafavīd state, was good enough reason for this initiative. But as Hamid Algar has shown,[63] there were possibly political motives behind it too: Nādir's ambitions to rule over an empire extending beyond Iran's frontiers, his need to maintain the loyalty of his troops who were mostly Sunnīs, while offsetting the effects of the continued, 'religiously motivated loyalty' of many Iranians to the Ṣafavīds as legitimate rulers of Iran, and the advisability of achieving a *modus vivendi* with the Ottomans. But however lofty his political ambitions may have been, his scheme for Sunnī–Shī'ī reconciliation, unlike that conceived by the Kubrawiyyah, was modest enough. It took the form of a twofold campaign, internal and external.

Internally, Nādir strove to put an end to those Shī'ī practices which perhaps more than any other aspect of Shī'īsm were provocative to the Sunnīs: *sabb*, public vilification of the first three Caliphs, and *rafḍ'* repudiation of the legitimacy of their Caliphate. These he formally prohibited, condemning them as 'vain and vulgar words' which cast discord and enmity among Muslims. Next, he tried to turn Shī'īsm into a mere school of law, shorn of its esoteric Imāmology. He therefore proposed that 'the separate identity and name of the Shī'ī *madhhab*' be abandoned, while 'part of its substance – that relating to *furū'āt* (branches of the law) be retained and renamed after Imām Ja'far aṣ-Ṣādiq'[64] the sixth Imām, the principal codifier of Shī'ī jurisprudence. In practice, this meant that Ja'far aṣ-Ṣādiq be treated on a par with the founders of the four Sunnī legal schools, so that there could be no doctrinal obstacle in Shī'īsm being eventually incorporated into Sunnī Islam.

Externally, Nādir demanded that the Ottoman Government, as the representative of Sunnī Islam, recognise Shī'īsm in its new garb, as the Ja'farī *madhhab*, and then give substance to this recognition by several practical steps: the erection at Ka'bah of a fifth *maqām* (ritual place) for the Shī'īs as the outward sign of the acceptance of their school on a par with the four Sunnī schools; the appointment of an *Amīr al-ḥājj* (pilgrimage leader) to accompany Iranian pilgrims travelling to Mecca by way of Damascus; the release of all prisoners taken during wars with Iran; and the exchange of ambassadors.

There was immediate opposition to Nādir's redefinition of Shī'īsm from those Iranian 'Ulamā' who justifiably considered that it destroyed the very essence of Shī'īsm by reducing it to a mere corpus of legal niceties. This opposition was ruthlessly suppressed by measures characteristic of the Nādirī style of government – execution of the chief Mullā, Mīrzā 'Abd al-Ḥusayn, and the confiscation of the endowments attached to the mosques and religious schools in Iṣfahān. But the whole project of a rapprochement with Sunnīsm foundered on the reaction of the Ottoman Government, which under the pressure of Sunnī 'Ulamā' rejected its principal points; the only positive element in its response was approval of

Nādir's prohibition of *sabb* and *rafḍ*! The episode ended with Nādir's assassination in 1747.[65]

From that year until the second half of the nineteenth century, when Islamic modernism appeared on the scene, no other attempt was made at reconciliation – at least none that was comparable, either in its political dimensions, or in its intellectual ingenuity, with those made by the Kubrawiyyah or Nādir. The climate was made even more inimical, if anything, for such efforts by the rise of Wahhābism in Arabia towards the end of the eighteenth century. Superimposing on Ḥanbalī rigorism a puritan militancy seeking to root out all 'innovations' in Islam, Wahhābism represented the greatest fundamentalist challenge to Shīʿism since the beginning of Islam. Although confined to a minority feared and denounced by most Sunnīs, its excesses, particularly the ravaging of the Shīʿī shrines, aroused lasting passions among the Shīʿīs, rendering them even more diligent in jealously guarding their separate identity.

* * *

On the face of it, the failure of the attempts described so far at Sunnī–Shīʿī reconciliation was caused by the stubborn refusal of one side or the other, for political or confessional reasons, to compromise on what it held to be an eternal principle. But whenever not simply actuated by mundane political calculations, this refusal was itself the effect of a much more profound and damaging disability – the sclerosis of religious thinking. So long as the exponents of both sects treated their received prejudices as revealed truths, there could be no real prospect of a reconciliation. This sclerosis was reflected primarily in the rarity of serious dialogue between the controversialists. More significantly, it was reflected in the absence of that imperceptible outcome of any dialogue which is the interpenetration of ideas and the slow transformation of a hitherto immutable system of thought through exposure to another system.

That is why, with modernistic trends gaining ground among religious circles in the Muslim world from the middle of the nineteenth century onwards, the barriers between Sunnīs and Shīʿīs gradually became less insuperable, allowing a good many cross-sectarian currents. The new situation held great promise, if not for concord, then at least for the diminution of age-old animosities. There were several reasons for this. First, in the altered moulds of political loyalties, the idea of the nation-state was replacing religious devotion as the ruling civic virtue of the modern age. This in itself had a dampening effect on sectarian divergences. Secondly, Islamic unity being one of the cardinal articles of their faith, the leaders of the first generation of Islamic modernists, notably Jamāl ad-Dīn Asad-ābādī (Afghānī) (d. 1897) and Muḥammad ʿAbduh (d. 1905), made strong pleas by Sunnī – Shīʿī unity. Of the two, Asad-ābādī was the more consitent, mainly because his own background was steeped in both Sunnī and Shīʿī traditions and because of his 'statelessness' he could afford to preach supra-confessional tolerance. ʿAbduh, having been brought up in a solidly Sunnī environment, could not conceal his dislike of heterodox movements, especially those instigated by the Iranians in early Islam.[66] This tendency became more pronounced in his disciple, Muḥammad Rashīd Riḍā, who, although committed to the modernists' ideal of Islamic unity, parted company with many of them by making anti-Shīʿīsm a major trait of his school, the *Salafiyyah*, after failing in his efforts to induce a Sunnī–Shīʿī conciliation.[67]

Third, unity was necessitated by other principles of modernism as well. Rationalism, which governed the better part of the modernist reformulation of the Islamic spiritual heritage, called for release from narrow parochial values in the interests of the universally applicable findings of reason: just as the Qur'ānic unitarian teachings liberated the Arabs from tribalism, Islamic modernism was expected to dissolve all sectarian bonds. The fight against Western domination too required the unity of all Muslims, irrespective of their subsidiary beliefs. It was therefore expedient to tolerate and even support heterodox trends in so far as they contributed to the anti-imperialist struggle. Thus Asad-ābādī called on the Indian Muslims to demonstrate in favour of the Mahdī of Sudan, even if his standing as a real Mahdī was dubious, because this united them in their fight against the British. But in the same breath, Asad-ābādī refuted the Qādīyānī reformist movement in India, because of its alliance with the British.[68]

Later, in the twentieth century, politics exercised further pacifying influence on the relations between the two communities through another development. This was the creation of multi-confessional states, particularly Lebanon and Iraq, whose political structure depended on the Sunnī–Shīʿī symbiosis. Preserving a minimum of mutual tolerance now became not so much a requirement of Islamic solidarity as a practical necessity. Equally restraining considerations stemmed from the diplomatic exigencies of maintaining normal and friendly relations between states with predominantly opposing confessional majorities. Thus the Saudi Arabs who in the eighteenth century considered the Shīʿīs as miscreants, and desecrated their shrines in Iraq, now not only treat the Shīʿī Iranians at least officially, as equal Muslims, but are also tolerant of their own Shīʿī subjects.

Islamic modernism, as construed by ʿAbduh's disciples, rapidly became identified with Sunnī Islam – and this in spite of their intention to make it a movement transcending all sectarian divergences. Its counterpart among the Shīʿīs started under different circumstances, and took a different form, which we shall survey in Chapter 5. But here also the modernists were agreed on the necessity of united action against the West. This was vividly illustrated by the attitude of the Shīʿī ʿUlamā' of Iraq, who, during the First World War, exhorted their followers to wage war against the British under the Ottoman flag, while in principle they considered the Ottoman rulers to be no more than 'usurpers' (*mughtaṣibūn*). They also led the national uprising in Iraq in 1920 against the British mandate, thereby forging closer links between the two sects.[69]

But the most ironical display of Shī'ī solidarity with the Sunnīs took place over the issue of the Caliphate – namely the very issue that had originally set the two communities apart. When in 1922 – as will be explained in the following chapter – Mustapha Kemal's drive to establish a modern state threatened the institution of the Caliphate in his country, the Sunnī Muslims outside Turkey, particularly in India, were greatly alarmed. But their concern was conveyed to the Turkish Government by two Indian Shī'īs – Sayyid Amīr 'Alī, and the leader of the 'extremist' Ismā'īlī sect, the Āghā Khān. After the abolition of the Caliphate in 1924, the Shī'īs kept up their campaign of solidarity: they took an active part in the Jerusalem Congress of 1931, held to discuss matters of common concern to all Muslims – including the fate of the Caliphate. In addition to the Yemeni delegate (the only ruling prince attending the Congress), the Shī'ī 'Ulamā' of Iraq sent an accredited representative; two Iranian Shī'īs attended, and the Muftī of the Shī'īs of Syria sent a message of sympathy. If one excepts the abortive Sunnī–Shī'ī consultations under Nādir, Gibb's remark in *Whither Islam?* is an apt description of the significance of this event. 'Never before in Islamic history,' he says, 'have the Sunnī and Shiites met together to deliberate on common problems, and while on the one hand the fact may be taken to illustrate the weakening of religious inhibition in political life, it no less truly indicates a growing realisation of the common interest of all Moslems in the modern world.'

Although Islamic modernism failed to realise most of its principal aims, its least achievement was to remove many of the inhibitions and taboos which prevented Muslim intellectuals from verifying the sources of conventional views. Owing to this factor, as well as the relative enlightenment induced by the advancement in educational standards, and growing contact with the outside world, Sunnī–Shī'ī controversy also started to be viewed in a different light. Some Sunnī writers studied the controversy less in a spirit of sectarian self-righteousness than as part of a critical reassessment of Islamic history. In this, they were largely influenced by the judgements of Western orientalists. The comments of the Egyptian Aḥmad Amīn (d. 1954), author of a multi-volume history of the Muslim civilisation since its earliest times, has drawn the widest response from Shī'ī apologists. Much of the style and content of the Sunnī–Shī'ī controversy in the present century has been determined by his attacks on Shī'īsm, which, contrary to those by such orthodox critics as Maḥmūd Ālūsī and Rashīd Riḍā, signify heavy borrowing from Western sources, and sometimes an uncritical acceptance of the views of authors such as Dozy and Wellhausen. To be sure, on most issues Amīn follows well-trodden paths, repeating the arguments of the traditionists: that vilification of the first three Caliphs is both blasphemous and an upshot of prejudice; that adulation of the members of the Prophet's house and the notion of the Imāmate as an inherited office run counter to many Qur'ānic verses teaching that only good deeds, and not descent, should determine the social grading of men; that the doctrine of '*iṣmah* is a replica of the Sassanian myth of kingship;[70] and that Shī'īsm has served as a refuge for 'all those who wanted to destroy Islam out of rancour and enmity, and wanted to inject into it the teachings of their forefathers, from Judaism, Christianity, Zoroastrianism and Hinduism.'[71] Oddly enough, the main difference between Amīn's sweeping condemnations, and Ibn Taymiyyah's strictures of Shī'īsm is that Amīn barely differentiates between moderate and extremist Shī'īs.

Amīn tries to simplify a complicated debate on these points by reducing the exclusive features of Shī'īsm, as against Sunnīsm, to four major principles: *'iṣmah*, Mahdīsm, *taqiyyah*, and the Return (*raj'ah*) of the Imām. Beneath most of Amīn's observations on these four issues lie the criteria of a modern, liberal mind. He objects to the Shī'ī theory of the Imāmate, not because he disbelieves the authenticity of the Ghadīr tradition (which, as he admits, is accepted even by some Sunnī historians), but because it violates the modern conceptions of democracy. 'In Shī'ī eyes,' he says 'the Imām is beyond any reproach. His nature and actions put him above the people. He is both the legislator and executor, but is never questioned over what he does. He is the measure of good and evil: what he does is good, what he forbids is evil. He is the spiritual leader, his spiritual authority being superior to that of the Pope in the Catholic Church. So, prayer, fasting, paying alms, and pilgrimage are of no avail without devotion to the Imām, just as the [good] deeds of an infidel are futile, until he believes in God and his Emissary.' The most harmful result of such a political theory is that it stultifies Man's critical powers, killing in him any inclination to rise up against injustice and corruption: 'Shī'īsm thus paralyses reason and deadens the mind, conferring on the Caliph, or Imām, or the Sulṭān, limitless powers; so he can do whatever he wills, and nobody has the right to protest, let alone to rebel, against him, nor claim having suffered injustice, because justice lies with the Imām.' The Shī'ī doctrine, claims Amīn, is thus the antithesis of true democracy, which establishes the 'sovereignty for the people, in the interest of the people, and assesses all actions against the criterion of reason, and makes the Caliph, the Imām and the King the servants of the people, so that the day they do not serve them, they cease to deserve remaining in authority'.[72] Amīn likewise disclaims the Shī'ī Mahdist ideas for their practical results, in 'leading people's minds astray, subjugating them to absurdities', and provoking successive upheavals in Islamic history, with the masses rallying in every age to a person claiming to be the Mahdī, causing the disintegration of the Islamic state, and the demise of its power.[73]

On the Shī'ī practice of *taqiyyah*, much reviled by the Sunnīs in the past as well as present, Amīn is surprisingly less critical, describing it merely as an expedient method used by the Imāms either to ensure the survival of their followers under hostile regimes, or to mobilise them in secrecy for revolts against the Caliphs. He also contrasts it with the Khawārij's vaunting of their opinions in the face of their foes because they invariably put their faith above everything else: most of Khawārij held that if a man saying his prayer saw another man stealing his property he should not disrupt his prayer to catch the thief. More significantly, he admits that the Sunnīs too have practised *taqiyyah* – though with a difference: for them, a Muslim who fears that his life may be in danger because of his faith should do all in his power to migrate to another land; only when this proves impossible should he practise *taqiyyah*, but strictly 'to the extent that is necessary'.[74]

As can be seen, Amīn's criticisms of Shīʿīsm are in essence different from those made by the medieval Sunnī polemists. This is perhaps to be expected. But what is more noteworthy is that – as was hinted earlier – they are also different from the line taken by such contemporary Sunnī writers as Rashīd Riḍā, Ālūsī, and many others who are still absorbed in ritual and legal squabbles. By contrast, Amīn's remarks are addressed to issues of a broader concern: the relationship between the rulers and the ruled, the rights of subjects to protest and revolt against tyrannical rulers, and the impact of religious beliefs on political culture.

The Shīʿī response to this new brand of critique is accordingly a mixture of theological hair-splitting and macro-politics. While some authors repeat the same old arguments, albeit supported by freshly culled evidence, others try to grapple with the larger questions raised by their creed in the relationship between the individual and the state. There is a fairly neat discrepancy between the educational background of the first group and that of the second: the former, which may be identified by the adjective *scholastic*, is stoutly traditionist both in its mentality and methodology, while the latter, the 'revisionist' or 'semi-revisionist', matches a thorough grounding in Islamic culture with either a formal training, or a serious interest, in one or other of the modern sciences. Among the 'scholastic' authors, the best known are ʿAbd al-Ḥusayn Sharaf ad-Dīn al-Musawī, the leader of the Shīʿī community in the Lebanon until his death in 1958 (and succeeded in 1961 by Mūsā aṣ-Ṣadr), noted both for his scholarship and active participation in the nationalist struggle against the French mandate;[75] the Iraqi-born Muḥammad Ḥusayn Kāshif al-Ghiṭā', distinguished by his conciliatory views on the dispute with the Sunnīs;[76] and the Iranian ʿAbd al-Ḥusayn Amīnī, whose thirteen-volume *Al-ghadīr* contains one of the most detailed contemporary accounts of the Shīʿī case for ʿAlī, and its related problems.[77] Among the representatives of the 'revisionist' or 'semi-revisionist' group, one must particularly mention Muḥammad Jawād Mạghnīyah, a prolific Lebanese scholar and writer,[78] and two more Iranians: Murtaḍā Muṭahharī (d. 1979), an original thinker and one of the intellectual leaders of the Iranian Islamic Revolution of 1978–9 and ʿAlī Sharīʿatī (d. 1977), a French-educated sociologist whose widely read books now constitute the ideology of Islamic radicalism.[79]

Many strands of Shīʿī modernism are traceable to the response of these authors to current Sunnī criticisms. However, though the credit for this should go largely to the 'revisionists', the 'scholastics' too should have a share in it because of their efforts to make known the wealth of untapped classical material which has led to a better understanding of Shī'ī history and culture. Thanks to both groups, a whole new range of the key Shī'ī beliefs which have always been targets of Sunnī attacks – on the Imām's infallibility, the nature of his guardianship (*wilāyah*) as distinct from his friendship with God (*walāyah*), the practice of dissimulation, the doctrine of Mahdism, the meaning of anticipation of his Return and the significance of martyrdom – have been redefined or reasserted, with an eye to the impression they would make on the critic, the sceptic, and the uninitiated. These are points which will be discussed in another chapter, so here we content ourselves only with explaining a few important ramifications of Shī'ī modernism in relation to Sunnīsm.

There is now a clear tendency among most Shī'ī authors to tone down the criticisms of the first three Caliphs. Even when such criticisms are repeated, the vilification of these men is condemned both as a sin against Qur'ān (6 : 108), and disruptive of Islamic unity. Conventional criticisms are refined by separating the case of Abū Bakr and 'Umar from that of 'Uthmān, with the more severe objections levelled against the latter, on the grounds that, first, he was an Umayyad, and could therefore be presumed to have had good cause to act maliciously towards the 'Alīds, and, second, he pursued a 'racialist' policy by allowing his tribal preferences to dominate his political appointments.[80] Fairness is occasionally shown towards Abū Bakr and 'Umar by admitting that their 'political integrity' could not be doubted, and 'Umar in particular is praised for his contributions to the expansion of the young Islamic state through military conquests.[81] None of these concessions are, however, allowed to blunt the main accusation against all of them – that they committed a grave offence by denying 'Alī's right to be Muḥammad's immediate successor.

Conversely, the arguments in support of extolling 'Alī and his descendants have been reshaped, with the emphasis plainly shifting from their supernatural to the more down-to-earth qualities. The Imāms are now more often admired for their statesmanship ('Alī),[82] political realism (Ḥasan),[83] and revolutionary foresight (Ḥusayn),[84] even aṣ-Ṣādiq's aloofness from politics is shown to have judicious political considerations behind it.[85] As regards the Imāms' supernatural qualities (infallibility, foreknowledge, etc.), these are said to be indicative, not of their social and political superiority over other Muslims, but merely their worthiness of a higher station in the hereafter; in the sensible world, all the faithful are equal, and any superiority is due, not to supernatural qualities, but to pious deeds.[86]

Differences with the Sunnīs are played down as secondary issues which arise from the legitimate diversity of opinions (*ikhtilāf*). The Sunnīs are assured that if some Shī'īs, including such towering authorities as Kulaynī, have contradicted their creed, this should not be taken as the universal view of Shī'īs, just as if some Sunnīs are hostile toward the members of the Prophet's House, the Shī'īs should not take this as indicative of the opinion of all the Sunnīs.

Islamic unity is cherished as an ideal which at times appears to transcend all differences of creed, however fundamental these may be. Even if one dismisses the Shī'īs' protestations of loyalty to this ideal as empty rhetoric, one cannot deny their significance in view of the Shī'īs' élitist statements in earlier periods, which seem to indicate a contrary desire to uphold doctrinal probity as a more noble value than expedient unity. Whereas before the Shī'īs took pride in their isolation from the erring majority, there is now a growing wish among them to overcome their centuries-old aversion to "swimming with the tide", and join hands with their co-religionists in the struggle against common external enemies.

If the changing attitude towards the Sunnīs has acted as one of the factors of Shī'ī modernism, with the Sunnīs the reverse is very much true: here, modernism has stimulated a re-evaluation of the pristine notions about all 'heterodox' sects, including Shī'īsm. For the Shī'īs, any rethinking was bound, sooner or later, to touch upon their disagreements with the majority sect, disagreements which are all bound up with the *raison d'être* of Shī'īsm. For the Sunnīs, rethinking implied no inescapable necessity of an excursus into the relationship with the 'heterodox' sects, at least not in the beginning, since its most pressing concern was a frontal assault on the problems posed by modernisation. Apart from the affirmation of Islamic unity as an overriding objective shared with all other Muslims, Sunnī modernism has brought about a change in two essential areas of religious thinking – first, on the principle of *ijtihād*, or the exercise of individual judgement, and second, on the relevance of the past (history) to the problem facing Islam today.

We saw before that *ijtihād* was one of the causes of dispute, because the Shī'īs hold it to be not only permissible, but also a permanent, imperative duty of the learned as the principal means of extracting the religious rules from the Qur'ān, the Tradition and the consensus, while the Sunnīs have repudiated it ever since the ninth century as an aberration leading to intellectual disarray and legal void. The teachings of Asad-ābādī (Afghānī), 'Abduh, Muḥammad Iqbāl and other modernists on the necessity of reconstructing Muslim thought gradually generated an atmosphere in which *ijtihād* could rid itself of much of the opprobrium formerly attached to it. Later, the advent of state ideologies requiring the orthodox legitimisation for public acceptance became another contributory factor: governments put pressure on the 'Ulamā' to justify the various reforms they were carrying out in the name of nationalism or socialism, and the 'Ulamā' could give their blessings to such reforms, which violated the traditional sanctity of ownership, the standing of women, and the jurisdiction of religious courts, only by seeking the liberating intervention of *ijtihād*.[87] A convergence has thus slowly taken shape between the positions of both sides, and, in theory, the Shī'īs should now draw comfort from the Sunnīs' conversion to their view that *ijtihād* is indispensable to the proper understanding of the religious rules. But this may be merely a superficial impression. So long as the two sects differ among themselves about two of the four sources of these rules, with the Sunnīs believing in analogy and consensus, and the Shī'īs rejecting analogy in favour of reason, and making the validity of the consensus dependent on its inclusion of the Imām, admission of the merits of *ijtihād* is by itself of no consequence. (There is apparently no dispute about the other two sources, the Qur'ān and the Tradition, but these too can give rise to discord, because of the disagreement over the first two – i.e. analogy or reason, and consensus – as well as over the methods of the interpretation of the Qur'ān, and authentification of the Tradition.)

The second change, namely the reassessment of past history, has posed an equally potent challenge to the intellectual resources of Sunnīsm. The hallmark of all innovative thought in contemporary Sunnīs has indeed been a critical reviewing of the past, with the intention of identifying factual inaccuracies, false premises and unwarranted generalisations governing the Sunnī judgement on some of the outstanding figures of Islamic history. This type of rewriting of Islamic history is usually associated with the name of the Egyptian scholar and critic Ṭāhā Ḥusayn, who has always emphasised his 'Cartesian' approach to the sources.[88] Its most tangible result has been a fairly objective reappraisal of both the positive and negative deeds of men like Abū Bakr and 'Umar, whose behaviour was always supposed to be impeccable, but is now subjected to the incisive scrutiny of an increasing number of writers – religious as well as secular.[89] It denotes a marked retreat from the time-honoured Sunnī axiom that all the Prophet's Companions had unimpeachable characters. The other outcome of this revision of the past has been a romanticisation of early Islamic history, from which the familiar heroes of both Sunnīsm and Shī'īsm have benefited, because it depicts not only personages like Abū Bakr and 'Umar but also Ḥasan, Ḥusayn and Fāṭimah as the archetypes of progressive Muslims.

The revival of *ijtihād* and the new school of historical revisionism among the Sunnīs have affected the Sunnī–Shī'ī dialogue by encouraging individual initiative for effecting some measure of reconciliation. In February 1959, the official review of the University-Mosque of al-Azhar in Cairo published a *fatwā* (opinion or responsum) by its Rector, Shaykh Maḥmūd Shaltūt, authorising instruction in Shī'ī jurisprudence. This was tantamount to the recognition of Shī'īsm as on an equal footing with the four orthodox legal schools in Sunnīsm. When Shaltūt gave his *fatwā*, Shī'ī studies had been absent from the curriculum of that university for over nine hundred years. Although al-Azhar was created in 361/972 by an Ismā'īlī Shī'ī, the Fāṭimid Caliph al-Mu'izz, two centuries later the Sunnī

Ayyūbīds turned it into a centre of orthodox scholarship. Thus rather than constituting a simple case of curriculum reform, Shaltūt's *fatwā* indicated a major psychological breakthrough.

Under the title 'Islam, the religion of unity', the *fatwā* is prefaced by two arguments in its justification, one historical, the other pragmatic. The historical argument is a reminder of the spirit of mutual respect and tolerance which permeated the relationship between the legal schools in early Islam. At that time, says Shaltūt, *ijtihād* was a source of plurality of ideas, but not discord, because the different schools were united by their belief in the paramount authority of the Qur'ān and the Tradition. The motto of the founders of all schools was: 'When a *ḥadīth* is proved authentic, it is my opinion; 'and do not care at all for my word' (*iḍribu bi-qawlī 'urḍ al-ḥā'iṭ*).' This enabled all groups to co-operate with one another – the Sunnīs among themselves, on the one hand, and the Sunnīs with the Shīʿīs, on the other – for the development of Islamic jurisprudence as a whole. It is obvious that in this argument, Shāltūt is using the term *ijtihād* in the sense of the exercise of collective judgement (*al-ijtihād al-'āmmah*), because he goes on to say that legal plurality degenerated into antagonism once the individual form of *ijtihād* (*al-ijtihād al-khāṣṣah*) was introduced. Subordinated as it was to personal whims and wishes, *ijtihād* then became a factor of dissension, to be later exploited and intensified by the imperialist enemies who fostered enmity among the Muslims, setting every group against another.

Shaltūt's second argument is simply a denunciation of prejudice or bigotry, and its harmful practical impact on the search for the best possible solutions to the present social problems of Muslims. He says that the legal schools of all persuasions should now be ready to accept from one another any idea which conforms to Islamic principles, and can best ensure the welfare of family and society. By way of example he mentions his own *fatwās* in favour of the Shīʿī rejection of the validity of 'suspended divorce' and divorce by triple repudiation in one sitting.[90]

Shaltūt advanced similar arguments in a more explicit *fatwā*, confirming the 'validity of worship according to the Imāmī Shīʿī doctrine'. (The word *sect* was deleted from the official document on the grounds that in 'Islam proper there are no sects, but only schools or doctrines'.) Combined with other conciliatory gestures such as the publication of 'Āmilī's *Wasā'il ash-shī'ah*, one of the most authoritative sources of traditional Shīʿīsm, and Ṭabarsī's *Majma' al-bayān*, a Shīʿī commentary on the Qur'ān, both with al-Azhar's blessings, and a series of friendly communications between Shaltūt and two Shīʿī leaders in Iraq, Muḥammad Khāliṣī and the aforementioned Muḥammad Ḥusayn Kāshif al-Ghiṭā', these *fatwās* established a distinct trend towards greater Sunnī–Shīʿī understanding. The credit for this should be largely put down to Shaltūt's generally temperate vision of Islam. But also instrumental in bringing about this trend were the activities of the *Dār at-Taqrīb al-Madhāhib* (the Organisation for the Bringing Together of Schools) based in Cairo. Created in 1947 at the initiative of an Iranian Shīʿī, Muḥammad Taqī Qummi, *Dār at-Taqrīb* soon became a forum in which, to quote Shaltūt himself, 'the Ḥanafī, the Mālikī, the Shāfiʿī and the Ḥanbalī sit next to the Imāmī and Zaydī round one table 'discussing' literary accomplishments, Ṣūfism and jurisprudence, in an atmosphere pervaded by a spirit of fraternity, a sense of affection, love and comradeship.'[91]

Paradoxically, another devlopment which was to bring Shīʿīsm close to the mainstream of Sunnī Islam in the years to come took place in a world far removed from the euphoric atmosphere of these pious, speculative exercises – in the conflict between Jamāl ʿAbd an-Nāsir's Arab nationalism, and Iran's pro-Western stance. In July 1960, Egypt broke off diplomatic relationship with Iran in retaliation for Iran's *de facto* recognition of Israel. In August, at a meeting of Al-Azhar, 150 ʿUlamā' issued a proclamation calling on Muslims throughout the world to adopt an attitude of *jihād* against the Shah of Iran for his pro-Israeli policy.[92] Three years later, the Shah launched his 'White Revolution', purporting to carry out reforms requiring the expropriation of large landowners, and female emancipation. This provoked a popular religious opposition, led by the hitherto relatively unknown Āyatullāh Ruḥullāh Khumaynī, who condemned what he regarded to be the illegality and falsity of these reforms as well as the Shah's connections with Israel and the United States.

The community of interests between this opposition in Iran, and the Nāṣirite Arab nationalist campaign against the Shah called into being a 'united front' between Iranian Shīʿīsm and Arab Sunnīsm. Almost overnight, the militant Shīʿī hierarchy of Iran was accorded in the Arab–Sunnī circles a respectability rarely known in living memory.[93] It is beyond the scope of this study to pursue the vicissitudes of this 'front' that lasted until recent times. Suffice it to say that with the triumph of Khumaynī's Islamic Revolution in 1978–9, Sunnī–Shīʿī co-operation was placed under severe strain when sectarian passions were aroused both outside and inside Iran, and some Sunnīs displayed fears of a Shīʿī revivalist threat to Islamic orthodoxy. This makes one doubtful about the ability of such limited Sunnī–Shīʿī concord as has been surveyed in this chapter to survive a massive confrontation between Iranian and Arab nationalisms, of which the Iran–Iraq war of 1980–81 is but one catastrophic example. But the whole episode throws a revealing light on the extent to which religion can become a handmaid of politics, rendering any sectarian peace vulnerable to the unpredictability of international relations.

If the Sunnī–Shīʿī concord has thus been proved to be dependent on political fortunes, Sunnī–Shīʿī unity comes up against some more verifiable, but also more daunting obstacles. In the first place, so long as sectarianism is closely intertwined with nationalist idiosyncrasies (Shīʿīsm with Iranian culture, Sunnīsm with Arab nationalism, Pakistan's Islamic identity, Kurdish separatism, etc.) any hope of unity is unrealistic. But the problem goes deeper than politics. It was shown in the Introduction that the difference between Shī'īsm and Sunnīsm is something more substantive and more far-reaching than pedantic squabblings over ritual, legal and even theological matters: it impinges on the way in which the Qur'ānic injunctions are applied to the nature of Man, the method of interpreting and conveying the divine message, the meaning of justice, and the philosophy of history. Thus as Algar points out, 'Sunnīsm and Shī'īsm are two parallel orthodox perspectives of the Islamic revelation that cannot converge, in their exoteric aspects, for reasons inherent in the nature of each. No project of political motivation could alter this fact, although a conciliation of the two perspectives is possible, both at the level of action and, more importantly, at the level of the esoteric.'[94]

The analysis in this chapter has shown that some progress has been made in the course of the present century towards this 'esoteric conciliation', as a result of one or two fundamental changes in the outlooks of both sides. The Sunnīs have allowed a greater scope than in the past to individual judgement, and this has prompted a diversity of opinion which can take in its embrace many a Shī'ī feature formerly discarded because of their real or presumed incompatibility with the dictates of orthodoxy or expediency. The single most important of these is a movement away from the wonted realism of the past towards an idealism which greatly relishes the élitist and historicist undertones of Shī'īsm. The glorification of some members of the Prophet's family, particularly Ḥusayn, has taken its cue from the same idealism. For their part, the Shī'īs have tempered their idealism by pruning it of those metaphysical and mystical elements which make their creed unsuitable for coping with the plight of Muslims in the modern world. At the same time, there has been much deprecation of the schismatic attitudes of the past, and appeals for conforming to majority norms in the performance of these rituals, like pilgrimage to Mecca (in October 1979 Khumaynī issued a *fatwā* exhorting the Shī'īs to abandon their age-old reluctance to say their prayers behind Sunnī leaders at the ceremony). Such trends are by no means universal among either Sunnīs or Shī'īs: one can still easily find Sunnīs branding the Shī'īs as renegades,[95] or reproving *ijtihād* as a back-door for heresy and latitudinarianism,[96] and Shī'īs refusing to tone down their particularism,[97] with 'moderators' admonishing both.[98] But the fact remains that 'unitarian' ideas are often expressed by authors who set the tone of current debates, and whose arguments for the moment carry great authority among the rising generation. What, then, differentiates the present phase of limited Sunnī–Shī'ī concord from the past is that, apart from being necessitated by the political expediency of maintaining a united front in the face of external enemies, it is accompanied by a considerable degree of intellectual harmony.

2 The crisis over the Caliphate

Sunnī political thought reached a turning-point in modern times with the abolition of the Caliphate by the decision of the Grand National Assembly of Turkey in 1924. This was one of those rare symbolic events in history which mark, however belatedly, the demise of time-honoured institutions. Coming at a time when religious modernism as initiated by Asad-ābādī (Afghānī) and 'Abduh had lost its impetus, it nevertheless was the apogee of a long period of intellectual ferment among Muslims which had started at the end of the eighteenth century. It precipitated a vigorous debate between the modernists and traditionalists, and, for a time, promised the formation of a synthesis of their opposing views as the beginning of a real regeneration of Islamic political thought. But soon bitter polemics, coupled with reactions to the secularisation of Turkey, led to an even sharper confrontation which redounded to the advantage of traditionalists, and eventually, by pushing the Muslim mind in the direction of an alternative to the Caliphate, became one of the factors stimulating the call for the Islamic state.

In reality, the Caliphate was something of a misnomer for the institution which stood at the summit of the Ottoman political hierarchy. There was the unconfirmed story that Sulṭān Salīm I had arranged in the sixteenth century for the Caliphate to be transferred to him by the last 'Abbāsid Caliph Mutawakkil.[1] But whatever the truth of the matter, Sunnī jurists refused to recognise the title Caliph for the Sulṭān either on the grounds that real Caliphate existed only under the Rightly-Guided (*Rāshidūn*), which was the view of the Ḥanafī jurists whose school was under the protection of the Sulṭāns, or because descent from the Arabian tribe of Quraysh was held by others to be an essential qualification of the Caliphs. Hence the title Caliph was not officially used for the Sulṭāns until the eighteenth century, when, for reasons of state, the Ottoman put all doctrinal and legal niceties aside and declared their Sulṭān a Caliph. The definitive instrument registering this innovation was the Treaty of Kuchuk Kainarja concluded in 1774 between the Ottoman Turks and Russia, in which the Sulṭān undertook to recognise the complete independence of the Tartars of the Crimea and Kuchan, which had hitherto formed part of the Ottoman Empire. Since the Empress of Russia, so Arnold tells us, claimed to be the patroness of the Christians of the Orthodox church dwelling in the Ottoman territory, the Ottoman plenipotentiaries called the Sulṭān – among other things – the 'sovereign Caliph of the Mahometan religion' in order to equip him with a commensurate spiritual authority over Muslims.[2] In the course of time, religious doctors provided ample arguments to defend this piece of Realpolitik, their case being strengthened later by the necessity of maintaining Muslim unity in the face of Western expansionism.

The circumstances leading to the abolition of the Caliphate arose from the Ottoman defeat in the First World War, and the efforts of Mustapha Kemal (Atatürk) – the founder of modern Turkey – to establish a secular state. He was helped in his designs by the disrepute brought upon the Sulṭānate-Caliphate as a result of its association with the foreign invaders of Turkey, as well as with internal reactionary forces. Here we are more concerned with the impact of that development on religio-political thought.

The abolition of the Caliphate took place in two stages. First, in November 1922, the Grand National Assembly decided to separate the Sulṭānate from the Caliphate, and then to replace the Sulṭānate with a republican regime. This was inevitable in view of the Constitution accepted by the Assembly in January 1921, which had declared that 'sovereignty belongs unconditionally to the people. The administration derives from the principle that the people control their destiny in person and in fact.'[3] The Sulṭānate being a hereditary institution had no place in this system. Thereupon, Sulṭān Vahideddin was deposed, and his cousin, Abdulmecid, was elected by the Assembly as the Caliph of all Muslims. This was an even more anomalous situation, which could not be tolerated for long. It was a return to the days of the Buyids and the Saljūqs, when a shadowy Caliphate existed in Baghdad, but the real power lay in the hands of potentates in Rayy and Iṣfahān. The new Ottoman Caliph was similarly 'shorn of all real authority or concern in the political and administrative affairs of the country; he was invested with the mantle of the Prophet, just as his ancestors had been, but he was deprived of the power of the sword.'[4] At this stage, Mustapha Kemal was still trying to meet his Muslim critics on their own ground, substantiating his retort to them by examples from Islamic history. Soon the contradictions inherent in the new arrangement started to rankle in his mind. Not the least of these was the fact the Caliph was supposed to be entitled to the obedience of Muslims throughout the world, but in practice only enjoyed the allegiance of the Turks. Mustapha Kemal must have expressed the feelings of many modernised Muslims when he declared just before the abolition of the Caliphate:

> Our Prophet has instructed his disciples to convert the nations of the world to Islam; he has not ordered them to provide for the government of these nations. Never did such an idea pass through his mind. Caliphate means government and administration. A Caliph who really wants to

play his role, to govern and administer all Muslim nations [finds himself at a loss] how to manage this. I must confess that in these conditions, if they appointed me as the Caliph, I would immediately have resigned.

But let us return to history, and consider the facts. The Arabs founded a Caliphate in Baghdad, but they also established another one in Cordova. Neither the Persians, nor the Afghans, nor the Muslims of Africa ever recognised the Caliph of Constantinople. The notion of a single Caliph, exercising supreme religious authority over all the Muslim people, is one which has come out of books, not reality. The Caliph has never exercised over the Muslims a power similar to that held by the Pope over the Catholics. Our religion has neither the same requirements, nor the same discipline as Christianity. The criticisms provoked by our recent reform [separating the Caliphate from the Sultanate] are inspired by an abstract, unreal idea: the idea of Pan-Islamism. Such an idea has never been translated into reality. We have held the Caliphate in high esteem according to an ancient and venerable tradition. We honour the Caliph; we attend to his needs, and those of his family. I add that in the whole of the Muslim world, the Turks are the only nation which effectively ensures the Caliph's livelihood. Those who advocate a universal Caliph have so far refused to make any contribution. What, then, do they expect? That the Turks alone should carry the burden of this institution, and that they alone should respect the sovereign authority of the Caliph? This would be expecting too much [of us].[5]

Mustapha Kemal's annoyance with what he thus held to be the hypocritical attitude of non-Turkish Muslims towards the Caliphate must have partly incited him to proceed to the second stage of its abolition. In November 1923, the text of the appeal by two distinguished Indian Muslims leaders, the Shīʿī Amīr ʿAlī and the Ismāʿīlī leader Āghā Khān, to which we referred in the previous chapter, was published in Istanbul. This pointed out that the separation of the Caliphate from the Sulṭānate had increased the significance of the former for Muslims in general, and called upon the Turkish Government to place the Caliphate 'on a basis which would command the confidence and esteem of the Muslim nations, and thus impart to the Turkish state unique strength and dignity'. According to Bernard Lewis, it was the crisis touched off by such protests that ended with the abolition of the Caliphate, because they all served to stress the links of the Caliphate with the past and with Islam, and this tightened Mustapha Kemal's resolve to remove it.[6] W. C. Smith alludes to a more emotional factor – the anger felt by some Turks at the protest of such 'unorthodox' figures over their action: 'It really was rather ludicrous to have a Shīʿī...and a Khojah (religiously ultra-heretical) telling the Turkish Muslims how to behave.'[7] But as Nallino has noted, more fundamental reasons could have also contributed to the *dénouement*. These arose, to put it briefly, from the incompatibility between Turkish nationalism and Pan-Islamism: the conflict between the concept of a modern Westernised state, based on the will of the people, and the notion of a supra-national Muslim state, resting on the bonds of the religious community; the contradiction between the nature of a modern state requiring the equality of all its citizens, irrespective of their beliefs, and that of an Islamic state presupposing the superiority of believers to non-believers; and, finally, the absurdity of a Caliphate deprived of temporal authority.[8] Some of these problems were not unprecedented in recent Islamic history: we shall see in chapter 5 how the issues arising from the conflict between the *Sharīʻah* and man-made law had been faced before by the Shīʻī leaders of the Iranian Constitutional Revolution in 1906. But most other issues, particularly the conflict between a universal Islamic state and a modern national state, and the relevance of the Caliphate to the political requirements of the age, presented a new challenge to Sunnī political thought.

Some religious thinking preceded the decision of the National Assembly. This is attested by a document which it subsequently published, giving its main reasons for the abolition. Some of the essential arguments of the document have been given elsewhere,[9] but here we will refer to one or two points that need our special attention. The most significant aspect of the document is its attempt to reconcile secular and religious theses on the nature and functions of a state. We do not know who its actual authors were, but as it stands its content gives cause to presume that a constructive discussion must have taken place prior to its redaction between some religionists and secularisers – an occurrence with rare parallels in the history of the modern Middle East, which has often been marked, especially in times of crisis, by complete rupture, if not bitter confrontation, between the two camps. The only other important exception which comes to one's mind is the Iranian Constitutional Revolution of 1906, following which groups of the 'Ulamā' and Westernised intellectuals co-operated in drawing up the first Constitution of the country. Neither in the Turkish nor Iranian case, however, did this co-operation survive the strain of subsequent political vicissitudes. In both, the secularisers emerged victorious – although in the Iranian case this proved to be temporary.

The text of the Turkish document has therefore an intriguingly hybrid character, drawing alternately on classical works of Sunnī jurisprudence and modern concepts of national sovereignty, social contract and general will. While most influential writings by Westernised intellectuals on democracy and representative rule in Turkey, Egypt and Iran roughly from the twenties onwards reveal – or affect – ignorance of Islamic history and culture, the authors of the Turkish document have made abundant use of the technical terms and formulae of Islamic public and private law in an obvious attempt to disarm their orthodox critics.

The document is also significant because of its pioneering value in modern discussions on the Caliphate: nearly all the outstanding critics and supporters of the Caliphate after its abolition seem to have done no more than develop its broad propositions. Particularly the critics, as we shall soon see, have almost repeated its main points: that the Caliphate, far from being divinely ordained, was simply a utilitarian institution, designed for the most judicious administration of the Muslim community; that the 'real Caliphate' lasted only for thirty years after the death of the Prophet; that what prevailed for the best part of Islamic history was a 'fictitious' Caliphate sustained by sheer force; and that with the Caliphate having outlived its purpose, the Muslims were now free to choose whatever form of government was suitable to their present needs and conditions. Thus, although the immediate issue before the Turks was the separation of the Caliphate from the Sulṭānate, the Assembly realised that such a decision could not be rationally explained without venturing into a reappraisal of the Caliphate itself, exploding in the process a number of myths about the sanctity of traditional political institutions, and the absolute duty of the faithful to obey rulers. The document is, therefore, equally noteworthy as a critique of classical Sunnī political theory. While the pathfinders of modernism, Asad-ābādī (Afghānī) and 'Abduh, in their effort to release the Muslim mind from the fetters of 'imitation', contented themselves with general strictures on the political submissiveness of the masses, the Turkish authors felt that the moment had arrived to openly challenge some of the specific doctrines responsible for this quietism; hence their refutation of the ideas of such authorities as at-Taftāzanī and Ibn Himām on the legitimacy of the 'Abbāsid Caliphate. They also displayed a keen historical sense by imputing the pro-Caliphate opinions of classical theorists to their unawareness of other forms and mechanisms of government, which are known only to the peoples of our time. A point made both implicitly and explicitly throughout the document is that the Assembly, embodying the Islamic principle of consultation (*shūrā*), was fully authorised to make any decision ensuring the proper conduct of the nation's affairs, and that withdrawing the political functions of the Caliph was one such decision. But whether in disproving conventional beliefs, or suggesting novel ideas, the authors were careful to rely persistently on the resources of the *Sharī'ah*, repeatedly quoting the *ḥadīths* and canonical maxims prescribing justice, expediency, common sense and the simplicity of good religion.[10]

Next the effect of the crisis on the Islamic thought outside Turkey has to be considered. Leaving the Westernisers aside, the abolition of the Caliphate came to one distinct group as the fulfilment of an old, though not always consciously cherished, desire: the Arab nationalists. As the representatives of one of the subject nations of the Ottoman Empire, they had, ever since the end of the nineteenth century, held the Ottoman Caliphate to be a mere subterfuge for perpetuating the Turanian hegemony, as well as the travesty of an office which by right belonged to the Arabs. This opinion was all the more interesting because it was expressed by both the Muslim and Christian Arabs. The Syrian 'Abd ar-Raḥmān al-Kawākibī

(d. 1902), well-known for his authorship of a pithy tract against (Turkish) despotism in 1900, enumerated the virtues of the Arab rulership in Islamic history, and used this as a justification of his scheme for installing a Qurayshī Arab as Caliph in Mecca. Nationalist reasoning ranked as high as religious considerations in his scheme: the Arabs, he said, were the founders of the Islamic society, and this, combined with their innate qualities such as pride, group solidarity, steadfastness and resilience in the face of physical hardships, should pre-empt the Caliphate for them.[11] But in the utopian state that he delineated, the Caliphate has purely spiritual authority, since he wanted it to be preoccupied solely with religious affairs;[12] but this did not tally with his strong views in the same tract, and in another well-known treatise on the 'Nature of Despotism' (*Ṭabā'i' al-istibdād*), which all imparted his conviction in the indissoluble link between religion and politics in Islam.

The Christian Najīb 'Āzūrī (d. 1916) who, like many Arab nationalists at the turn of the century, had close connections with the French designs on the Ottoman Empire, similarly visualised an Arab Caliphate with spiritual authority over all Muslims, but ruling a territory composed of only Ḥijāz and Medina:[13] such an Islamic counterpart to the States of the Church was his suggested solution to the thorny problem of the separation of the temporal and spiritual powers in Islam. If there was ever any chance of such innocent projects coming to fruition through Arab-Turkish understanding, it was destroyed by the growing hostility between the two nations, culminating in the Arab Revolt of 1916. By that time, Arab nationalists had lost interest in the Caliphate, and had become concerned either with the grandiose ideal of Arab unity, or with the machinations for establishing separate Arab states after the First World War. For this reason, reaction to the abolition of the Caliphate seems to have come mostly from non-Arab Muslims. Only a handful of 'committed' religious writers like Rashīd Riḍā and some of the Azharites (whose views will be subsequently examined) felt strongly enough to comment on the event.

In the eyes of the secularists, the end of the Caliphate was a logical sequel to the collapse of the Ottoman Empire, and the result of an anachronism maintained by force. But for the religionists, the matter was more complex, and had to be explained within the legal categories of orthodox Islam. This was not the first time in history that the Sunnī theorists had to face the ordeal of resorting to casuistry to prescribe the attitude of the faithful towards the collapse of religio-political authority. Eight centuries earlier, the overthrow of the 'Abbāsid Caliphate in Baghdad, in 656/1258, had placed them in an almost similar quandary. To the jurists with a flair for historical reminiscence, that precedent cautioned against hastily concluding that the fate of the institution itself had been sealed. After the Mongol invasion, in the words of Suyūṭi (d. 911/1533), 'the world went through three and a half years without a Caliph'.[14] But at the end of that interregnum, a cousin of the last Caliph was reinstated in Cairo as the new occupant of the office, which, however shadowy its reality, acted as the legitimising authority of the Mamlūk rulers of Egypt for the next three and a half centuries.[15] So in the present crisis too, in 1924, there were some Sunnī jurists who argued that the decision of the Turkish authorities had changed nothing in the situation, and that the Muslims were still bound in allegiance to the Caliph Abdulmecid.

The Indian Muslims, numbering about seventy millions, and forming numerically the most important part of the Muslim world at the time, had long taken a strong interest in the Ottoman Caliphate. In the nineteenth century, although the Ottoman Empire was progressively weakened by loss of more territories inhabited by the Muslims to non-Muslim powers, the Sulṭān's claim was consolidated because of the growing strength of religious movements of solidarity against Western domination. India and Russia, with large Muslim minorities, were among the most active centres of pro-Ottoman campaigns. Later on, during the mutiny of 1857 in India, the British further boosted the Ottoman Sulṭān by obtaining a proclamation from him urging the Indian Muslims to remain loyal to the British. And again during the Crimean War 'the British themselves had magnified Turkey in the Indian eyes. In the second half of the nineteenth century, Sulṭān 'Abdul 'Azīz's claim to be the universal *Khalīfa* of Islam was generally accepted by the Indo-Muslim middleclass intelligentsia. It can be safely assumed that he was the first Ottoman sultan in whose name the *khuṭba* was read in Indian mosques.'[16] The momentum of the pro-Ottoman movement was kept up by the rise of the nationalist fervour in the second half of the nineteenth century. By that time, an intellectual dimension was added to the movement by the Muslim middle classes, who gradually overcame their dependence on the imperial system, and began to express their discontent against the British in sophisticated ideological and literary forms. It was from among them that the Muslim leaders of India's struggle for independence arose: Abu'l-Kalām Āzād, Muḥammad 'Alī and his brother Shawkat 'Alī. When the First World War broke out, pro-Ottoman feeling had ironically become a robust anti-British vehicle. Britain was soon to be condemned not only for such imperialist brutalities as the Amritsar massacre, but also for its complicity in the disintegration of the Ottoman Empire, and the weakening of its Caliphate.[17]

In 1919, all-India 'Khilāfat (Caliphate) Conferences' were organised, and aroused Muslims' emotions in favour of the Ottoman Caliph. These were soon followed by the formation of the Khilāfat Committee which, under the vigorous leadership of Muḥammad 'Alī and others, mobilised the whole theological weight of Indian Islam in an anti-British campaign. This established an organic link between Indian nationalism and 'Khilāfatism', which ensured Muslim–Hindu co-operation in the struggle for India's independence until the years immediately before the Second World War. But the Khilāfatists were soon to face bitter frustrations. Already many of the nations of the Empire had achieved their independence from the Sublime Porte. This had not deflected the determination of the Khilāfatists, who strove sanguinely to re-establish the Ottoman suzerainty over the lost territories.[18] But then came the decision of the Grand National Assembly of Turkey to replace the Sulṭānate with republicanism, and maintain the Caliphate only as a spiritual office. We saw that the Indian Muslims' expression of concern over this development only helped to expedite the abolition of the Caliphate, and secularisation of Turkey. From then onwards, the appeal of the movement started to decline, and the majority of educated Indian Muslims concentrated their efforts on internal problems. In 1925, the Khilāfat movement announced that 'it had turned its attention to the communal welfare of the Indian Moslems', and even turned down the invitation to attend the 1926 conference in Cairo to discuss the future of the Caliphate.[19]

This waning of enthusiasm, however, did not affect the dogmatic position of the hard core of the movement. Its most articulate representative, Abu'l-Kalām Āzād, was distinguished from others not only because of his belief in the necessity of the 'reconstruction' of Islam, but also by his mastery of Islamic theology. His views agreed with those of Mustapha Kemal so far as he too considered the Ottoman Caliphate to be different from the Papacy. But Āzād's reasoning was his own: in Islam, 'spiritual leadership is the due of God and his Prophet alone'. So obedience to the Caliphate was binding on all Muslims, though not in the same degree as submission to God and his Prophet'.[20] In all this he was reproducing, with only occasional alterations Māwardī's theory. It is, therefore, difficult to imagine that men like him simply changed their mind overnight to swim with the tide of secularism, and supported the abolition of the Caliphate. On the other hand, we could not find conclusive evidence to judge with certainty the response of the Indian Muslim thinkers – as distinct from the masses – to the abolition. The only substantial evidence is provided by the work of Muḥammad Iqbāl, the most sophisticated of Islamic modernists in India, who gave a clear judgement in favour of the Turkish move. But then Iqbāl was deeply influenced by the Western modes of thought, and in any case could not be regarded as the representative of the 'orthodox' trend.

Iqbāl also approved of the abolition of the Caliphate primarily on the same grounds as those we just quoted from Mustapha Kemal: the Ottoman Caliphate, he said, had long become 'a mere symbol of a power which departed long ago', because the Iranians always stood aloof from the Turks in view of their doctrinal differences; Morocco 'always looked askance at them, and Arabia has cherished private ambition'.[21] The idea of a universal Caliphate was a workable idea when the empire of Islam was intact, but it had now become an obstacle in the way of a reunion of independent Muslim states. But how could the abolition of the Caliphate be justified in terms of the Sunnī political theory?

Iqbāl's basic answer to this question was that the Turks had merely practised *ijtihād* by taking the view that the Caliphate could be vested sometimes in a body of persons, or an elected assembly. Although 'the religious doctors of Egypt and India had not yet expressed themselves on the point', he personally found the Turkish view to be 'perfectly sound': 'the republican form of government is not only thoroughly consistent with the spirit of Islam, but has also become a necessity in view of the new forces that are set free in the world of Islam'.[22] He further cited two examples of earlier Sunnī adaptation of the Caliphate to political realities: first was the abolition of the condition of Qarashiyat (descent from the tribe of Quraysh) by Qāḍī Abū Bakr Bāqillānī (d. 403/1013), for the candidates of the Caliphate, in deference to the 'facts of experience', namely the political fall of the Quraysh and their consequent inability to rule the world of Islam. The second was Ibn Khaldūn's suggestion, four centuries later, that since the power of the Quraysh had vanished, there was 'no alternative but to accept the most powerful man as Imām or Caliph in the country where he happens to be powerful'. Iqbāl concluded from all this that there was no difference between the position of Ibn Khaldūn, who had realised 'the hard logic of facts', and the attitude of modern Turks, who were equally 'inspired... by the realities of experience, and not by the scholastic reasonings of jurists who lived and thought under different conditions of life'.[23]

These were brave words at the time, expressive of an enlightened spirit impatient with the backwardness of the Muslims and the obscurantism of their religious leaders. But if they were meant to persuade those leaders to change their attitude, and come to terms with the modern world, they proved to be self-defeating. This was partly because they were based on the sanguine assumption that the abolition of the Caliphate did not necessarily mean the severance of Turkey's links with Islam as the state religion, and their persuasiveness was therefore soon sapped by events. But the more important reason was Iqbāl's constant resort to arguments resting on 'facts of experience', 'realities of experience', and 'hard logic of facts'. Now it is quite possible to find the equivalents of these notions in the Sunnī legal devices of *istiḥsān*, evading a fixed code in the interests of 'what is better', and *istiṣlāḥ*, doing the same 'for the sake of general benefit to the community'. But even these genuine dispensations for occasional departures from established norms, let alone Iqbāl's philosophical escapades, must have shocked the orthodoxy, when the point at issue was not the infraction of minor rules of the Islamic commercial or penal law but the fate of the highest institution in the political structure of Sunnī Islam. Iqbāl's appeal for the revitalisation of political thought in Islam was further weakened by his attack on the 'Ulamā' as scholastic jurists bent on perpetuating legal anachronisms. However, if his appeal was to have had any chance of success beyond the tiny circle of Westernised Muslims, it would have been thanks to the blessing of the same 'Ulamā', and their readiness to convey it to a wider audience. He was undoubtedly aware of his need for the traditionalists' support. This is clear from his attempt to seek legitimacy for his modernism in the views of two figures from the past – Bāqillānī and

Ibn Khaldūn. These precedents were of dubious value to his case. Baqillānī's opinion did carry some weight with the conservatives; but it could not go very far in silencing their criticisms of the Turks, because suggesting the elimination of only one prerequisite of the Caliphate was different from endorsing its total demise. Ibn Khaldūn was even less effective, since, however eminent his position as a founder of sociology, he occupies no place in the pantheon of Sunnī theology or jurisprudence.

Outside India, the only authoritative religious response to the abolition came from Egypt – from a group of religious scholars, who held a session to discuss the matter, under the chairmanship of the Rector of al-Azhar, Shaykh Muḥammad Abu'l-Faḍl al-Jīzāwī, and the President of the High Religious Court, Muḥammad Muṣṭafā al-Marāghī, and attended by the representatives of the principal legal schools of Sunnīsm. The gathering of such figures, particularly at a time when the revivalist legacy of Muḥammad 'Abduh stood at a very low ebb among the Azharites, could hardly be suspect of harbouring any modernistic, let alone secularist, intentions. Nevertheless, the resolution of the scholarly gathering shows that even in this body, despite its orthodox pronouncements, there was a willingness to come to terms with the new development. This is apparent, first, from its refusal to be drawn into the dispute over the theoretical justification of the Caliphate. Whereas the traditional exponents of the Caliphate have mostly insisted on its canonical obligatoriness (*wujūb shar'ī*), the resolution merely defined the Caliph or Imām as 'the representative of the Prophet in guarding the religion, and implementing its precepts, and administering the affairs of the people in accord with the religious law' – a standard definition, but one which made no claim about the Caliphate being necessitated by the divine revelation. This could be conducive to a more flexible framework to deliberate on its future. Second, the resolution criticised those Muslims who still felt themselves bound by the oath of allegiance to the deposed Caliph and regarded obedience to him as a religious duty. It is interesting that although its authors belonged to Arab culture, the resolution did not base its criticism of such Muslims on the belief that the Turks were wrong in arrogating the Caliphate to themselves. Instead, it merely argued that the oath of allegiance had been illegal in the first place, because it had been taken to a Caliph who did not deserve this title in so far as he lacked temporal power. Third, the resolution accepted the abolition of the Caliphate as a *fait accompli*, and although noting the consternation and anxiety that it had caused among Muslims, thought that it was now time to hold a congress to decide the future of the Caliphate 'on a basis which would not only conform to Islamic tenets, but would also fit the Islamic arrangements to which the Muslims had consented for their government' – a clear reference to the modern political systems adopted by various Muslim nations in recent times. The authors also conceded that this could be done only after recovering '[our] composure, after deliberation and awareness of different viewpoints'.[24]

In view of such evident clues to the readiness for accommodation with non-traditionalists, the rest of the story of the debate over the Caliphate in Egypt – and in Sunnī Islam – is a frustrating tale of deadlocked polemics. Because, although the name of the next critic of the Caliphate, 'Alī 'Abd ar-Rāziq (d. 1966), marked the highest point in the debate, it also marked a vociferous orthodox reaction which quashed all hopes for the debate being brought to a conclusion, or to a synthesis of opposing views. 'Abd ar-Rāziq was certainly the most controversial theorist thrown up by the crisis. He took advantage of the abolition of the Caliphate to launch a forceful attack on the entire traditional school of Islamic political thought. On this point, he contested the views of not only the orthodox 'Ulamā', but also modernists like Rashīd Riḍā, who, despite differences, shared his anti-dogmatic feelings. All this was somewhat paradoxical, because he had a deeper immersion in traditional education: he had completed all his studies at al-Azhar, and acted for some time as a judge of the Religious Court. Having attended, at the new Egyptian University, lectures by Nallino on literature, and those by Santillana on philosophy, and having spent some time in Oxford pursuing studies in law and economy (which he had to leave unfinished because of the outbreak of the First World War), he was also familiar with Western culture. But contrary to those of Iqbāl, his writings did not indicate much absorption of Western thought – this, in fact, was his strong point in so far as his ideas were meant to influence moderate religious opinion. In his principal work *Al-Islām wa uṣūl al-ḥukm* ('Islam and the Fundamentals of Government') he also made greater use of the legal and historical antecedents of the Sunnī political theory. So in presenting his ideas 'Abd ar-Rāziq enjoyed a vantage-point to contribute to a new Sunnī consensus on the relationship between Islam and the modern state.[25] His central argument was that the Caliphate had no basis either in the Qur'ān, or the Tradition, or the consensus. To prove each part of this argument, he dealt in some detail with the major pieces of evidence which are normally drawn from these three sources in establishing the 'obligatoriness' of the Caliphate. He rightly said that the Qur'ān nowhere makes any mention of the Caliphate in the specific sense of the political institution we know in history. As he says, this is all the more puzzling in view of what God has said in it: 'We have neglected nothing in the Book' (6:38). All the verses which are commonly supposed to sanction the Caliphate do in fact nothing of the sort: they merely enjoin the Muslims to obey God, the Prophet and the 'Holders of Authority'. It is the term 'Holders of Authority' (*ulu'l-amr*) which is alleged by some Sunnī writers to mean the Caliphs. But the great commentators of the Qur'ān have expressed a different opinion: according to Bayḍāwī it means the Muslim contemporaries of the Prophet, and according to Zamakhsharī, the 'Ulamā'.[26] Nor can any convincing proof be extracted from the sayings attributed to the Prophet: 'The Imāms [should be] from the Quraysh' or 'He who dies and has no obligation of allegiance [to the Imām] dies the death of ignorance': 'even when', says 'Abd ar-Rāziq, 'one assumes these *ḥadīths* to be authentic, they do not prove that the Caliphate is a religious doctrine, and one of the articles of faith'. Christ has said: 'Render unto Caesar what is Caesar's, and unto Christ what is Christ's'; but this cannot be taken to mean that Christ has regarded Caesar's regime to be necessary for his followers. Similarly, Islam has called upon the Muslims to respect and help the poor, or emancipate slaves, but this does not signify the obligatoriness of poverty and slavery.[27]

To dispose of consensus as the last, conceivable sanction, 'Abd ar-Rāziq argued that, judging from concrete historical instances, consensus, whether in the sense of the agreement of the Prophet's Companions and their followers, or that of the 'Ulamā' or the entire Muslim community, has never played any role in installing the Caliphs – except in the case of the first four. The Caliphate has always been established by force, and maintained by oppression: it is for this reason that political science has always been a barren discipline, and political writings have been so scant among the Muslims. If there has been any consensus serving as the legitimiser of the Caliphate in history, it has been of the kind that the Muslim jurists refer to as 'the consensus of silence' (*ijmā' sukūtī*). Being himself an expert on Islamic jurisprudence,[28] 'Abd ar-Rāziq felt confident enough to declare that consensus in this sense can never be used to deduce 'religious proof and canonical rule'. To underline the perils of 'consensus of silence' he mentioned the example of the enthronement of Fayṣal, the son of Sharīf Ḥusayn, as the King of Iraq, after the First World War, which was justified by the British claim that 'the people who loose and bind' (*ahl al-ḥall wa'l 'aqd*), namely the religious and political leaders, had consented to it. From a strictly legal point of view, he said, the British were right: there had indeed been an election of sorts, in the form of consultation with the tribal chiefs and the 'Ulamā' – but this was as valid a form of consensus as the one arranged by the Umayyad ruler, Mu 'āwiyah, to receive the oath of allegiance to his son Yazīd: in the year 55/674 he summoned all the representatives of Muslims to an assembly in which he obtained their agreement to Yazīd's succession at the point of the sword.[29]

Thus far, 'Abd ar-Rāziq's reasonings could be excused by many a traditionalist as a legitimate expression of an unconventional opinion on the Caliphate – especially at a time when that institution was completely discredited. But he then doomed his book to orthodox damnation by introducing an issue which, although being related to the question of the Caliphate, was tangential to his immediate concern. This was the question whether Islam, as a system of religious doctrines, necessitated the creation of government at all. No sincere Muslim can answer this question in the negative without exposing himself to serious inconsistency. 'Abd ar-Rāziq accordingly admitted that contrary to the Caliphate, the creation of government has in fact been envisaged in the Qur'ān as an essential instrument to administer the affairs of Muslims, and protect their interests: when God says that he has elevated certain individuals above others

(43:32), or when He orders the Prophet to adjudicate among people according to the Book, and not to follow individual vagaries (5:48), He is indeed proclaiming the necessity of government. But this again does not mean that government is a fundamental principle of religion. True the Prophet, during his period of messengership, also performed some political acts, such as conducting wars, appointing officials, collecting alms-tax and distributing spoils of war, but none of these acts was directly related to his Prophetic mission. Even *jihād* cannot be considered as a function of prophecy, because according to 'Abd ar-Rāziq's reading of the Qur'ān, God has instructed the Muslims to propagate their religion only through peaceful persuasion and preaching. Whenever the Prophet resorted to acts of war, it was not for the sake of disseminating the religious call, but 'for the sake of state [or kingdom, *mulk*], and towards consolidating the Islamic polity. And there is no state which is not based on the sword, and sustained by virtue of violence and subjugation'.[30] This should mean that all the other verses in the Qur'ān enjoining, for instance, the Muslims to strike the infidels wherever they find them, should be interpreted in the same vein – although 'Abd ar-Rāziq does not explicitly say so. What is significant is that he thus draws a distinct line between the Prophet's position as a responsible statesman, and his position as a religious or spiritual teacher. Hence, all the Prophet's political acts should be explained in terms of the requirements of maintaining an emerging state, but any attempt at relating them to the essence of his divine mission is totally unjustified. Ironically, a crucial reason mentioned by the author in support of this argument is the principle of individual responsibility in Islam – that is, one of the main points used by modern, radical writers to encourage the Muslims to take a more active part in the political life of their societies: had God wanted the Prophet to undertake the political as well as religious leadership of the Muslims, He would not have warned the Prophet repeatedly against acting as the 'agent' (*wakīl*), 'guardian' (*ḥafīẓ*), or 'holder of absolute authority (*musayṭir*) over the Muslims, while reminding him that his sole function is to communicate (*al-balāgh*) the divine message through wise words, sermon and dialectics.[31]

The conclusion of all this debate was the most subtle part of 'Abd ar-Rāziq's arguments – and one which has been most misunderstood by many of his critics and expositors alike, with damaging results for the overall impression that his work made on religious thinking. This conclusion can be stated in two propositions: first, political authority and government, however indispensable for implementing Islamic ideals, do not belong to the essence of Islam and specifically do not constitute any of its cardinal principles.[32] Second, Islam, if properly understood, leaves the Muslims free to choose whatever form of government they find suitable to ensure their welfare. The opposite belief that in Islam, religion and politics form a unified whole, is wrong so far as it associates politics primarily with the Caliphate, and then with the despotic regimes that have ruled the

Muslims throughout history. 'Abd ar-Rāziq considers the currency of this belief to be the result of both the observations of well-meaning, 'realistic' historians like Ibn Khaldūn. who have erected an existing state of affairs into a dogmatic axiom, and the cynical insinuation of the despots themselves who wanted to give an appearance of sanctity to their rule.[33] The final remark of the book summed up the author's urge to see his conclusions turned to the service of political activism among Muslims today: 'There is nothing in the religion which prevents Muslims from competing with other nations in the field of social and political sciences, and from demolishing that antiquated order which has subjugated and humiliated them, and to build up rules of their state and the organisation of their government on the basis of the most modern achievements of human reason, and on the most solid experiences of nations as to the best principles of government'.[34]

It is possible that if the essential ideas of the book had not been dressed in such a provocative language, they would have been received differently by the orthodox establishment – at a time when it was reeling under the blows of the Turkish secularisers. It is an indication of the tendentious spirit in which the book was treated by the orthodox 'Ulamā' that, in their most authoritative statement denouncing its contents, they singled out a neutral reference to Bolshevism by the author as evidence of his Communistic beliefs. 'Abd ar-Rāziq's actual remark had been that if the Muslims jurists, in establishing the necessity of the Caliphate, merely wanted to demonstrate the necessity of government in general, then what they said was true: 'Promoting the religious symbols', he said, 'and ensuring the people's welfare do indeed depend on the Caliphate, in the sense of government – in whatever form and kind the government may be, absolutist or conditional, personal or republican, despotic constitutional or consultative, democratic, socialist or bolshevist.'[35] Apparently seizing on this sentence, the Special Court of al-Azhar, set up to pass judgement on the author, declared: 'In addition to negating the religious foundation of the Islamic (state), and revolting against the repeated cases of the Muslims' consensus with regard to their form of government, he takes the position of licensing the Muslims to instal a Bolshevic state.'[36] The more draconian measure was taken by another court, composed of twenty-five prominent scholars of al-Azhar, which, invoking a law enacted in 1911 binding the institution to prosecute the offenders against the prestige of the 'Ulamā', deprived 'Abd ar-Rāziq of both his Azharite diploma and judicial appointment.

All this was understandable in the emotionally-charged atmosphere prevailing in the Sunnī world in 1925. But the regrettable fact was that when passions subsided, instead of such anathemisations giving way to a more sober judgement, the work itself fell into oblivion, except in the studies of a few Western scholars – until recent times. The orthodox 'Ulamā' were not, of course, short of arguments against the work, so far as they ignored 'Abd ar-Rāziq's distinction between Caliphate and government, and presumed that if they could prove the legitimacy of both on the basis of Muslim historical practices, that should be enough to prove the 'obligatoriness' of both too. The special Court of al-Azhar peremptorily dismissed the work in these terms: 'It is evident that the bases of government, and the sources of legislation with the Muslims are the Book of God, the Prophetic Tradition, and the consensus of the Muslims. For Muslims, there can be nothing better than these. Shaykh 'Alī ['Abd ar-Rāziq] wants Muslims to demolish what is based on these foundations.' Another religious scholar, Shaykh Muḥammad Bakhīt, in a voluminous rebuttal, overlooked all the nuances in the author's case by reducing it to a simple claim that 'the system on which the government of Abū Bakr, and three other Rightly-Guided [*Rāshidūn*] Caliphs was based is ineffective and antiquated because of its disconnection with the social and political sciences, and that the achievements of human intellect are sounder and better than it.' He further simplified the debate by saying that 'this amounts to the author's negation of the principles of Islamic government, and of what was set up by the Emissary of God . . . compared with which nothing can be better and sounder, emanating as it does from the light of God.'[37]

The tenor of recent criticisms of 'Abd ar-Rāziq is different. Echoing the growing modernist urge for the integration of religious fervour with political action, these assail him less for his challenge to an institution long revered by the Sunnī Muslims than for his denial of the inseparability of religion and politics in Islam.[38] This line of criticism is justified to the extent that its aim is to prove that Islamic ideals cannot be realised only through persuasion and moral example. But it still does not disprove 'Abd ar-Rāziq's central contention that neither the Caliphate nor government constitutes an article of the Muslim faith. More significantly, what both the traditional and modern critics fail to appreciate is that the main lesson which he tries to convey to his readers through the more explicit of his conclusions is less concerned with the depoliticisation of Islam than with showing the main cause of the poverty of political thought and the atrophying of the critical faculties among Muslims. He holds this cause to be the sacrosanct character that the Muslims have historically attributed to their regimes, and their resultant belief that any revolt against rulers is tantamount to a revolt against the fundamental principles of Islam. This view is certainly not invalidated by the occasional dispensations that the jurisconsults have made for legitimate rebellion against unjust rulers, since in practice the ultimate authority for ascertaining the legitimacy of any rebellion is itself beholden to the rulers.

E. I. J. Rosenthal has raised a different objection that might be similarly levelled against 'Abd ar-Rāziq from an orthodox standpoint, which is inherent in any conception of Islam as an all-inclusive system of temporal and spiritual precepts. This is the relationship between state and law in Islam. The Imāmate or Caliphate, he avers, 'is incomprehensible and meaningless without recognising the place and function of law in it. The student of Islam from the time of the Caliphate to the modern age is aware that the question of a religious or a lay state depends on the place of the *Sharī'ah* in a state created by and for the Muslims. The source (divine or human) and the extent of the law of such a state determine its character. The law in force makes it a religious or a lay state.... By definition, then, a state whose criminal and private law is not based on the *Sharī'ah* is not an Islamic state, even where Islam is the state religion and the personal status law is the *Sharī'ah*-law, be it entirely traditional or modernised in varying degree, and whether this personal status law is administered by judges under religious or state authority.'[39] It is true that any real or presumed discretionary power vouchsafed by God and the Prophet to the Muslims in shaping their political institutions is limited by the imperative necessity of enforcing the provisions of the *Sharī'ah* in the penal and private domains. But one must not forget that despite the *Sharī'ah*'s grasp of nearly all aspects of individual and social life, there is no such thing as a unified Islamic legal system, enshrined in integrated codes, and accepted and acknowledged unquestionably by all Muslims. There are confessional and sectarian divergencies over a wide spectrum of issues, ranging from the forbidden varieties of wine to the rules of the holy war. Added to this is the possibility of personal interpretation of the law, a possibility which, so far as Sunnī Islam is concerned, has been enhanced ever since the birth of modernism in the teachings of 'Abduh. And finally, when it comes to the application of the law, the willingness and readiness of the state is a determining factor, and this in turn is a function of its ideological and political underpinnings. This is particularly borne out by the emergence of a number of states in the twentieth century which have aimed at making Islam the sole, or the predominant, basis of their social, economic and political orientation. Saudi Arabia, Libya, Pakistan, and the Islamic Republic of Iran have all equally valid claims to be considered as Islamic states. But this has by no means resulted in their adoption of a uniform system of penal or private law. This is illustrated by the divergent ways in which they have treated the seemingly straightforward Qur'ānic punishment of amputation of hands for theft. The differences in legal systems can be at least partly put down to the specific nature of a ruling sect (Wahhābism in Saudi Arabia), a certain synthesis of Islam and socialism (Libya), the need of a military regime for legitimacy (Pakistan), and the wide scope allowed to the individual judgement of religious leaders under Shī'ism (Iran). In none of these cases is there a direct correlation between the commitment to Islam and the nature of the regime as embodied in its legal system. To the extent that any doctrinal or ideological element has been instrumental in moulding the political and juridical institutions in each country, it has stemmed directly from what its leaders perceive to be genuine Islam – a perception which is determined by a host of psychological, social and historical factors.

But if the installing of the state, far from being a religious duty of Muslims, is merely a contingent act of political wisdom, how can the attainment of Islamic ideals be guaranteed? ‘Abd ar-Rāziq’s reply to this question is implicit in his repeated descriptions of Muḥammad’s messengership as a spiritual, rather than political, leadership: the simplicity of the Prophet’s political arrangements for conducting the affairs of the Islamic state, and his refusal to leave behind any set of detailed administrative directives for the future Muslim generations, testify to his wish not to see his ministry associated too closely with the arts of statecraft. As Rosenthal has noted, he thus asserted ‘the purely and exclusively religious character of Islam’.[40] If it had been allowed to develop in a free and honest debate, it would have eventually involved an overdue analysis of an area of Islamic culture which has always been vulnerable particularly to Western criticism – the question of the self-subsistence of moral values. The crux of any exaltation of the Prophet’s spiritual, as opposed to his political or military leadership is that it is also an exaltation of individual conscience versus forcible, collective conformism. This is not a vision alien to Islam – witness all those Qur’ānic verses absolving the Prophet from responsibility for the salvation of individual Muslims, something which is essentially the fruit of their own actions. The systematised form of this vision is a moral philosophy which values good deeds only in so far as they are anchored in the fulfilled conscience of their agents, and not in the fear of any external sanctions, immediate or eschatological.

‘Abd ar-Rāziq did not have the opportunity to develop his views into such explosive conclusions. Even if he wanted to do so, violent orthodox reaction made sure that he would not.

Such was the inconclusive end of the first, and perhaps the most important, controversy in twentieth-century Sunnī political thought. The abolition of the Caliphate was outwardly a great victory for the modernists – Muslim ‘revisionists’ no less than secularisers – since it removed the last visible symbol of an outworn power structure. But the real victor at the end of the day was the orthodoxy which had effectively prevented a momentous change in the political reality from leading to a corresponding adjustment in the conventional notions of political legitimacy. Its success was facilitated to a large extent by the over-confident, intemperate mood of some of the modernists, which made them insensitive to whatever potential for reform existed inside the religious community. Instead of developing this potential by adopting a more discriminating approach, the modernists launched an offensive which, simultaneous as it was with the secularisation of Turkey, lent plausibility to the traditionalists’ charge that what the modernists sought was not a simple modification of religious attitudes, but the very eradication of Islam as an all-inclusive system of moral, social and political guidelines. The ideological conflict between the two groups was later compounded by a cultural gap: while in the twenties the Turkish or Egyptian opponents of the Caliphate still expressed themselves in the conventional terms and concepts of the orthodox theory, the later generations of modernists increasingly tended to use terms and concepts borrowed from Western schools of political thought.

3 The concept of the Islamic state

I Muḥammad Rashīd Riḍā

As was hinted at the beginning of the last chapter, the crisis over the Caliphate had one subsidiary, doctrinal result: it introduced the idea of the Islamic state as an alternative to the Caliphate, which was now being declared, either implicitly or explicitly, not only by the Turkish secularists but also by Muslims of such diverging outlooks as 'Abd ar-Rāziq, Rashīd Riḍā and the 'Ulamā' of al-Azhar to be impossible of resuscitation. But soon the idea moved into the centre of religio-political thinking. What prompted this shift was a combination of circumstances arising from the traditionalist response to the secularisation of Turkey, the aggressiveness of some Western Powers, the setbacks to secular–liberal ideologies in Egypt, and, last but not least, the consequences of the Palestinian crisis. The concept was at first vague and general, but it grew in clarity and hardness as these circumstances made themselves felt, and militant Muslims stepped up their efforts to assert Islamic values in the face of Western inroads. The chief vehicle through which the concept was actively canvassed was fundamentalism, the most political manifestation of religious thought from the mid-twenties onwards. Fundamentalism was at first the meeting-ground between the puritanism of the Wahhābī founders of Saudi Arabia, and the teachings of the *Salafiyyah* movement (from *salaf*, meaning forerunners), which, drawing inspiration from Muḥammad 'Abduh, preached a return to primeval Islam conceived as a religion in perfect harmony with the humanism and rationalism of modern Man. These twin wings of fundamentalism later on drifted apart, with the *Salafiyyah* being increasingly represented by activist and revolutionary trends, and Wahhābism by a staunch conservatism. This chapter is devoted to an exposition of the ideas of Muḥammad Rashīd Riḍā (d. 1935), in many ways the founding theoretician of the Islamic state in its modern sense, and their continuation in the doctrines of later fundamentalists.

As a direct disciple of 'Abduh, Rashīd Riḍā has exercised great influence in shaping the activist ideology of the Muslim Brothers in Egypt and elsewhere in the Sunnī-Muslim world. Besides, he was certainly the only Muslim thinker of note at his time who formulated his views on the Islamic state as part of his observations on the dissolution of the Caliphate clearly and courageously, but unlike 'Abd ar-Rāziq – with whom he shared some of his conclusions – not in a way which would aggravate the traditionalist resistance to change. His thesis provides an instructive starting-point to gauge the degree to which the modern concept of the Islamic state has changed from its earlier spiritual character to its present, totally political nature.

It was explained in the previous chapter how in the final days of the Ottoman Caliphate Arab nationalists welcomed its weakening, and intensified their campaign for the restoration of the Caliphate to the Arabs. The aftermath of the First World War, however, had a sobering effect on some of them. After the war, the only Arab candidate for the Caliphate was Sharīf Ḥusayn of Mecca, but his connections with the British discredited him in Muslim eyes. When in March 1924, after the abolition of the Caliphate in Turkey, he declared himself the Caliph of the Muslims, only the representatives of Iraq, Ḥijāz and east Jordan swore the oath of allegiance to him; but the Muslims of India and Egypt rejected him as a British agent. This made the Arab advocates of the Caliphate – as an institution – very cautious in making any suggestion for the future occupant of the office, without first finding the right candidate.[1]

Rashīd Riḍā's important treatise on the Caliphate (*Al-khilāfah aw'al-imāmat 'al-uẓmā*, the Caliphate or the Supreme Imāmate, 1922–3) was published on the eve of the abolition of the Caliphate. Nevertheless, it gives vivid expression both to this caution, and the tension between the demands of Arab nationalism, and religious loyalty to the Caliphate. It is a work which should obviously be appreciated against the background of Riḍā's intellectual development – his change from an advocate of the Ottoman Caliphate in the name of Islamic universalism, to a relatively objective commentator on its decline – as well as in conjunction with his modernist ideas on the necessity of *ijtihād* (independent judgement), legislation, and fighting ignorance and superstition among Muslims.[2] He belonged to that generation of Syrian *émigrés* who made Egypt their home and centre of intellectual activity at the end of the nineteenth century, and were therefore able to take a broader view of things.[3] He condemned ethnic and racial prejudice, and criticised Ibn Khaldūn for glorifying '*aṣabiyyah*, or group solidarity and clan partisanship, as the motivating force of polities, dynasties and even prophetic missions. Notwithstanding all this, he was an active spokesman of Syrian Arab nationalism. In 1920 he became President of the Syrian National Congress that elected Fayṣal as King of Syria. It is perhaps this oscillation between Islamic universalism and Arab nationalism which is behind his undogmatic, at times ambivalent, views on the Caliphate and the Islamic state – a feature which is all the more striking because of the unshakeable tone of conviction imparted by his other, innumerable articles in his periodical *Al-Manār*.

Riḍā brings up the subject of the Islamic state after dealing with the problems of the Caliphate. He does this in three stages: (1) first he traces the foundations of the Caliphate in the Islamic political theory; (2) then he demonstrates the cleavage between that theory and the political practice of

Sunnī Muslims; (3) finally he advances his own idea of what an Islamic state should be. Each of these stages will have to be described in some detail.[4]

(1) In the first stage, his introductory résumé of the classical theory of the Caliphate is ostensibly aimed at establishing its 'obligatoriness' (*wujūb*), which he holds to be based on the religious law (*shar'*), and not, as the Mu'tazilah contended, on reason (*'aql*). To prove his point, he relies heavily on the Prophetic sayings (*ḥadīths*) and consensus (*ijmā'*), but not on the Qur'ān. This, and his extensive quotations from Māwardī, Ghazālī, al-Ījī and Sa'd ad-Dīn at-Taftāzānī, at first create the impression that he has subscribed to a legalistic approach to the question. But it soon becomes obvious that his main objective is to show that the classical theory sets such high standards for the right conduct of the Caliphate that the institution which has come to be known under this name to Muslims in history should unhesitatingly be rejected as a monstrous deviation. In the light of this conclusion, his quotations from authoritative sources of the past transpire to be no more than precautionary lines of defence against possible orthodox attacks.

He differentiates between what he calls the *ideal* Caliphate, which as is agreed by most Muslims existed only under the *Rāshidūn* (Rightly-Guided) and a few exceptional pious rulers like the Umayyad 'Umar Ibn 'Abd al-'Azīz, and the *actual* Caliphate, under which the Muslims lived for the best part of their history. Subdividing the actual Caliphate into the Imāmate of Necessity (*al-imāmat' aḍ-ḍarūrah*) and Tyranny, or conquest by force (*at-taghallub bi'l-quwwah*), he again summons the past jurists to his aid to demonstrate that these varieties of the Caliphate were permitted and tolerated only as temporary expedients, in special circumstances. The Imāmate of Necessity was allowed in cases when all the essential prerequisites of the Caliph, especially justice, efficiency, and descent from the Quraysh could not be found in one person, and the electors had therefore to settle for a candidate who possessed most of these qualities. The Imāmate of Tyranny was simply installed by force, and rested on the family or tribal solidarity of its founders, with no room left for the approval of the electors. But the jurists' permission to the Muslims to tolerate or obey these regimes, Riḍā asserts, was not supposed to be more than a dispensation; by no means did it absolve the believers from the duty of striving towards establishing a proper Caliphate. The Imāmate of Necessity had to be obeyed because its alternative was chaos. Less dignified was the obedience to the Imāmate of Tyranny, because it belonged to the same category of actions as the eating of pork or the flesh of animals not killed according to ritual requirements, and in cases of unavoidable necessity. Riḍā gives equal weight to the jurists' detailed descriptions of the conditions under which the Caliph forfeits his rights, and can be deposed. After quoting all the cases which, according to Māwardī, give cause for the deposition of the Caliph (loss of moral probity, physical disability, insanity, captivity, apostasy and unbelief), he dwells on the right to revolt against unjust rulers. He considers this problem in the case of a properly constituted Caliphate, because the Imāmate of Tyranny obviously falls outside any such discussion, and is governed by the maxim 'the necessities make the forbidden things permissible' (*aḍ-ḍarūrāt tubīḥ al-maḥḍūrāt*).[5]

In his desire to prove the soundness of the theoretical Caliphate, Riḍā simply avers that the past authorities have imposed the obligation to resist injustice and oppression on *ahl al-ḥall wa'l-'aqd*, 'the people who loose and bind'. This term, which we have come across several times before, covers all varieties of the representatives of the community, particularly the 'Ulamā'. The vital condition which should be observed by this group in exercising its right to resist injustice 'even if by war' is that the 'advantages of such an act should outweigh its disadvantages'.[6] Riḍā again quotes classical jurists in support of this, but what he fails to do is to examine questions left unanswered in the principal sources of classical theory. In the first place, the qualifications laid down for the exercise of the right to revolt can, in practice, evidently be more constrictive than vague phrases like 'advantages outweighing disadvantages' would imply. The urge to revolt must always be weighed against the fear that it might result in anarchy. This fear acts as an ever-present deterrent to rebellion by making the *status quo*, compared with probable ensuing civil strife, appear as 'the lesser of the two evils'. Then there is the problem of defining exactly what constitutes injustice and oppression, and what is equally important, determining whether they have been committed with a frequency and on a scale which would warrant revolt. Presumably occasional contraventions of the canons of justice cannot give cause for rebellion, since they fall into the category of *ma'ṣīyah*, or individual sin, which, contrary to *kufr* (unbelief), is a controversial ground for disobeying the Caliph; some authorities maintain that in such cases he should merely be advised to correct his behaviour.[7] And finally, there is the procedural problem of locating the authority for settling the foregoing questions. This, in fact, is part of the larger problem of the accountability of the Caliph or ruler in general which we shall discuss in the following chapter. In Riḍā's analysis, the only people qualified to pass judgement on the conduct of the rulers are again those who 'loose and bind'.[8] In the absence of any tradition of political thinking outside the framework of the *Sharī'ah*, however, these leaders can do no other than follow the advice of the 'Ulamā', or the *mujtahids*. So ultimately everything turns on the ability and integrity of the 'Ulamā' to voice their honest opinion on vital political issues. When one remembers that in classical theory the Caliph was also supposed to be a *mujtahid*,[9] the challenge posed to the 'Ulamā' by an offending Caliph seems all the more daunting.

But, like 'Abdūh,[10] Riḍā diagnoses the corruption of the 'Ulamā', and their subservience to rulers, as one of the main causes of the distortion of the Caliphate, from its ideal form under the *Rāshidūn* into an apparatus serving the basest interests of the despots and dynasts, thus making tyranny the normal form of government in Islamic history.[11] Hence the very people who are charged with the task of preserving the justness of the system prove to be the mainstay of its abuses. The vicious circle is complete – freedom from injustice is not possible without the 'Ulamā' taking the lead, but the 'Ulamā' themselves perpetuate injustice by giving it an air of divine providence. The conundrum is not exclusive to the theory of the Caliphate, but is inherent in any political system shielded by an ideology, since this is bound to produce after a while self-appointed guardians of its 'truth', ready to hurl accusations of heresy at all potential or actual rivals.

Interestingly enough, when it comes to mentioning specific cases from history of how the Muslims have used their legitimate right to revolt against unjust rulers, Riḍā mentions only the example of the Turks overthrowing the Ottoman Sulṭānate.[12] This is strange, not only because the subsequent secularisation of Turkey greatly diminished the value of any argument that the Turkish decision to overthrow the Sulṭānate had been a simple exercise of the right to resist, or revolt, against injustice, but also because – as was noted before[13] – the Turks had justified their decision by denying both the canonical obligatoriness and primacy of the Caliphate – a view diametrically opposed to that taken by Riḍā in the earlier sections of his treatise.[14] But perhaps such laconic remarks in favour of the Turkish decision constitute a more reliable indicator of Riḍā's real feelings on the subject than the quotations from the orthodox jurists. Perhaps these quotations were really meant to ward off the accusations of heresy, in order to make his suggestion for the future of the Caliphate palatable to orthodox tastes. One thing certainly casts doubt on the seriousness of Riḍā's debate about the right to revolt. He quotes all the principal jurists on the matter, except one who otherwise enjoys his unstinting admiration: Ibn Taymiyyah. It was, as was mentioned in the Introduction, Ibn Taymiyyah who, with more authority than any other orthodox jurist, sharpened the Muslims' consciousness of the excruciating choice they have to make between anarchy and injustice, every time they feel oppressed by a tyrant. It was with him that endurance of the *status quo* acquired the dignity of a pious act. His warning against the evils of anarchy has to be treated seriously because it comes not from a pseudo-intellectual cynically preaching doctrines favourable to the interests of the ruling classes but from a devoted religious thinker who had the interests of the Muslims at heart, and paid for his convictions with his freedom.

But this omission might also be to Riḍā's credit, because it denotes his awareness of a major pitfall in Sunnī political theory. He undoubtedly knew that so long as the authority of a government, whether called Caliphate or otherwise, is supposedly sanctioned by religious tenets, no rebellion against it can be easily justified. Quoting Ibn Taymiyyah would have faced him with the necessity of engaging in a great deal of sophistry to explain it away, or make it consonant with his other arguments. He therefore saw the way out of the vicious circle created by the 'Ulamā's double role as both the defenders and monitors of the *status quo*, by concentrating on the familiar safeguards against the abuse of power: unfailing enforcement of the principle of consultation (*shūrā*) between the ruler and the 'people who loose and bind',[15] full assumption by the latter group of its responsibility for the sound conduct of public affairs, and what for him seemed to be the most important of all, restoring the pristine standards of simplicity, humility and frugality in the lifestyle of the rulers, so that those attaining high positions are not motivated by the desires of self-aggrandisement and hegemony. Of these suggestions, only that on the necessity of reactivating the 'people who loose and bind' is both crucial and practical, and we shall later consider its implications. Consultation is also feasible, provided it is clearly defined and, as Riḍā himself realised, guaranteed by solid constitutional arrangements. The last proposal, on the rulers' modest living, is obviously purely moral, and relies heavily on the good faith of the rulers, although one shrewd way of ensuring it, which he advises on the Prophet's authority, is to debar from office those who display willingness to occupy it (*ṭālib al-wilāyah la yuwallā*).[16]

(2) The second stage of Riḍā's advance towards the idea of the Islamic state is to examine a number of practical difficulties hindering the rehabilitation of the Caliphate – especially finding the right person to become the Caliph of all Muslims, as well as the right city for his capital. Surveying the political scene, he rules out the most ambitious candidate for the Caliphate at the time, Sharīf Ḥusayn of Mecca, for his despotism, lack of canonical knowledge, pro-British sympathies, and opposition to reformism. Turks are also naturally excluded, since they were at the time opposed to the concentration of all spiritual and political powers in the hands of one man anyway. He is silent on the Egyptian candidates. Only Imām Yaḥyā of the Yemen enjoys his approval because of his mastery of the religious law, moral probity, efficiency, political semi-independence, and Qurayshī descent. But he admits that the Imām could become the Caliph of all Muslims only if, first, the people of Ḥijāz, Tihāmah and Najd agreed to take the oath of allegiance to him, and, second, if the Imām himself undertook to observe the rules of *ijtihād* by allowing all groups of Muslims to follow their particular rites. In point of fact, laying such conditions was another way of stating the impracticality of the whole scheme, for the simple reason that the Imām belonged to the Zaydī sect of Shī'īsm. Although, as Riḍā rightly points out, compared with other Shī'īs, the Zaydīs are the closest to Sunnī, especially Ḥanafī, Muslims in canonical matters, it is hard to imagine how the majority of Sunnī Muslims could have brought themselves to obeying a Shī'ī caliph, of whatever denomination.[17]

So he arrives at the sad conclusion that there really is no candidate to meet the ideal requirements of the Caliphate. For more or less the same kind of reasons he finds both Ḥijāz and Istanbul unsuitable as the seat of a restored Caliphate. Ideally, he says, the Caliphate should be revived through the co-operation between the Turks and the Arabs of the Peninsula, who between themselves possess the essential qualities required for the regeneration of Islam. The Turks occupy a place between the rigidity of the Arabs of the Peninsula and the undiscriminating, Westernised outlook of those who seek to dispense with the religious and historical constituents of the Islamic community; the determination, tenacity and courage of Turkey's new leaders, and their skill in military techniques, ensure their success in reforming Islam by establishing a Caliphate equipped with both the material strength and moral virtues necessary to protect the Muslims from Bolshevism and anarchy. The Arabs of the Peninsula, on the other hand, are the 'substance' and 'root' of Islam; there is no trace of heresy and Westernisation in their midst, their only defect being 'ignorance of the ways of administering and developing the land'.[18] He also praises the Arabs because of the pivotal place of their language in Islam; this has nothing to do with national or racial prejudices, but is cleverly incorporated into his reformistic doctrines: Islamic revivalism depends on *ijtihād* in religious law, and *ijtihād* is impossible without proper understanding of the sources of the law, for which knowledge of Arabic is an indispensable tool. Again the realist in him takes over; he confesses to his lack of confidence in both the Arabs and the Turks, because neither of them has reached the requisite degree of progress, and neither is showing any readiness to co-operate in such an enterprise.[19]

He then makes a suggestion which, although sounding as utopian as the previous one, gives him the opportunity to set forth his principal ideas on the nature and future of the Caliphate: it should be installed, so he proposes, in an 'intermediary zone' between the Arabian Peninsula and Anatolia, where Arabs, Turks and Kurds live side by side; for instance in Mosul, which at that time was the bone of contention between Iraq, Turkey and Syria, and moreover he wants the adjoining territories, which were also being claimed by Syria, to be annexed to it. He hopes that once the area is declared neutral, as the seat of the Caliphate, the parties would stop quarrelling over it, and Mosul would be truly 'worthy of its name (in Arabic, *mauṣil*, literally, the place of re-union)... serving as the spiritual link (*rābiṭah waṣl ma'nawī*)' at a geographic borderline.[20]

The metaphor 'spiritual link' is in fact the key to Riḍā's vision of a regenerate Caliphate – and of an Islamic state. He elaborates this vision in his proposal on the organisation of the Caliphate. For him, this presented a simpler problem than the previous issues, not least because he could approach it free from the fear of offending any national susceptibilities. What he suggests is not in essence different from what the Turks had already done, namely, the transformation of the Caliphate into a spiritual office, serving mainly as a symbol of the unity of all Muslims, settling canonical disputes, but also overseeing the general adherence to Islamic rules among his followers. This is proved not only by the kind of remark just quoted on the character of the Caliphal realm, but also by his heavy emphasis on the moral and scholarly qualities of the candidates. True, one can point to some of his remarks, requiring the acknowledgement of a properly elected Caliph as 'the just Imām, representing the Prophet... in upholding religion and temporal politics (*sīyāsat 'ad-dunyā*)',[21] to argue that what he had in mind was more than a purely spiritual pontificate. But the opposite testimony of other features of his scheme is overwhelming: his lengthy discursus on the virtues of 'independent knowledge' (*al-'ilm al-istiqlālī*) or *ijtihād* and other related juridical talents, which takes up almost the whole of the section on the 'institutions' of the future Caliphate[22] leaves the reader in little doubt that these are for him the most essential qualifications of the Caliph. His reticence on efficiency, courage and other civic and political virtues which he himself enumerates in the first phase of his argument in the manner of classical theorists may not mean their exclusion, but does mean their relegation to a lower rank. His proposed procedure of electing the Caliph is also isulated against political considerations by confining the candidates to the graduates of a special university to be set up to train not only the future Caliphs but also religious judges and *muftīs*. The courses which he recommends for the curriculum of such a university are all certainly useful to widen the trainees' general knowledge, but hardly to produce practical politicians: international law, heresiography, universal history, sociology and study of papal, episcopal and patriarchal institutions. Lastly, the proposed administrative offices of the Caliphate were all of a consultative, supervisory and apostolic nature – which, even though carrying immense political weight, were not exactly the same as the attributes of a fully-fledged Caliphate.[23]

When these suggestions are read in the context of Riḍā's reformism – his attack on 'fossilised jurisconsults', his praise of modern sciences and technology, and his repeated pleas for the revival of *ijtihād* – their innovative import, and proximity to 'Abd ar-Rāziq's conclusions, becomes more visible. But again unlike 'Abd ar-Rāziq, he could not be accused of having denied the canonical origins of the Caliphate, or having pleaded the separation of religion and politics in Islam. He had, after all, demonstrated his earnestness by paying attention to some of the practical obstacles to the restoration of the Caliphate in its traditional form – a feature missing from the works of most Muslim writers of the period, who concerned themselves with speculative generalisations. After identifying these obstacles, he had arrived at a conclusion which was not very far from that reached by the Turks and 'Abd ar-Rāziq – although, compared with the latter, from different premises. The conclusion was that, however much the Sunnī Muslims, himself included, piously wished otherwise, it was impossible to revive the traditional Caliphate, and hence it would be better to devise the nearest alternative to it.

(3) It is here that Rashīd Riḍā turns from the question of the Caliphate

to that of the Islamic state – a subtle, and almost imperceptible, transition. However paradoxical it may sound, the term he uses for the Islamic state (*ad-dawlah*, or *al-ḥukūmat al-Islāmiyyah*)[24] is, at least in its modern sense, a new addition to Islamic nomenclature thanks mainly to the Ottomans. In classical Islam, state or government (the distinction between the two is a recent refinement) was known, if not as Caliphate or Imāmate, then under such terms as *imārah* (amirate), or *wilāyah* (guardianship or governorship). Riḍā does not give a definition of the Islamic state, all the time implying that it is synonymous with the Caliphate. Sometimes he uses compounds such as the 'Islamic Caliphate' (*al-khilāfat al-Islāmiyyah*), or the 'government of the Caliphate' (*ḥukūmat al-khilāfah*),[25] which are rather tautological. Hence the many ambiguities in his plan, which is nominally offered in the name of the reorganisation of the Caliphate, but actually proposes a new entity, since some of its functions and institutions (for instance, legislation and propaganda) are unprecedented. It is another evidence of his pragmatic disposition that his plan for this reorganisation makes a direct assault on two vital issues: the principle of popular sovereignty, and the possibility of man-made laws. Schemes for the Islamic state which take no account of these two questions are empty expressions of utopian goals – and there have been many such schemes offered to Muslims even after Rashīd Riḍā proposed his. He and his master 'Abduh deserve great credit for having at least initiated the debate over them.

Of the two issues, the first is treated lightly. All that Riḍā says on the subject is what most contemporary Muslim writers – whether traditionalist or modernist – charitably recommend: that once the government implements the principle of *shūrā*, or consultation between the rulers and the ruled, and the provisions laid down by the jurisconsults on the right to resist injustice, democracy is ensured for Muslims.[26] But consultation depends on the good faith of the rulers, and the vicious circle created by the provisions against injustice has just been hinted at. A further guarantee of democracy for Riḍā is the predominance of the 'Ulamā' who, in his view, are ideally placed to act as the natural and genuine representatives of Muslims. In saying this, he is manifestly inspired by the performance of the Shī'ī 'Ulamā' of Iran, whom he admires as being the only men of their class living up to this expectation by their leadership of the famous Tobacco Rebellion of 1892 and the Constitutional Revolution of 1906.[27] The second issue – on legislation – is treated more fully, and by leading up again to the function of the 'Ulamā' links with his discussion on the first issue, and in a way makes up for its shortcomings.

If political philosophers have normally understood law in terms of a rational requirement of orderly social life, the Salafī proponents of the Islamic state have more often tended to conceive of it as a testing ground for measuring the Muslim community's cultural and moral integration. It was 'Abduh who argued cogently against the Muslims' adoption of foreign, mainly Western, laws and institutions. He put the blame for this firmly at the door of orthodoxy for its impervious juridical outlook: by ignoring the *Sharī'ah*'s boundless resources for legal renovation, orthodoxy fostered the misconception that Islam by its very nature is incapable of coping with the growing complexity of modern life, and Muslims had therefore to have recourse to foreign laws. Pursuing the same point, Rashīd Riḍā likens the legal system of every society to its language: just as no language should allow the grammatical rules of another language to govern its syntax and modes of expression, if it wants to keep its identity, no nation should adopt the laws of another nation without exercising its independent judgement and power of adaptation for adjusting them to its beliefs, mores and interests, otherwise it will fall prey to mental anarchy, and forfeit its solidarity and independence. The Muslims have not only borrowed foreign laws, worse still, they have done so without any sense of discrimination. They can now achieve cultural and moral redemption only by liberating all the latent agents of dynamism in their religion. For 'Abduh, the main methodological tools for bringing this about were first, the principle of *istiṣlāḥ* or *maṣlaḥah*, the supremacy of public interest as the guiding norm to deduce laws from the Qur'ān and Tradition, and second, the method of *ikhtīyār* (selection) or *talfīq*, namely comparison and synthesis of the good points of all the four Sunnī legal schools, and even the opinions of independent jurists not adhering to any of them.[28]

As *muftī* of Egypt, 'Abduh applied these principles to a number of his rulings and decisions on issues which were seemingly trivial, or peripheral to the tension between tradition and modern political ideas, such as whether Muslims could wear European hats or eat the flesh of the animals slaughtered by Christians and Jews, whether the painting of human figures was permitted by religious law, whether polygamy was good or bad. Riḍā's departures were also of the same nature, and have been criticised because, with the exception of his concession on credit, and his interpretation of *ribā* (usury) as a compensation for service, following Muḥammad 'Abduh and Ibn Qayyim Jawziyyah, and his decision that art (music and painting) is canonically permissible hardly 'touch any of the more vital aspects of a modern state and society, such as the position of women'.[29] But such criticisms overlook the ability of orthodox forces to mount a successful resistance against any innovations of a more substantial scope, with devastating consequences for the further advance of religious modernism – witness their vociferous reaction against Ṭāhā Ḥusayn's critique of pre-Islamic poetry, with its implied threat to all traditional thinking,[30] and 'Abd ar-Rāziq's liberationist tract against the Caliphate. As it happened, the peripheral reforms of 'Abduh and Riḍā played, in the long run, a more effective part in transforming the attitudes of ordinary Egyptians towards modernity.

From the premise that the independence of the legal system is an essential bulwark for the Muslims against cultural alienation and moral anarchy, Riḍā not only draws the obvious conclusion that the *Sharīʿah* must be preserved or revived in its proper form, but also infers that the civic rule (*ḥukūmah madaniyyah*) can neither survive nor function without legislation. The term he uses for legislation is *ishtirāʿ*, which again is a neologism in the sense he has in mind, because although it is derived from the root *sharʿ* (literally meaning law, but specifically, Divine Law), in his usage, it means both the actual law-making and the ability to deduce law (*istinbāṭ*) from the *Sharīʿah*. He stresses that the essence of these rules is their adaptability to meet the exigencies of every time and place, and fit the religious and political characteristics of every nation.[31] The final criterion, however, against which such laws should be judged remains the *Sharīʿah*.

This is by no means an original idea, since one could find its precedents and counterparts in the history of the Ottoman legal reforms,[32] or in the controversies during the Iranian Constitutional Revolution.[33] But in expressing it, Riḍā comes amazingly close to the secularists when he states the canonical reasons for the Muslims' freedom of legislation in non-religious matters. The most important of these, according to him, is as always the necessity of *ijtihād*. But there are also two other reasons. He adduces one of these from the well-known division in the *Sharīʿah* between the rules governing devotional or ritual acts (*ʿibādāt*), and those governing social relations or mundane transactions (*muʿāmalāt*). He redefines the nature of the latter category, which is primarily relevant to the task of legislator. He says that relations governed by such rules are only subject to certain general religious principles, such as the individuals' respect for one another's rights, honour, lives and properties. But outside this proviso, all administrative, juridical, political and military acts, in which the main intention is not 'nearness to God', belong to the 'branches' (*furūʿ*) of the *Sharīʿah*, provided they are performed in good faith. This means that they are fit to be the subject of novel, man-made laws.[34] The other reason results from the distinction between religion (*dīn*) and the law (*sharʿ*). It is true, Riḍā says, that Islam consists of both, and in traditional sources the terms for both are used interchangeably. But they can give rise to two separate sets of rules. Borrowing a term from logic, he describes their relationship as one of the Universal (religion) to the Particular (law).[35] He does not pursue his analogy, and his imprecision again lends considerable potential to his argument as a defence of secular legislation. In logic, the relationship of the Universal to the Particular can be one of two kinds: absolute (Animal to Man), and particular (Man to White man). Riḍā does not say to which of these two kinds the relationship of religion to law in Islam belongs. If it is of the first kind, all provisions of the law, however irrelevant they might be to Man's spiritual needs, have to be under the aegis of religion. But if it belongs to the second category, then large areas of the law can be independent of religion.

In addition to these general considerations, there are also specific legal formulae which Riḍā cites as further licence for a modern legislator to make public interest his paramount aim. They all emanate from the notion of necessity. He mentions only two of these (we will know of more in our discussion on socialism in the next chapter). First is the principle of protection against distress and constriction (*'usr wa ḥaraj*), which applies essentially to social relations or transactions, but only rarely to acts of devotion and worship, because in these a certain degree of discomfort and even painful effort is necessary to cultivate discipline and purity of the soul, whereas social relations contain the religious element only to the extent described before. Second is the principle of refraining from causing loss or harm to oneself or to others (*lā ḍara wa lā ḍirār*).[36] Hence one might say that even in the absence of any textual injunction in the Qur'ān and Tradition on *ijtihād*, the principle of necessity would have been enough to furnish a canonical basis for independent legal deductions.

Legal dynamism thus turns out in Riḍā's description to be the cornerstone of the Islamic state in the modern world. In his mind, so long as such a state is able, thanks to the intellectual vitality of the 'Ulamā', to seek solutions to problems hitherto unforeseen in the *Sharī'ah*, not by going beyond its provisions but by making full use of its inherent mechanism for renovation, there is no danger of the Muslims losing faith in the excellence of their religion. For this reason, although Riḍā identifies the *Ummah* or community as the locus of national sovereignty,[37] he uses this democratic fiction to bolster the position of its representatives – *ahl al-ḥall wa'l-'aqd*, 'the people who loose and bind'. It will be recalled that this term includes the 'Ulamā', which in the present context means the jurisconsults or the jurists who, according to Riḍā, should possess, in addition to a thorough grounding in the traditional sources of the *Sharī'ah*, a lively critical mind for independent judgement. But for him, what should distinguish them most markedly from other experts in the application of the *Sharī'ah* is their moderation: they must strike a balance between the Westernised élite and the hidebound, dogmatic, orthodoxy.[38] As we saw, Riḍā himself tried – although not always successfully – to practise this moderation in his observations on the state of the Muslims of his time: his critique of both Arabs and Turks for their faults, while recognising their merits; his admiration of the Iranian Shī'ī 'Ulamā' as the true spokesmen of their people in both religious and political matters, while criticising some of their doctrines for apotheosing their Imāms; his sympathies for the fundamentalism of the Ḥanbalī school,[39] while advocating flexibility in its application,[40] and finally, some of his utilitarian legal teachings as exemplified by the counsels mentioned before. The negative side of moderation is his occasional unwillingness to make a clear-cut stand on controversial issues, or to think out the full implications of his reformism. This may be the result not so much of a 'tendency to dash off in all directions',[41] as of the honest doubts afflicting a reformer who leaves the safe corner of abstract speculation for the hectic arena of practical politics.

We can now summarise our discussion on Rashīd Riḍā by drawing together the main strands of his idea of the Islamic state. The broad ideological orientation of such a state, contrary to what is suggested by the label of Riḍā's own brand of reformed Islam – fundamentalism – is not a total return to the origins of Islam. It is a return to only those elements of early Islamic idealism which are untarnished by mundane, ethnic and sectarian prejudices. The political, social and economic affairs of the state are regulated by a constitution which is inspired in its general principles by the Qur'ān, the Tradition and the historical experience of the *Rāshidūn* caliphs. Since *ijtihād* is an imperative attribute of all legal thinking, these primordial sources are not likely to present many insuperable obstacles to any measure designed to promote public welfare. This is further ensured by the provision that the Head of State – Caliph or Imām – should himself be a *mujtahid*, and aided in his juridical capacity by 'the people who loose and bind'. These people form the most powerful group in the state and are the guardians of its Islamic character. They share many of the theoretical functions of their traditional forerunners: they elect the Caliph and represent the community. It is in consultation with them that the decisions of the state acquire a religiously binding force. But what is new in their case is their power to legislate. It is thanks to this feature that law-making, as an ongoing effort to find rational and systematic solutions to unprecedented problems, is no longer an innovation. The *Sharī'ah* continues to have overriding authority, but there is also a body of 'positive law' (*qānūn*) subordinate to it, in the sense that if there is conflict, it is the *Sharī'ah* which is valid, but otherwise positive law is accepted and with a binding force which derives ultimately from the principles of Islam.'[42] The Caliph is elected by the representatives of all Muslims from a group of highly trained jurisconsults who should also have impeccable reputations; but he is not required to have any specifically political and military qualities. There is ambiguity about the nature of his authority and leadership, but whatever it is, he is not a temporal ruler. This does not mean that his office is apolitical, but since positive law occupies such a pivotal place in the state, there is an overwhelming emphasis on his status as the moving spirit of the legislative process.

The Head of State or Caliph is the elected leader of all Muslims – (Twelver) Shī'īs, Zaydīs, Ibāḍī (Khārijīs) and the four schools of Sunnīsm, but seeks neither the abolition of their differences nor a forced integration of their creeds, but simply a recognition of doctrinal pluralism as a legitimate manifestation of free individual judgement. The Caliph should be obeyed only to the extent that his decisions conform to the principles of Islam, and have a bearing on public interests. The community, through its representatives, has the right to challenge his decisions whenever these are seen to contravene those principles. Every individual is entitled to learn for himself all the requisite techniques of understanding the Qur'ān and Tradition without any intermediaries, either past or present. There is no religious domination (*as-sulṭat ad-dīniyyah*) in Islam;[43] faith is an individual matter which can be the subject of only guidance and education, but not edict and regimentation. Nobody, whether powerful or weak, is authorised to spy on anyone's beliefs. Women are equal to men at all levels of social activity, except in the headship of household, the supreme Imāmate, and leadership in prayer, which are exclusive to men. The minorities – Christians and Jews – enjoy security of worship and business; they can even engage in activities which are allowed in their own religions but forbidden in Islam, provided that such acts do not harm others. On this score they are in a sense more privileged than Muslims, in whose case apostasy is punishable (but not by death, which has been required by the consensus only, and has no basis in the Qur'ān). The spirituality of the office of the Caliph does not obviate the need for a temporal authority which should 'complete the wisdom of law-making' by creating a centralised system of sanctions and punishments against law-breakers. The exact relationship between this temporal authority and the Caliphate is not known. Obviously Rashīd Riḍā could not work out the details of this relationship, and remove the numerous ambiguities and inconsistencies in his scheme, while the debate on the Caliphate was still going on at the time of the publication of his treatise. Even so, his outline of the Islamic state embodies many features which make it acceptable to a large cross-section of the Muslim community all over the world; especially, in spite of his vehement polemics against the Shī'īs, the historical arguments which he adduces in support of his plan appear to make many concessions to their political theory: his criticism of the method of candidature of Abū Bakr on the ground that it had not been preceded by consultation with all the parties concerned, of 'Umar's appointment by Abū Bakr, because it was later misused to institute hereditary rule, and of Uthmān's weakness which allowed the Umayyads' encroachment upon the interests of the community, together with his admission that the Caliphate in its proper form thus existed only partially under the *Rāshidūn*, and disappeared altogether after them, all amount to a virtual endorsement of the Shī'ī case against the Sunnī Caliphate. It is noteworthy that in recent years, about half a century after the publication of Rashīd Riḍā's treatise, when some Iranian Shī'ī leaders – the architects of the Islamic Revolution – produced their initial ideas on an Islamic state as an alternative to submission to tyrannies in anticipation of the return of the hidden Imām, there were strong similarities between their pronouncements and those of their Sunnī adversary: in both, the 'Ulamā' have prime responsibility for leading the popular struggle for establishing the new state; *ijtihād* is the main intellectual means of upholding and reviving the *Sharī'ah*; the head of state is distinguished more by his jurisprudential and exegetical competence than his political skills; sectarianism is discarded in favour of an irenic, 'unitarian' Islam just as nationalism is deprecated in the name of universalism; and perhaps most important of all, resisting the cultural offensive of the West is the implied objective of all political, educational and legal reforms. The only significant difference between the two is that while the Sunnī scheme has an air of finality about it, the Shī'ī model is, even if tacitly, temporary, since it is not consciously aimed to supersede the doctrine of the Return of the Imām.

Having said all this, the fact remains that the Islamic state as perceived by Rashīd Riḍā is far from being an all-powerful system regulating every detail of the social, political and cultural life of Muslims. Whether because of some obscurities and contradictions in his scheme, or an underlying conviction that a religious prescription of the totality of human life is impossible in the modern age, the main conclusion from his outline is, as Rosenthal remarks, 'the parallel existence of a religious and political state, despite the emphasis on the former and condemnation of the latter'.[44] This dichotomy did not last very long in the subsequent evolution of the message of the *Salafiyyah*, when it was exposed to the strong undercurrents of mass politicisation, from the twenties and thirties onwards in Egypt, Syria and Pakistan. The tensions which were slowly gathering momentum in that period soon resulted in a sharp ideological polarisation. Movements seeking to use religion as an instrument of struggle in these circumstances have always been in danger of sliding into authoritarian militancy. An orderly dialogue might possibly have slowed down, if not stopped, such a drift. But a complex of factors made such a dialogue impossible: an atmosphere poisoned by the bitter political feuds of the 'twenties and 'thirties, the cultural gap between the disputants, and the resultant absence of a *rapport*, not only between the modernist critics of the Caliphate and the entrenched orthodoxy, but also among the modernists themselves. Such were the conditions surrounding the rise and development of the movement of the Muslim Brothers – the continuators of the teachings of Asad-ābādī (Afghānī), 'Abduh and Rashīd Riḍā in the field of active politics – whose ideology marks the break of fundamentalism with the notion of the parallel existence of religion and politics and insists on the subordination of the former to the latter.

II Fundamentalism

The movement of the Muslim Brothers, although forming so far the only organised Islamic trend which has had a following all over the Muslim world – particularly Egypt, Syria, Iran, Pakistan, Indonesia and Malaysia – by no means presents a homogeneous front. Its ideology, temper and style of activity in each country have been largely determined by the strategy and requirements of the national struggle, whether for independence, democracy or redeeming the vanished identity of the national culture. Accordingly, the strength of its demand for the Islamic state, and the motives and reasons for this demand, have varied greatly from country to country. Before the Islamic Revolution of 1979 in Iran, the strongest appeal came from Pakistan, where the idea of the Islamic state has always generally exerted a compelling attraction, for the simple reason that it was Islam that brought Pakistan into existence as a state. The drive in Egypt and Iran had been no less vigorous, but it was often distracted by the powerful competition of secular ideologies – nationalism, liberalism, socialism and Communism. The degree of intellectual sophistication in the formulation of the demand has similarly not been uniform – with Pakistan again taking the lead. Here we consider some of the broad characteristics of the movement in Egypt, Iran and Pakistan as examples of modern Islamic fundamentalism – in contradistinction to the traditional type exemplified by the Saudi model.

The Brothers' movement in Egypt, founded in 1928 by Ḥasan al-Bannā' (d. 1949), was the product of one of the most complex phases of its modern history. This complexity, in the words of Bannā' himself, resulted from the 'disputed control of Egypt between the Wafd and Liberal Constitutionalist parties, and the vociferous political debating, with the consequence of "disunity", which followed in the wake of the revolution of 1919; the post-war "orientations to apostasy and nihilisms" which were engulfing the Muslim world; the attacks on tradition and orthodoxy – emboldened by the "Kemalist revolt" in Turkey – which were organised into a movement for the intellectual and social emancipation of Egypt', and the non-Islamic, secularist and libertarian trends which had pervaded the entire academic and intellectual climate of Egypt.[45] The significance of this statement by Bannā' is that, while some fundamentalists today may claim their creed to be a natural outgrowth of the truth and the inherent resilience of Islam, he thus admits to a direct correlation between the Brothers' movement and its surrounding social, cultural and political factors. His own response to this prodigious range of threats to the Islamic character of Egyptian society was at first moral and didactic. He merely strove for a time to awaken his limited audience to the dangers by preaching and writing. But as his Society spread and came into conflict with opposing forces in the country, it moved towards growing militancy and political action. The factors prodding it along this course were again motley, and often sprang from Egypt's internal political development, especially its struggle against British imperialism before and after the Second World War. But one factor requires special mention here because it figures with unfailing regularity in the history of the Brothers' movement in most other Muslim countries as well. This was the impact of the Palestinian crisis, and the ensuing Arab–Israeli hostilities. The simultaneity of a number of turning-points in the history of the expansion of the Society with those in the drama of the Arab–Zionist conflict furnish yet another proof of the truism that political radicalism thrives on nothing better than the threat of an external enemy. This became evident on at least three occasions between the date of the creation of the Society, and its dissolution, once in 1948, and again in 1954.

The first was the transformation of the Society from its modest beginnings as a youth club into a potent political force. This coincided with the first phase of the open conflict between the Arabs and the Zionists, culminating in the Arab general strike of 1936–9, which provided the Society with an unprecedented opportunity to relinquish its pious campaign of 'propaganda, communication, and information' in favour of political activism. The Brothers' contribution to the Arab cause in Palestine must have played a decisive role in encouraging Bannā' to decide in 1939 on turning the Society into a political organisation. What is of more interest to us is that the Brothers redefined their ideology for the next phase in a way which stressed the ability of Islam to become a total ideology, since they now declared their programme to be based on three principles: '(a) Islam is a comprehensive, self-evolving (*mutakāmil bi-dhātihi*) system; it is the ultimate path of life, in all its spheres; (b) Islam emanates from, and is based on, two fundamental sources, the Qur'ān, and the Prophetic Tradition; (c) Islam is applicable to all times and places.'[46] Bannā' then declared his movement to be the inheritor, and catalyst, of the most activist elements in the Sunnī traditionalist and reformist thinking by describing it as 'a *Salafiyyah* message, a Sunnī way, a Ṣūfī truth, a political organisation, an athletic group, a scientific and cultural link, an economic enterprise and a social idea.'[47] The programme of the Society consisted of two items. One was the 'internationalisation' of the movement: it stressed the necessity of a struggle not only to liberate Egypt, but the whole of 'the Islamic homeland' from foreign control. The other was the duty 'to institute in this homeland a free Islamic government, practising the principles of Islam, applying its social system, propounding its solid fundamentals, and transmitting its wise call to the people'. It then went on to add that 'so long as this government is not established, the Muslims are all of them guilty before God Almighty of having failed to install it'. This betrayal, in 'the bewildering circumstances' of the time, was a betrayal, not only of Muslims, but of all humanity.[48] The Brothers could hardly be more explicit in their demand for an Islamic state.

The second instance of the impact of the Palestinian crisis had an even more radicalising influence on the Brothers' political ideology and activity. It was precipitated by the United Nations' resolution on the partition of Palestine in November 1947, and the first Arab–Israeli war. Even before that, with the increasing bitterness of the political mood of the country, and the sharpening of the struggle against the British, violence had become a normal feature of political life, with various groups using it both against one another and the Government. The stresses and frustrations caused by the war, and the Arab defeat of 1948, incited the activists to fresh violence inside Egypt, but most of the blame for this was put on the Brothers, whose society was consequently dissolved in December 1948.[49] After the assassination of Bannā' in 1949, the moderate wing of the Society tried to retrieve its legal status by electing as its leader Ḥasan Ismā'īl Ḥuḍaybī, a judge of more than twenty years standing, and an outspoken opponent of violence and terrorism. But this was a temporary diversion, and the militants soon took over again. The first war with Israel affected the fate of the Brothers – and through them, Egyptian politics – in another way too: it put them in touch with the Free Officers, the nationalist group in the Egyptian army which overthrew the monarchy in 1952. Although marred at times by an ambiguity that characterised the Society's position towards all political groups, these links were of a special nature, forged as they were by the common hardships of the two groups at the Battle of Fālūjah. Apparently, while the Brothers helped to indoctrinate the Free Officers, the latter helped the Brothers with military education (Nāṣir was once accused of having trained the Brothers in the use of arms).[50] One reason for such intimacy may have been the fact that while the Society's tactical co-operation with political circles was often planned and effected 'from above', its alliance with the Free Officers was made possible by the shared idealism, and joint action 'at the bottom'. This rift between the leadership and the rank and file – which is perhaps an inherent disability of all political parties committed to ideologies – later on badly damaged the Society as Egypt's political crisis deepened. However, the common feelings and experiences of the past must have aroused among the Brothers an expectation that, with the Free Officers establishing themselves as rulers of Egypt, the realisation of Islamic ideals was within easy reach. When the Officers proved to be much less doctrinaire than they had appeared on the battlefield, and too pragmatic for the Brothers' taste, conflict developed fast, and with all the intensity and violence that mark the feuds between erstwhile comrades. Such reversals turn out to be less puzzling when one notes that the rift between the leadership and the rank and file in the Society widened after 1952, as circumstances became temporarily more favourable to its activities. While at least some of the leaders seemed inclined to co-operate with the regime, and consented to a gradualist approach, the rank and file were becoming increasingly impatient with the slow pace of reforms, and suspicious of the Officers. It was thus that an unsuccessful attempt was made by the more militant Brothers on Nāṣir's life in October 1954, following which the Society was once again dissolved, and a number of its leaders and activists were executed, or condemned to long terms of imprisonment.[51] It is difficult to conceive how the relationship between the Brothers and the Free Officers could have followed such a tortuous course without the Palestinian crisis having acted as a major catalyst in the growing radicalisation of the Brothers' political thinking.

One can go on pointing to still more examples of the continuing link between the Brothers' radicalism and the Arab–Israeli conflict after 1954: the traumatic effects of the Arab defeat in the Six-Day War of 1967, however disastrous for Nāṣirism, were highly beneficial for the Brothers and their ideology. They dealt a mortal blow to the semi-secular Arab socialism, and created the right collective psyche for new attempts at vindicating the truth of suppressed or neglected traditional beliefs. This is what happens, thundered the review of al-Azhar, when Muslims discard their glorious heritage, and allow themselves to be enticed by fleeting, exotic ideas – a rebuke which would have had greater moral force if al-Azhar itself had not been obediently toeing the official line during the previous decade.[52] Although in the past al-Azhar had shared the Brothers' absolute faith in the unsurpassed ability of Islam to solve the social and political problems of Muslims, this was the first time after a long period that, in addressing the rulers, it was restating the same faith in the annoyed tone of a guide who had long suffered the aberrations of his wayward disciples. Like the Brothers, some of the Azharites interpreted the Arab–Israeli war in terms of a conflict between Islam and Judaism, and appealed for intensified religious education of the people as the most effective way of fighting Israel.[53] Both the Brothers and al-Azhar were helped in their bid for self-assertion by the religious fervour which was aroused in response to some of the consequences of the Arab defeat: the decision of the Israeli Government to declare the irrevocable annexation of Jerusalem, which is equally sacred for Muslims, the fire at al-Aqṣā Mosque, and the emergence of messianic vision and religious feelings in Israel itself. As if to concede the justice of the orthodox admonitions, the Egyptian Government released several hundred Brothers from prisons in April 1968, an act which marked a general relaxation of controls on the fundamentalist groups, at least for the time being.

The Brothers' concept of the Islamic state is an accentuated form of Rashīd Riḍā's. But its real distinguishing mark is that, as Nadav Safran rightly says, it is advanced by a militant and armed movement which does not simply 'express pious boasting or devotional cant', but reflects a 'messianic vision' which the Brothers seek to bring into being 'sword in hand'.[54] But this interpretation reveals only half the truth in so far as it does not take full account of the fact that the Brothers' political outlook was at least partly a reaction against what the Arab masses regarded as Israeli expansionism since 1948. Safran bases part of his stimulating criticism of the Brothers' doctrines on a well-known book, *Min hunā na'lam* (From Here We Learn), published in 1948 by one of their prominent leaders, Muḥammad Ghazzālī, who later defected from their ranks, but the ideas he expressed in that particular book and some of his other publications can still be treated as representative of the fundamentalist perception of the Islamic state. It is noteworthy that one of the arguments which Ghazzālī puts forward in this book to prove the case for the Islamic state – to which Safran makes no reference – is the example set by Israel. The Israelis, Ghazzālī muses with admiration, 'could have called their country the Jewish Republic, or the Jewish Socialist Union, just as their Arab neighbours have named their countries after the ruling families – [such as] the Mutawakkilite State of the Yemen, or Hashimite Jordan, or Saudi Arabia'. But they called it Israel 'which is the symbol of their attachment to their religion and reminiscences, and of their respect for their sacred values. The Jews who have done this are masters of wealth and knowledge, and leaders of politics and economy, and there have been people from among them who have taken part in effecting the nuclear fission, and in many inventions. Nevertheless, they have felt no shame in ascribing themselves to their religion, and have not thought of shirking their obligations.'[55] This tendency to taunt the Muslims for not emulating the Israelis in blending religion with politics must have received further moral stimulus from the later growth of the Judaic influences in Israel's political, military and educational institutions, as the new state consolidated itself.

At the other end of the spectrum, there are authors like Richard Mitchell, who have tried to make the Brothers' political doctrines less distasteful to Western audiences by denying that they ever aimed at installing an Islamic state, in the sense of the Caliphate or a theocracy. Mitchell's argument is that one should distinguish in the Brothers' political writings between the concept of the Islamic state, and that of the Islamic order (*an niẓām al-islāmī*); according to him the Brothers merely sought the former and not the latter.[56] This view cannot be reconciled with the kinds of statement that we quoted earlier from the Brothers' programme of 1939. But it is true that under Bannā's leadership, so long as there was any hope of achieving power through constitutional means, the Society, either out of wavering or for purposes of camouflage or politicking, often avoided a stance which would indicate a revolutionary rejection of the *status quo*. It is with respect to such vacillations that one is inclined to agree with the Egyptian critic of the Brothers, Raf'at as-Sa'īd, in describing their ideology as 'politics without programme'.[57] But as prospects for their imminent accession to power receded, both as a result of official suppression and the tremendous popularity of Nāṣirism from the Suez crisis of 1956 onwards, their ideas became more and more rigid – and lucid. This process was strengthened by external factors as well: the more the West and Israel appeared to be aggressive the more strongly the Brothers felt confident to fall back on the neglected Islamic heritage, and to delineate the state that should be grounded on it. So in the eyes of the new theorists of the movement, the silver lining to all its setbacks was the greater receptivity of the 'real' public to their protests and aspirations. The extent to which they perceived the psychological climate to have changed in their favour can be gauged by their attitude to the Caliphate. If in 1924, as we saw before, Rashīd Riḍā lauded the Turkish measures against the Caliphate as a timely exercise of the religiously sanctioned right to revolt against unjust rulers, in 1950 Ghazzālī deprecated the abolition of the Caliphate as a cowardly submission to the desires of the imperialist West which was aware of the symbolic value of that institution for millions of Muslims scattered all over the world.[58] For him, the Western hostility to Islam is a continuation of the Crusades. Some people, he says, are misled by appearances, and believe that the Europeans have discarded religion altogether; they therefore doubt that Europe's stand against Islam is motivated by Crusader feelings. But the truth is otherwise, 'the official title of the British sovereign is the Defender of the Faith, and the first item on the programme of the Conservative Party is the establishment of a Christian civilisation, and the ruling party at the moment in Italy...is the Christian Democratic Party'.[59] All this amounts to a negative justification of the necessity of the Islamic state. Muslims should set up such a state, so Ghazzālī seems to be arguing, because Israel and the West are clinging to their religions, hell-bent on the destruction of Islam. True, Ghazzālī also offers positive justifications, although these are largely the repetitions of the arguments already quoted from Rashīd Riḍā, and the critics of 'Abd ar-Rāziq. But even these assertions are studded with frequent references to European history – to the example of the French and Russian revolutionaries: just as they did not rest content with mere preaching of their egalitarian ideals but proceeded to attain political power as a necessary goal of their activities, so too Muslims cannot divorce their spiritual and moral values from politics without depriving themselves of the possibility of promoting those values.[60]

As regards the actual principles and characteristics of the Islamic state, although these are not spelled out by Ghazzālī beyond the broadest generalities, they differ from those in Rashīd Riḍā's outline in a number of important respects. First and foremost is the absence of any serious debate on the necessity or permissibility of human legislation – a subject which had engaged Rashīd Riḍā's particular attention. Conversely, the all-pervasiveness of the *Sharī'ah* in terms of judicial provisions for every conceivable area of social, economic and political life is emphasised. Second, whereas Rashīd Riḍā readily admitted the variety and complexity of human experience as an argument for the diversification of the sources of laws, the impression produced here is one of a monochrome, monolithic world, governed by a uniform, indivisible law which is revealed by the Qur'ān and the Tradition. The sole lawgiver is God; all human beings are equal in their subjection to his ordinances. There are numerous laws, but all of them enjoy a certain organic unity among themselves, with none having any precedence over the others. By the same token, while in Rashīd Riḍā's scheme the religious and the political coexisted happily but independently, here there is a total integration of both under the aegis of the *Sharī'ah*. This is rendered inevitable because of the necessity of enforcing the injunctions on the holy war (*jihād*), retribution (*qiṣāṣ*), and alms-tax (*zakāt*), which as the highest civic functions in Islam can neither be left to private initiative nor carried out by individual means alone. Ghazzālī underlines the cardinal place of these functions by calling them 'social worships' (*'ibādāt ijtimā'iyyah*), thereby suggesting that in terms of rewards they enjoy the same status as the ritual acts of prayer, fasting and pilgrimage.[61]

The indivisibility of the legal system, however strict it may appear, has at least one comforting implication for liberal opinion. Such severe punishments as the amputation of the thief's hands or the flogging of the adulterers have to wait until all the conditions of a proper Islamic state have been fully realised – a pre-condition which would have met Rashīd Riḍā's approval too. But while Riḍā, at least for a period, admired the Saudis for their pure understanding of the *Sharī'ah*, Ghazzālī lashes out at their formalistic application of the penal law, and their disregard of the total spirit of Islam: 'When the Muslims,' he says, 'recently awakened and resolved to return to Islam in their laws and beliefs, they started their search for the truth at the wrong end, seeking to restore the "branches" before the principles. They called for the re-establishment of retribution and punishment before making sure that the political circumstances that had allowed the ruler to throw away the *Sharī'ah* would not prevail again.'[62] He pursues the same theme under the title 'Are there religious governments today?': 'It might be thought,' he says, 'that the religious rule offers us clear evidence of its aims and methods by its manifestations in the Arabian Peninsula. . . . This is because only in these countries is the thief's hand cut off and the adulterer flogged. That is to say, they are the only Muslim governments which insist on the application of these laws in an age which has renounced, and intensely abhorred them. We do not dispute that these prohibitions are part of Islam, but we find it strange that they are considered to be the whole of it. We wish to see the punishments enforced so that the rights and the security and the virtues may be preserved, but not that the hand of a petty thief be cut off while those punishments are waived . . . in the case of those who embezzle fantastic sums from the state treasury.' Ghazzālī's conclusion is that so long as the evils of despotism and economic disparities between the ruling rich and the masses persist in the Arabian Peninsula, and so long as its states are still struggling to assure their sheer existence, there can be no talk of the application of Islam as a religion and a state in these lands.[63] We shall see presently how some Muslim fundamentalists have found it extremely difficult to reconcile these ideas with the hard facts of practical politics once they have achieved power.

But nowhere in Ghazzālī's account does the character of the Islamic state assert itself more forcefully than in the domain of female rights and obligations. Against the background of the brief history of the feminist movement in Egypt, Ghazzālī's ideas on the subject seem to be a definite retrogression. Almost half a century before him, Qāsim Amīn (d. 1908), a disciple of 'Abduh, had launched a modest campaign in favour of female emancipation in Egypt. At first Amīn was careful to formulate his appeal for securing women's education, and an end to their seclusion, by reference to the Qur'ān and the *Sharī'ah*. But later, when he came under attack from the orthodoxy, he abandoned the Islamic framework, and adopted modern civilisation as the warrant for transforming the life of Muslim women.[64] About two decades later, Rashīd Riḍā carried on the same debate, but restored it to its Islamic setting. Although harping on the natural inequalities between men and women to justify male preponderance, and warning against the corrupting influences of modern life on family morality, Riḍā argued on the whole in support of greater female participation in the communal life of Islam.[65] But neither Amīn nor Rashīd Riḍā lived amidst the kind of social and moral strains that bedevilled urban, and particularly metropolitan, life in Egypt, as in other 'developing' Muslim countries, after the Second World War. Never before had the congeries of attitudes, beliefs and values which give that distinct tang to the collective life of a Muslim people been felt to be so threatened by popular infatuation with the trappings of Western civilisation. If the chief issue for Amīn was how to overcome the inertia and ignorance of the female half of the population, for Ghazzālī and men of his formation it was how to prevent the fibre of family life from disintegrating under the weight of spreading promiscuity. To dismiss this alarm at the immoral consequences of female emancipation as a mark of sheer bigotry is to run the risk of ignoring its deeper social causes. A glimpse of these causes can be obtained from a cursory glance at the function of entertainment in any of the modern Muslim states caught between the opposing poles of traditionalism and superficial modernity. If, in Ghazzālī's definition of the Islamic state, concern about the way the Muslims occupy themselves in their leisure time looms as large as issues of high politics, this is not necessarily owing to misplaced priorities. In societies which lack sufficient educational organisations as well as recreational facilities for the vast majority of people, but the appetite for both is whetted by the direct or indirect contact with the countries that enjoy them, the scarce, available outlets of entertainment – mainly the cinema, newspaper-reading, and informal gatherings – become doubly influential as moulders of collective outlook and tastes: they serve the functions of both a refuge from daily cares and 'ersatz' educational agents. While this may hold true of some Western countries too, the crucial point about such Muslim countries as Egypt and Iran, is that in their case these popular modes of entertainment often foster needs and values which are not even remotely connected with objective social and political conditions. This defect is aggravated by the absence of such corrective institutions as voluntary, cultural associations and a free press. Irrelevance to the real or concrete internal problems and needs at the individual or social levels has not, of course, detracted from the popularity of some of the most hackneyed products of Western culture, especially films, among the urban masses in the Muslim world, a popularity which has often tenaciously outlived vigorous spells of political hatred of the West. Whether in Nāṣir's Egypt, or Sukarno's Indonesia, or Qadhāfī's Libya, or Khumaynī's Iran, carefully cultivated anti-Americanism has hardly made a dent in the popular addiction to Hollywood films, or worse still, to their homespun imitations.

More than any other social group, Muslim women have suffered –

materially, morally and politically – from this combination of circumstances. No doubt a major part of their suffering can be said to have resulted from some of the provisions of the *Sharī'ah*, particularly the laws of inheritance which heavily favour men. But at least in the period of nascent Islam this did not prevent a number of women from achieving prominence as political leaders ('Ā 'ishah, the Prophet's favourite wife), or compelling examples of implacable idealism (Fāṭimah, his daughter), or heroines of revolutionary resistance (Zaynab, 'Alī's daughter). It was the increasingly one-sided interpretation of the *Sharī'ah*, concomitantly with the rigidity of certain trends of Muslim thought, which was used by the ruling monopolists throughout history to confine women to a secluded, passive life of subordination to men. As victims of a twofold deprivation – sexual and social – women are therefore doubly vulnerable to the alienating effects of cultural imports. In Western democracies, anxiety about public morality, whether with regard to female behaviour or any other issue, is often associated with campaigns by right-wing fringe groups. This is not always the case in the Muslim East, where debates on moral issues often lead on to a problem non-existent, at least to the same extent, in the West: the side-effects of the borrowing of a foreign culture. Accordingly the views of Ghazzālī, and other intellectual spokesmen of the Brothers' movement, have two clear components: a cultural censuring of the blind imitation of Western patterns of behaviour, whether by men or women, and a set of moral prescriptions for tackling the problems arising from this imitation, or from the process of modernisation in general. While the moral statements give rise to disagreements with the secularists, there is a surprising degree of unanimity between writers of both groups on the cultural score. Thus some of the apologetics of the Egyptian liberal thinker 'Abbās Maḥmūd al-'Aqqād against Western detractors of Islam are, in spirit, indistinguishable from the writings of Sayyid Quṭb; similarly, the tirades of the Iranian controversialist Jalāl Āl Aḥmad against the Westernisation of Iran have been recast in many of the slogans of the Islamic 'cultural revolution' in that country.

After urging the removal of what he considers to be temptations to a dissolute life (seductive appearance, unchaperoned outings and journeys, etc.), all heightened by the Westernised way of life, Ghazzālī's main concern is to advise an educational system for women geared essentially to family responsibilities. This is stated with some subtlety. He is at pains to prove Islam's insistence on an active social and political life for women.[66] But he then modifies this insistence by trying to justify the prohibition on women occupying ministerial and judicial positions, not only because, in his view, female sentimentality militates against impartial judgement, but also on practical grounds: female judges or solicitors have to investigate all sorts of crime, including those violating every standard of decency, and effect cross-examinations which sometimes require them to put aside their sense of shame, and ask embarrassing questions; they may also have to be transferred away from home, with all the disruption this would entail for family life.[67] He warns against concluding from all this that Islam holds men to be intrinsically superior to women, and admits that there are some women who are superior in intellectual and moral qualities just as Mary and 'Ā'ishah were in their times.[68] The tradition that keeps women in a state of permanent inferiority by virtue of their physical pecularities is not of Islamic but of oriental ancestry, he says.[69] Islam attempts to strike a balance between this stultifying legacy, which forces women to be used exclusively as an agent of animal reproduction, or an instrument of sensual pleasure, and the unrestrained freedom which is afforded them in the West. So the Islamic state releases women both from bondage to sensuous men and exposure to the enticements of Western civilisation, while providing every opportunity for them to fulfill their talents, and thus gradually overcome the frailties wrought in their nature by centuries of unnatural segregation and enslavement. There is, however, a limit to this process of liberation, which is revealed by Ghazzālī's plan of female education. For reasons already stated, he is opposed to any curriculum designed to train women to become secretaries, or heads of departments, or cabinet ministers, and instead recommends education principally as a means of cultivating virtues: women should be educated, not to achieve a career, but because education is good for its own sake. As a subsidiary benefit, education will also enable women to carry out their duties towards their families, and to assist men to perform their mission.[70] The philosophy behind this plan obviously kills any hope of an Islamic state being able to produce female political leaders: a woman's role, he says, is far greater than that of a man if she stays at home. So while Rashīd Riḍā, as was mentioned before, had forbidden only three offices for women in his state (those of prayer-leader, head of family, and head of state), Ghazzālī blocks all careers to them.

* * *

The Muslim Brothers have not been able so far to become the ruling party in Egypt, and one cannot predict the final shape of their ideas, if and when they accede to power. But at least a glimpse of this was furnished when the Iranian variant of their movement, called *Fidā 'īyān-i-Islām* (the Devotees of Islam), gained a share in Iran's ruling hierarchy after the victory of the Islamic Revolution of 1978–9. The Devotees became an active force on the political scene after the Second World War.[71] Their first important public campaign was to mobilise popular support in Iran in favour of the Palestinians at the time of the first Arab–Israeli war. But the history of their movement has differed from that of the Brothers in Egypt mainly on two counts: first, they never became a mass movement, always remaining a coterie of zealots dedicated to violent pursuance of their aims, although some of their anti-imperialist slogans did at times become popular; second, they have so far produced no protagonist either of the political perspicacity of Ḥasan al-Bannā', or the intuitive gifts of Sayyid Quṭb, or the erudition of the Pakistani Abu'l A'lā al-Maudūdī. The founder of the movement, Sayyid Mujtabā Navvāb Ṣafavī (d. 1956), of Ṣafavīd descent on the maternal side,[72] was a man of enormous personal charisma, capable of inspiring immense loyalty in his immediate entourage and reportedly enjoying even the respect of some of the high-ranking 'Ulamā' in Iran, particularly Shaykh 'Alī Akbar Ilāhīyān, himself a mystical man renowned for his esoteric pursuits.[73] Nonetheless, Navvāb Ṣafavī always remained a figure on the sidelines of the community of religious scholars. Until the Islamic Revolution, the Devotees claim to fame rested on their self-confessed part in a series of political assassinations between 1945 and 1963, rather than on any contribution to religious and political debate. The Egyptian and Syrian Brothers too have resorted to violence – or been accused of having done so: but for the student of religio-political thought, this has to be set against their intellectual record: the fairly systematic teachings of Bannā', or the ideological writings of Ghazzālī, or the socialistic theorising of Muṣṭafā as-Sibā'ī.

All this highlights a characteristic which distinguishes the religious community in Iran from that in other Muslim countries, that is, the plurality of the 'poles' of Shī'ī leadership, and by indirection, the availability of alternative patterns of religious experience, and if need be of alternative outlets of activism. This naturally decreases the chances of a single religio-political trend, even in extraordinary circumstances, to supersede the multiple shades of opinion on an issue or a set of issues which give cause for national concord – unless such a trend is epitomised by a figure of such commanding prestige, political or otherwise, as to eclipse all other religious leaders. But even in these exceptional circumstances the fundamental multiplicity remains intact, albeit in a latent state, ready to re-emerge at the first opportune moment. The distinctness of the Iranian case is thus evident. In Egypt, with al-Azhar's standing as an independent political force irredeemably compromised by its commitment to the state, and with occasional challengers to the orthodoxy like 'Abd ar-Rāziq and Khālid Muḥammad Khālid seemingly disrupting the consensus on the unity of religion and politics in Islam, the Brothers offered, over a long period, the only reliable forum for religious militancy and idealism. The Devotees never achieved such advantage in Iran, and whenever they became the focus of national attention they had to hang on to the coat-tails of any national religious leader available at the time to thwart the suppression of officialdom, or the hostility of other political groups: in the forties and fifties it was the Āyatullāh Sayyid Abu'l-Qāsim Kāshānī who acted as their patron for a time; in the seventies it was Khumaynī.

The Devotees have always been non-intellectual, in every sense of the term. This has relatively immunised them against any internal dissension. But it has also deprived them of the opportunity to proselytise outside the centres of religious education, or traditional foci of support for religio-political movements, such as the bazaar and a few industrial complexes, to subject their ideas to the rejuvenating test of dialogue with their opponents. It has also intensified their fundamentalism whenever they have had to go underground – namely, for the greater part of the period from 1951 to 1979 – or carry on their activities in the absence of a charismatic leader, as from 1956 (after the execution of Navvāb Ṣafavī) until 1979 (when Shaykh Ṣādiq Khalkhālī became their best-known spokesman). But avoidance of intellectualism has allotted an almost unique place to the Devotees in the history of secret or semi-secret oppositional religious groups in Iran. Whether in the form of the encyclopedist circle of *Al-Ikhwān aṣ-Ṣafa'* (the Brethren of Purity) in the fourth (tenth) century, or the armed conclaves of the Sarbidārī Ṣūfīs in the eighth/fourteenth century, or some of the secret societies during the Constitutional period, the political agitations of these groups were always tempered by one kind of intellectual, esoteric activity or another. The Devotees would have none of it, not out of any deliberate hostility to speculative thought, but simply because of their total dedication to political action. This uncommon feature goes some way towards explaining why, of all the contemporary Shī'ī religio-political groups in Iran, the Devotees have been the only one to establish doctrinal, and, reportedly, organisational, connections with their Sunnī counterparts in the Arab world. During the last decade or so many of the works of Sayyid Quṭb, Ghazzālī and as-Sibā'ī have been translated into Persian, and published by the Devotees or their supporters. In view of the Devotees' unswerving adherence to Shī'īsm, and the fact that these authors have expressed strong Sunnī views, such manifestation of a supra-sectarian spirit on the part of one of the most militant groups of contemporary Shī'īs is rather remarkable.

The judicial philosophy of the revolutionary regime of the Islamic Republic of Iran can be put down in no small measure to the Devotees' concept of Islamic justice. This concept has materialised itself in the punishments meted out by the revolutionary courts, not only to the agents and supporters of the overthrown monarchy, but also to persons accused of various moral offences. While explanation of some of these punishments in political terms as requirements of the survival of a young regime in the face of counter-revolution cannot be easily refuted in a world dominated by power politics, their justification on religious grounds has provoked a debate which, if sustained in a free atmosphere, can have great bearing on the identification of the attributes of an Islamic state in one crucial respect. The generic terms invariably used by the courts in describing the offences of the accused have been 'fighting God and his Apostle' (*muḥārabah bā khudā va rasūl*) and 'corrupting (or causing disorders) on the earth' (*mufsid fi'l-arḍ*). These terms have not so far been judicially defined, but have been taken from the Qur'ān: 'The recompense of those who war against God and his Apostle, and go about to commit disorders on the earth shall be that they shall be slain or crucified, or have their alternate hands and feet cut off, or be banished the land' (5:33). 'This [is] their disgrace in the world, and in the next a great torment shall be theirs. Except those who, ere you have them in your power, shall repent; for know that God is Forgiving, Merciful' (5:34).

Beyond the objections levelled against the working of the courts by liberal and some left-wing intellectuals, doubts have also been expressed on religious grounds as to the applicability of the verse to the charges in question. Even before the issue was raised by the establishment of the Islamic Republic in Iran, the verse appears to have long been the subject of controversy, indeed ever since the beginning of Islam. Since the offences mentioned in the verse are vague, Muslims must have realised early in their history that any misinterpretation can turn it into a lethal instrument in the hands of tyrants against their opponents. Hence the attempts either to remove the ambiguities in the verse, or to restrict its application to specific crimes. This is borne out by the Qur'ānic exegetics which indicate that difference of opinion arose over basically four issues: first, whether the verse in its entirety, irrespective of any other controversy resulting from it, applies to the crimes committed only by Muslims, or the People of the Book (Christians, Jews, etc.), or the infidels; second, what exactly is meant by the phrases 'fighting God' and 'corrupting (or causing disorders) on the earth'; third, does the fact that several punishments are enumerated in the verse (slaying, crucifying, etc.) denote that the judge has the power to choose whichever punishment he deems fit at his own discretion, or does it mean that the crimes themselves have different grades, and each punishment depends on the nature and severity of the crime? The conflicting answers to these questions reflect primarily the Muslims' extreme caution in taking the verse at its face value. Thus, while some commentators and jurists think that the verse lays down a general rule about all offenders against the public order, whether Muslim or non-Muslim, others believe that it is meant to provide only against Muslim offenders; still a third group, relating the verse to its historical 'cause of revelation', believe that it refers only to those infidels and People of the Book who defaulted on their covenant with the Prophet Muḥammad.

The most widely accepted definition of 'fighting God and his Apostle', and 'corrupting (or causing disorders on) the earth' in the classical commentaries is highway robbery, and, more specifically, killing and plundering people on the highways and thoroughfares, and pillaging and destroying the harvest. Both Sunnī and Shī'ī authorities agree that the two phrases signify two constituents of a single crime, the second supplementing the first. They also agree that the principal condition for the realisation of the crime is the use of arms. But the Shī'ī commentators, in particular, have tended to take a restrictive view by identifying the crime with certain concrete acts. The sixth-/twelfth-century commentator Faḍl Ibn Ḥasan Ṭabarsī, who is respected by some Sunnīs as well, says that the 'fighter (against God) [*muḥārib*]' is whoever 'draws the sword and terrifies the highways'. This, according to the eighth Shī'ī Imām, ar-Riḍā, can take one of four forms, which, in descending order of gravity, are as follows: (a) murder and plunder, (b) murder alone, (c) plunder alone, and (d) terrorising.[74] The contemporary Iranian Shī'ī thinker Sayyid Muḥammad Ḥusayn Ṭabāṭabā'ī summarises these varieties as 'disrupting public order' which, he adds, 'both customarily and naturally, can only take place by the use of arms in a threat to kill'. But he admits that in its normal usage, the term 'fighting God' can also have a general meaning, which is to contravene 'any rule of the *Sharī'ah*, and also any act of injustice and transgression.'[75] It is the latter meaning which is stressed in Rashīd Riḍā's commentary, since he says that the verse enjoins punishment of 'all those who commit acts injurious to public order, against individual lives, properties and honour in Islamic countries, and in so doing, rely on their force'.[76] Such acts are not obviously confined to those mentioned in verse 33, but, as he says, can take innumerable shapes according to different times and places. That is why the punishments have not been set out in detail, leaving the matter to the judgement of authorities in every age. He defends the general harshness of the punishments by describing them as deterrent, or, again in the favourite terminology of all the apologists of Islamic penal law, as a 'blocking of the means' (*sadd dharī'ah*) of transgression and corruption, comparable to the maximum preventive penalties prescribed by the legal systems of all states. To expose the unfairness of the Western criticisms of Muslims on this point, he cites the Dinshāwī affair which in 1906 had caused acute national humiliation for the Egyptians. A group of British soldiers who were shooting pigeons in the delta fought with the villagers of Dinshawi. Several officers were injured, and one died of shock and sunstroke. In retaliation, the British soldiers killed a peasant; later on, fifty-two Egyptians were also arrested, and in the ensuing trials, held under the presidency of the Christian Minister of Justice, Buṭrus Bāshā Ghālī, four were sentenced to death, and the rest to terms of imprisonment with hard labour or flogging. The sentences were executed on the following day with a certain display of ruthlessness.[77] Rashīd Riḍā says that although the incident did not constitute either a rebellion against the authorities or a case of causing corruption on the earth, the British showed particular ruthlessness in dealing with it so that nobody would dare in future to defy their military presence. Rashīd Riḍā compares the British Government's connivance in the affair with the second Caliph 'Umar's equitable treatment of the Muslims and Copts in Egypt,[78] to provide further evidence of Islam's unflagging sense of justice, and, by implication, of the correctness of his interpretation: all states inflict harsh punishments on those who challenge their authority, but an Islamic state would do so more judiciously and fairly.

The Devotees' understanding of the verses in question seem to be nearer to Rashīd Riḍā's than to that of Shī'ī commentators of the past or present.

In indicting alleged offenders, they make frequent use of the term 'causing corruption on the earth' because presumably it admits more easily of facile application to any offence against public interest. This enables them to include a vast variety of misdeeds, ranging from sodomy to embezzlement of public funds to high treason, among crimes punishable by death. It also involves a casuistry which avoids the necessity of proving the incidence of the first element of the crime of 'causing corruption on the earth', namely, 'war against God and his Apostle', which, as we saw, requires evidence of the use of arms, because, for them, any accusation of causing corruption on the earth automatically presumes the guilt of having waged war against God and his Apostle, even if the accused has not committed any armed offence. This also solves the last problem raised by commentators, that is, determining the punishments. Once any moral and political offence can be defined as causing corruption on the earth, imposition of capital punishment becomes unavoidable. This is again a departure from the Shī'ī tradition, because in the same *ḥadīth* that was quoted before the eighth Imām ar-Riḍā, quotes verse 33 to establish a clear link between the severity of the crime and severity of punishment, the implication being that there is no single, blanket 'recompense' for all varieties of crimes. Verse 34 brings up the possibility of pardoning the culprits provided they repent before being caught; they may be pardoned both in the sense of being exempted from stipulated penalties, and forgiven by God in the hereafter. Ṭabāṭabā'ī seems inclined to stress the former meaning when he says that the verse represents 'one of the cases in which (divine) forgiveness pertains to worldly matters'. But perhaps the most important and the most decisive point about the punishments mentioned in verse 33 is that, as Rashīd Riḍā and Ṭabāṭābā'ī both emphasise, [79] the Prophet Muḥammad did not inflict these punishments on the infidels after defeating them. According to Rashīd Riḍā, the reason why 'Alī also acted likewise in the case of the Khawārij was that, despite their open defiance of his authority, he did not think that they were set upon destroying civilised life or public security, but knew that they were simply acting on their judgement and understanding of religion,[80] they were thus, in today's parlance, political offenders. Among the modernists too, at least one group, the Indian Qādiyānīs, although strongly defending the harshness of punishments as evidence of Islam's opposition to 'false sentiments' dealing with 'dacoits, robbers and thieves', hold that political offenders should be forgiven, 'if they repent and desist from further rebellion and other offences against the state'.[81]

As was noted before, merciless retributive measures by states in times of crisis may be justified by the convenient logic of extraordinary circumstances, or the demands of preserving a newly established regime against overwhelming odds. But what is of greater interest to us is that they point to a glaring paradox which can come to the surface when a fundamentalist group finds, for the first time in modern history, an opportunity for attempting to translate its vision of Islam into legal and political realities. On the face of it, the Devotees' approach has been draconian and retrogressive, especially with their insistence on adherence to rituals and norms of formal behaviour. But whenever they are criticised either on this score or for their deviation from the accepted interpretation of specific Qur'ānic verses, they accuse their critics of rigid, formalistic thinking, and by so doing admit the virtue of adapting religious precepts to changing circumstances; for while they do their best to extend the provisions of the verses beyond the 'highway robbers, dacoits and thieves' to include any and every offender against public interests, their opponents seem to be miserably shackled by the literal meaning of the verses. So they claim that it is they, not their critics, who are the real modernists. If one essential condition of modernism is a rejection of the literal interpretation of the Qur'ān, then this claim cannot be dismissed out of hand. But the Devotees and their doctrinal allies do not seem to be concerned about the fact that their espousal of the modernist cause at least on this score, by opening the way to non-literal interpretation of all sources of religious thinking, is bound to be harmful to the central tenet of fundamentalism – safeguarding the purity of Islamic teachings from the 'poison' of speculative exercises.

The foregoing brief survey of the Iranian version of the Muslim Brothers confirms and elaborates the point we already made about the place of law in the Islamic state. It is true that a state can be Islamic only by dint of its enforcement of the *Sharī'ah*. But the provisions of the *Sharī'ah* do not form a rigid code of laws accepted by all Muslims. Apart from the laws of personal status and what Iqbāl calls 'socially harmless rules relating to eating, drinking, purity and impurity', the nature of a substantial number of them depends on the mentality, and therefore on the intellectual, social and political climate, of those who try to extract them from the sources. A liberal-minded Muslim would try to deduce from the Qur'ān and the Tradition all the necessary guarantees of individual rights and liberties, and a socialist would be more keen on demonstrating the collectivist ethos of Islam. This truism proves that, so far as modern political trends in the Muslim world are concerned, a plea for establishing the Islamic state can neither be the unique feature of the fundamentalist ideology nor a conclusive proof of the conviction that Islam is heedless of any doctrine or principle outside the purview of the *Sharī'ah*.

* * *

How Islamic fundamentalism can face different doctrinal problems in its effort to turn itself into a state ideology is illustrated by the case of the *Jamā'at-i-Islāmī* in Pakistan.[82] We saw that both the Egyptian (or Syrian) Muslim Brothers and the Iranian Devotees conducted their activities in circumstances where Islam as a political ideology relevant to the modern world had become marginal in national politics. This was the ascendancy of secular, liberal and left-wing political parties and ideologies, following a long period of forced and superficial modernisation of laws and institutions. The situation was different in Pakistan where Islam was the *raison d'être* of the state. The sole justification for establishing the state of Pakistan was that its people belonged to Islam, to a religion different from that of the majority of the inhabitants of the Indian sub-continent. Islam has therefore always been at the very heart and centre of intellectual and ideological debate both among the Muslims and between them and the Hindus, both before and after the emergence of Pakistan. Whether in deference to Hindu revivalism, or to stand up to British imperialism, or in the drive for Muslim–Hindu unity, or to mobilise popular support for the Ottoman Caliphate, or, finally, to protect the Muslim minority against a Hindu-dominated state, Islam always kept its pivotal place in the political conscience of the Indian Muslim élite.

It is this overriding historical fact that can largely account for a distinct feature of the *Jamā'at* as compared with its Egyptian and Iranian counterparts: a greater political maturity, inspiring its contributions to the national debate over a wide range of issues faced by Pakistan in her long and arduous course of constitutional development. Whereas the Brothers and the Devotees had either to operate as ineffectual opposition groups, or conduct clandestine campaigns, or enter into dubious alliances with other political factions, the *Jamā'at* was allowed – and challenged – to state its ideas openly and officially in the discussions on the structure of the Islamic Republic of Pakistan. It did not always live up to this challenge, but its performance was undoubtedly more impressive than similar groups in other Muslim countries. The ideas that it set forth were in many cases more practical and to the point.

Side by side with these differences, however, there have been similarities too, otherwise the *Jamā'at* would have been completely cut off from the mainstream of fundamentalism.

Just as the perceived menace of Zionism has been partly responsible for the growing rigidity of the Brothers' ideology in the Arab countries, so too has the threat of Indian nationalism or bellicosity been instrumental in nourishing fundamentalist trends in Pakistan. This can be clearly seen in the history of her search for political order and constitutional development.[83] Since her formation in 1948, three constitutions have been adopted in that country – in 1956, 1962 and 1973. In addition to the problems concerning the distribution of powers between the centre and provinces, and the nature of the executive suitable for Pakistan, the relationship between religion and state has been a principal cause of this constitutional instability. It may be that as G. W. Choudhury has remarked, the Islamic provisions of these constitutions are merely 'high-sounding phrases'[84] which have no corresponding reality in the country's legal system or socio-political spheres. But however symbolic the value of such provisions may be, one cannot ignore their importance as an index to the relevance or urgency of Islam, both at the official and popular levels, as the ideological framework of the state. Thus, while in 1956, with the history of Hindu–Muslim conflicts still fresh in memories, the first Constitution understandably asserted the dominant place of Islam by determining the title of the country as the 'Islamic Republic of Pakistan' and through the famous Repugnancy Clause ('no law shall be repugnant to Islam'), and the prohibition of usury, drinking, gambling and prostitution, the Constitution of 1962 considerably watered down the Islamic character of the state. This was made possible partly by the high-handed method of government of Ayyūb Khān's military regime, but also partly by the changed atmosphere of the times due to dwindling religious fervour and a dawning realisation of the necessity of the country's development along modern economic and educational lines. The war with India in 1964, and the much more devastating Bangladesh war of 1971, resulting in the dismemberment of Pakistan, revived popular religious feelings, and this was reflected in the Constitution of 1973 which for the first time declared Islam to be the state religion.[85]

The theoretical predominance of Islam in the national politics is, no doubt, a crucial factor in giving some substance and urgency to the *Jamā'at*'s religio-political platform. But no less important has been the dedication of its founder and theoretician, Abu'l A'lā Maudūdī (d. 1979). It is an indication of his unique status in the fundamentalist movement that while men like Bannā' or Sayyid Quṭb in Egypt or Navvāb Ṣafavī in Iran were treated as outsiders or extremists by the religious establishment, Maudūdī has had close association with the 'Ulamā'. Given the fact that he himself was not strictly an *'ālim* by formation, but was self-taught in the Islamic sciences, and even in his twenties was semi-Westernised, this was no mean achievement. His views often reflected the 'Ulamā's' positions, particularly on constitutional issues. His relations with them were by no means free of personal rivalries and frictions. Binder has enumerated the differences between his fundamentalism and the 'Ulamā's' traditionalism: these basically boil down to the fact that while he believed in the necessity of *ijtihād*, they adhered to the age-old practice of *taqlīd* (imitation of authorities).[86] But Maudūdī has frequently tried to minimise this divergency by warning that *ijtihād* cannot be exercised outside the norms of the *Sharī'ah*, and this makes stringent demands on those who should qualify as *mujtahids*.[87] Much more significant has been his disagreement with them over women's rights to occupy high political offices, as will be explained below. Perhaps one reason why he was at times recognised as the 'Ulamā's' spokesman has been the latter's inability to produce any figure who would match his intelligence, talents and international standing: he is the only contemporary non-Arab Muslim fundamentalist whose works have been translated into Arabic.

Outwardly, there is nothing in Maudūdi's career which would suggest a revolutionary temper. In 1937 Muḥammad Iqbāl, as the President of the

Muslim League, invited him to co-operate in the codification of Muslim jurisprudence; in 1938, he became Head of the Islamic Research Institute at Lahore. Meanwhile, he acted as the Dean of the College of Islamic Theology at Lahore for two years.[88] His monthly review *Tarjumān al-Qur'ān* ('Exegesis of the Qur'ān', begun in 1932) bears further witness to a speculative disposition. In unison with the 'Ulamā', he was at first opposed to the movement for creating Pakistan, because he considered it inappropriate to use Islam[89] – a universalist religion – as the ideological underpinning of a nation-state (a problem which, as we shall see in the next chapter, was faced by the Arab nationalists as well). But he later changed his mind, seeing in the whole Pakistan movement a promise for the rebirth of Islam. It is true that after the Partition he came into conflict with government authorities, frequently being accused of fomenting trouble. He was arrested and imprisoned once in 1948 for his campaign against liberal politicians, and again in 1952 in connection with the disturbances against the Qādīyānī community. He was also blamed for student unrest in West Pakistan.[90] He and his followers always denied these charges, an attitude which contrasts sharply with that of radical Muslims elsewhere, who often welcome such imputations as evidence of their own revolutionary identity. Maudūdī did not allow official animosity to deter him from constitutional activities. He submitted proposals and comments on the Draft Constitution of 1956, and his followers acknowledged the legitimacy of the parliamentary processes by taking part, and gaining limited support, in the electoral campaigns.

And yet, in spite of this background, and of certain rightist traits in his teachings, it would be wrong to describe him as a conservative thinker. In fact, of all the fundamentalist authors who have achieved international fame, his is the only ideology which includes a fairly coherent theory of the 'Islamic revolution'. This is because he takes an uncompromisingly holistic view of the issue of the Islamic state. Ghazzālī and Sayyid Quṭb come close to this holism, the former in his doctrine of the indivisibility of the Islamic legal system, the latter on Islamic socialism; but since Islam has always been taken for granted in Pakistan as at least as one of the essential determinants of the country's political regime Maudūdī has been less hamstrung than them by the obligation to prove Islam's ability to supersede modern, secular ideologies. Instead, he has concentrated on demonstrating the rational interdependence of Islamic morality, law and political theory. His religious and political teachings thus offer the most comprehensive exposition so far of the nature of the Islamic state.

An Islamic state, without an Islamic revolution preceding it, is bound to founder on the moral infirmities of its citizens: this is the gist of Maudūdī's theory of 'the process of the Islamic revolution'. Some of his arguments in support of this proposition could have been adduced by any secular ideologue, since they are partly based on the analogies of the French, Russian and Nazi German revolutionary movements. None of these movements, says Maudūdī, would have succeeded without the backing of its appropriate type of social consciousness and moral atmosphere, and these can only be brought about through a revolution.[91] In this argument, the revolution is prescribed mainly as a spiritual prerequisite of the Islamic state, but he also pursues another line of reasoning which is sociological, emphasising the character of the state as something which is formed, not by artificial means, but as the product of the 'interplay of certain moral, psychological, cultural and historical factors pre-existing it'[92] – a notion which, although couched in modern or Marxian terms, can be traced back to Ibn Khaldūn: 'Until there is a change in the social fabric, no permanent change can be produced by artificial means in any state', he says.[93] Mindful of the controversy among the philosophers of history over the overestimation of social structure as a decisive factor of political change, he immediately adds that he does not thereby suggest the 'doctrine of determinism', denying the freedom of human will.[94] The success of his entire scheme of revolution hinges on the firm resolve, integrity and steadfastness of individuals in an untoward environment. To prove that such a suggestion is not utopian, he mentions the example of the Prophet Muḥammad and the small numbers of his followers: just as that tiny group gradually won the non-believers over to their side by their sacrifices and sufferings, so too there should now come forward a group of people who would sincerely believe in the call to the unity and sovereignty of God, ready to abandon the life of self-indulgence and accept the restraints of morality. It is this belief in the unity and sovereignty of God which is the ultimate protector of the revolutionaries against all deviations and distractions. Combined with a 'true understanding of Islam, single-mindedness, strong power of judgement, and complete sacrifice of personal feelings and selfish desires', it will give the revolutionaries the ability to withstand all hardships, and finally overcome public apathy or enmity.[95] What is interesting in the whole of this argument is that although in expounding its premises Maudūdī may sound like a social determinist, he ends up a voluntarist by stressing the element of individual will and initiative.

Is violence indispensable to an Islamic revolution? Maudūdī thinks not, and this is consistent with his conviction in the tremendous force of moral example, although like all fundamentalists he does not rule out force as an unavoidable means of dealing with evil in the world. Again he falls back on the analogy of incipient Islam: 'Historians', he says, 'have given such prominence to the religious wars of the Prophet that people have been misled into believing that his revolution in Arabia was brought about by violence and bloodshed, whereas not more than a thousand or twelve hundred men were killed on both sides in the course of all the wars.... If you recall the history of revolutions in the world, you shall have to admit that this revolution is fit to be called a "bloodless revolution"'.[96] One could contest this claim by pointing out that the place of violence in a social movement should not be judged solely by the number of people killed in its process, that even one person killed is always one too many, and that a more plausible criterion is whether violence is accepted in the corporate thinking as a legitimate means of realising social ideals. On this score, an Islamic revolution can certainly not be free of violence for the simple reason that Islam itself does not negate the use of force in the abstract. But perhaps a more pertinent observation is that unlike all the familiar protagonists of revolution, Maudūdī is obviously reluctant to preach recourse to force, and instead stresses the necessity of gradual, spiritual transformation of the society in order to inculcate 'the true Islamic mentality and moral attitudes'[97] in the people.

The state born of such a revolution is not, at least in form, dissimilar from the totalitarian regimes of modern times. It cannot be otherwise, since the revolutionary movement preceding its birth aims ultimately to effect the utmost uniformity and harmony of souls. 'It is essential,' he says, 'that a particular type of movement should grow up, permeated by the same spirit; the same sort of mass character should be moulded; the same kind of communal morality should be developed; the same kind of workers should be trained; (and) the same type of leadership should emerge.'[98] The responsibility for running the state will be vested in men who would seek to enforce, not their own will, but the divine law. They should then create the 'same mental attitude and moral spirit' among the people. Their system 'would produce Muslim scientists, Muslim philosophers, Muslim historians, Muslin economists and financial experts, Muslim jurists and politicans.[99] Sustaining this monolithic culture is the ideological character of the state, based as it is 'on a definite set of moral and spiritual principles, and ruled by a group of persons . . . of widely differing nationalities.'[100] These principles are subsumed under the formula 'submission to the sovereignty and unity of God'. Far from being disturbed by the totalitarian implication of making ideology the exclusive guiding principle of state actions, Maudūdī finds it the most reliable defence against the corrupting influence of power. He sounds absolutely sure of this, mainly because power for him means only a specific institutionalised form of it – the nationalistic state. The failure of the revolutionary regimes in the past, he says, has been due to their preoccupation with narrow, nationalistic pursuits.[101] But an Islamic ideology, by protecting the minds from all family, ethnic and racial prejudices, is the antithesis to nationalism, and therefore forestalls decline. What is overlooked in this reasoning is that power, in order to be corrupting, does not need to pursue nationalistic or ethnic aims alone. In fact it does not need to pursue any aim *at all* to be so. In many cases rulers have been infatuated with power *for its own sake*. The hope, or conviction, that rulers can be kept out of mischief by adhering to a certain set of doctrines, or leading an ascetic way of life, is as old as the notion of Utopia in human history. It is a noble idea, but one which has so far rarely worked in practice. Maudūdī does not provide any evidence that his ideological state would be an exception to this depressing observation of history. Since the case for the intrinsic power of ideology as a shield against corruption is thus unsubstantiated, his suggestion for immunising the Islamic state against the pest of nationalism – entrusting its government to a group of people of 'widely differing nationalities' – exacts too much credulity: he is over-confident of the ability of individuals to subordinate their immediate, emotional desires to long-term, rational ends.

Within the framework laid down by the Islamic revolution, no department of individual and social life is exonerated from the 'Islamic order'. No other fundamentalist advocate of the Islamic state presents as lucid a blueprint of it as does Maudūdī. His numerous writings and speeches deal with many of the details of the constitutional and legal features of the Islamic state – another reflection of the urgency of his theme in the context of Pakistan politics: the sources and methodology of law-making, the distinction between the permanent and unalterable part of the *Sharī'ah* (such as the prohibition of interest and wine-drinking) and the flexible (made possible through the device of *ta'wīl* or 'probing into the meaning of the injunctions found in the Qur'ān and Tradition', *ijtihād, qīyās*, or analogy, and *istiḥsān*, or 'juristic preference'), the functions of the legislative, judicial and executive organs of the state, and the position of the electorate.[102] His remarks on these issues are partly meant to repel doubts about the feasibility of the Islamic state in general, and partly incidental to the particular problems of Pakistan (for instance, his opposition to 'joint electorates' consisting of both Muslims and non-Muslims[103] becomes more comprehensible when one recalls the distinct significance of the Hindu community in Pakistan as India's neighbour, or the controversial status of the Qādīyānīs, who regard themselves as Muslims but are described by Maudūdī as non-Muslims).[104] However, as he himself notes, the whole question of the constitutional and legal characteristics of the Islamic state is subsidiary to a larger issue – that of the *Sharī'ah*, not as a body of laws, but as a 'complete scheme of life and all-embracing social order', without which Islamic laws can 'neither be understood nor enforced'. It is this scheme which he calls the 'Islamic order', and is a corollary to his theory of revolution. He finds it, not hidden in convoluted theological or juridical disquistions, but neatly encapsulated in fourteen Qur'ānic verses, all from the Sūrah *Banī Isrā'īl*.[105] These have to be quoted in full:

> Thy lord hath ordained that ye worship none but him; and kindness to your parents whether one or both of them attain to old age with thee; and say not to them 'Fie' neither reproach them; but speak to them both with respectful speech; [17:23]
> And to him who is of kin render his due, and also to the poor and to the wayfarer; yet waste not wastefully,
> For the wasteful are brethren of the Satans, and Satan was ungrateful to his Lord:
> But if thou turn away from them, while thou thyself seekest boons from

thy Lord for which thou hopest, at least speak to them with kindly speech:
And let not thy hand be tied up to thy neck; nor yet open it with all openness, lest thou sit thee down in rebuke, in beggary.
Verily, thy Lord will provide with open hand for whom he pleaseth, and will be sparing. His servants doth he scan, inspect.
Kill not your children for fear of want: for them and for you will we provide. Verily, the killing them is a great wickedness.
Have nought to do with adultery; for it is a foul thing and an evil way.
Neither slay any one whom God hath forbidden you to slay, unless for a just cause: and whosoever shall be slain wrongfully, to his heir have we given powers; but let him not outstep bounds in putting the manslayer to death, for he too, in his turn, will be assisted *and avenged.*
And touch not the substance of the orphan, unless in an upright way, till he attain his age of strength: And perform your convenant; verily the covenant shall be enquired of:
And give full measure when you measure, and weigh with just balance. This will be better, and fairest for settlement:
And follow not that of which thou hast no knowledge; because the hearing and the sight and the heart, – each of these shall be enquired of:
And walk not proudly on the earth, for thou canst not cleave the earth, neither shalt thou reach to the mountain in height:
All this is evil; odious to thy Lord.
This is a part of *the wisdom* which thy Lord hath revealed to thee.... [17:26–39]

It is noteworthy that in elaborating his idea of the 'Islamic order', Maudūdī mentions only these verses, with no reference to any *ḥadīth* or other secondary sources. This is perhaps meant not so much to minimise the importance of *ḥadīths* as to lend more authority to his scheme of 'order'. Besides, the verses he quotes have all clear and straightforward meaning, leaving little or no room for equivocation. These had to be quoted in full, because they not only show the exact canonical basis of the 'order', but also illustrate Maudūdī's preference for deducing the principles of his political thought straight from the Qur'ān. As he reminds us, the verses belong to the Medinan period of Muḥammad's messengership, namely, the period in which he received divine revelation of the moral, social, economic, political and cultural institutions of the new Islamic state and society. The underlying principles of these institutions, as derived from the foregoing verses, are as follows: (1) The ideology of the Islamic state is nothing but the thought that real sovereignty and lordship belongs only to God, and that it is His law which lays down the rules of human conduct, and the principles of government throughout the world. (2) Parental rights occupy the highest place in the scale of all human relationships. Respecting, obeying and serving one's parents is a religious duty. Hence the obligation of the Islamic state to establish its juridical, educational and administrative policies on the basis of protecting and strengthening family life. (3) People should not be content only with satisfying their minimum material needs, but ought to seek a prosperous life, without indulging in extravagance, and allocate a portion of their income towards the maintenance of their needy relatives and other fellow-citizens. Such is the way to promote the spirit of co-operation, self-sacrifice, and economic mutual help. These are not merely moral prescription, but ideas which can be turned into living realities through the institutions of obligatory alms (*aṣ-ṣadaqāt al-wājibah*), supererogotary alms (*aṣ-ṣadaqāt an-nāfilah*), testaments, inheritance and endowments. (4) Extremes of wealth and poverty should both be avoided. Poverty (or to use Maudūdī's euphemism, 'insufficiency of wealth') is not necessarily an unnatural phenomenon, because 'the inequalities which arise from natural causes, with no interference by artificial limitations' are not evil in themselves. (5) Birth control through 'killing the offspring, and miscarriage' is a crime. The remedy lies in constructive efforts for elevating the family's living standards. (6) Adultery should be prohibited, not only by outlawing the act itself, but also through eliminating all its 'means, causes, stimulants and accessories'. This is the aim of the Islamic bans on drinking, dancing, men's imitation of women (*takhannuth*), and women's imitation of men (*istirjāl*), as well as the various laws aimed at facilitating marriage, and preventing individual overspending and corruption. (7) No human being should be killed, except for a just cause, which consists of punishment for five kinds of crime: (a) murder, (b) hostility and war against Muslims, (c) attempt at overthrowing the Islamic order, (d) adultery, whether by men or women, (e) apostasy or high treason. In punishing those guilty of such acts, no transgression, no 'overkill'. and, especially, no torture should be allowed.[106] The state alone can be in charge of punishment. Individuals or families should not exercise the right of revenge on their own. (8) The rights of orphans should be protected. (9) Promises should be kept, and contracts implemented. (10) Business transactions must be conducted with complete honesty. (11) Individual and public policies should be based, not on doubts or presumptions, but only on solid evidence. Nobody should be arrested or harmed or imprisoned on mere suspicion. The same holds true of international relations. (12) Muslim behaviour should be free of all traces of arrogance and vanity.[107]

As can be seen, the elements of the scheme are not of the same nature or importance from a political standpoint: some deal with general principles of social life, some with interpersonal relationships; some are political, some moral. But this combination of the general and particular, of political and moral is the distinctive feature of all the manifestos of those modern fundamentalists who regard the creation of an Islamic state within the immediate capability of Muslims. But more particularly it serves to confirm the point we already made to refute the validity of any distinction between an 'Islamic order' and an Islamic state, as has been suggested by some authors, because it is unthinkable that a society be run along these lines in the political, social, penal and moral fields, without its government being fully committed to Islam.

When this scheme is considered in the light of Maudūdī's other writings, then the following broad strands of his political teachings become manifest: first, despite the revolutionary methods recommended by him to fulfil the prerequisites of the Islamic state, his perception of the structure of the state itself is 'conservative', in the sense of running counter to any weakening of the institutions of family and private ownership. Maudūdī is more specific on this point in his later writings, making it amply clear that the kind of revolution he is seeking is far from a total overhauling of social structure. 'Islam', he says, 'does not aim at an extreme revolution (*inqilāb mutiṭarrif*), transforming everything from the foundations, as does Communism, which militates against human nature, abolishing private ownership and instituting state control over individual properties. Islam eschews such a destructive reversal of (the order of) things, consonant as it is with human nature.'[108] Such qualifications of the appeal for the revolution can only be explained by the genuine fundamentalist misgiving, felt in Pakistan as elsewhere and particularly in the post-Bandung period, that Islamic radicalism may be exploited by left-wing movements. Allied to this loathing of abrupt and violent change, is the *second* basic element of his ideology – an opposition to all egalitarian doctrines which deny the natural inequalities of human beings. Any attempt, he asserts, to impose equality on entities which are naturally unequal is as unjust as fostering inequality among the equals.[109] This, of course, is a commonplace proposition with which one can hardly disagree, and certainly one admitted to be true by most fundamentalists, in Pakistan or elsewhere. Controversy arises over the context in which it is stated, and the aim it pursues; whether it is intended to condemn disparities of wealth and social status, or, conversely, to counter quasi-communistic notions of absolute equality. While sharing with Sibā'ī and Sayyid Quṭb their denunciation of unjustifiable social inequalities and immorally gained wealth, Maudūdī occasionally veers towards rightist espousal of the 'wisdom of inequality', notably when the point at issue is the sanctity of private ownership, and the right of the state to confiscate and manage lands in the name of the community. From this non-egalitarian stand flows the second conservative strand in his ideology – the rejection of the inevitability of class struggle. Class differences, he says, when being the result of 'natural' causes, do not constitute an evil in themselves. Rather than trying to eradicate the 'differential inherent in human society', an Islamic state should therefore merely attempt to prevent them from becoming 'an instrument of exploitation and injustice'. These mellow thoughts make Maudūdī more circumspect than his Arab or Iranian counterparts in the use of socialist rhetoric, while outlining his theory of revolution.

Third, although Maudūdī is more explicit than any other fundamentalist of his time in his stand for the principles of the electiveness of rulers, their accountability to the ruled, their obligation to consult 'the people who loose and bind', and the right of ordinary citizens to criticise all those in power, he is opposed to democracy in the sense of a particular system of government imported from the West.[110] One might explain this opposition by reference to the cultural puritanism of all fundamentalists who repudiate in principle any Western institution, or, alternatively, to the stereotyped notions about incompatibility of Western democratic values with Muslim attitudes. But in the case of thinkers like Maudūdī, it has more to do with an élitist streak in their mentality, despite the fact that their appeals for Islamic revivalism are often addressed to the masses. It is, of course, in the nature of any idealism, set upon swimming against the tide of public fascination with values opposed to its principles, to be authoritarian. Taking pride in the fact that their version of Islam is a 'stranger' in a world enthralled by ungodly attitudes is a common feature of all fundamentalists – from Muḥammad Ibn 'Abd al-Wahhāb to his direct opposite, the Āyatullāh Khumaynī.' 'Islam does not regard numbers as a criterion of truth and rectitude', says Maudūdī, ignoring that his fellow-Sunnī polemists have often used the reverse of this argument in denouncing the Shī'ī minority status. He also decries many of the institutions associated with democracy: the multi-party system, because it 'pollutes the government with a false sense of loyalties' besides being divisive; and electoral campaigns by candidates, for the same reason that Rashīd Riḍā had drawn from the Prophetic Tradition, prohibiting the rulership to all its aspirants. Moreover, there cannot be much scope for democracy in a state such as the one he champions where the most powerful organ is a judiciary charged with upholding not simply the law, but God's laws: 'In Islam, the judiciary is independent of the executive. The task of the judge is to implement God's laws.... He does not sit on the seat of judgement in the capacity of the representative of the Caliph or the Ameer, but as the representative of God.'[111]

We may add two other points which do not figure in the foregoing catalogue, but can be gathered from Maudūdī's other declarations: one is the severity of the punishments and penalties provided in the *Sharī'ah* for wrongdoers, and the second is the position of women. He defends the former with great vigour and cogency against its Western critics: it is not, he contends, the religious punishments which are barbaric, but rather the crimes which call them into operation. What is again reassuring to modernists is that for him the whole system of these punishments is primarily a deterrent, and in any case intended for a society which has already been revolutionised and reformed according to Islamic principles, where presumably the incidence of crime is reduced to the minimum, the implication being that their application before such a state of affairs prevails would be unjust. Islam, he says, 'does its best to save people from punishment, just as it lays down the strictest conditions for the admissibility of testimony as evidence of crime, and fixes a certain period of time to conduct investigations before applying punishments, so as to check any error that might have been made by the witnesses, and directs the judges to exert all in their power to ward off the punishments from the people.'[112] On the question of the proper behaviour and appearance of women and their social and political rights, there was no apparent theoretical disagreement between Maudūdī and other fundamentalists. He was, if anything, more demanding than many of them on the practice of *ḥijāb* (veiling), and on their being barred from high political offices. But in practice he turned out to be more liberal than any other well-known theoretician of his kind by supporting a woman candidate (Fāṭimah Jinnāḥ) in Pakistan's presidential election of 1965. This seems to have been largely a political move inspired by the *Jamā'at*'s vehement opposition to the incumbent president, Ayyūb Khān, on the grounds of his pro-Western policies. Whatever the motive, the fact is while a gathering of the 'Ulamā' produced a *fatwā* declaring that in Islam a woman could not be head of state, Maudūdī announced that a woman could attain this office, although it was not desirable.[113]

Islamic thinking in Pakistan is not, of course, exhausted by the theories of Maudūdī. Nor has the *Jamā'at* been the sole representative of Islamic activism, as evidenced by the fact that the decline in the *Jamā'at*'s power after its defeat in the general elections of 1969 did not mean the dwindling of the force and appeal of the concept of the Islamic state. Another distinguished Pakistani thinker, Muḥammad Asad, had his own plan of the Islamic state which deserves equal attention. But Maudūdī's ideas have been more germane to our study because of their influence beyond Pakistan, as well as their place in the nexus of fundamentalist utopianism.[114]

4 Nationalism, democracy and socialism

Contemporary discussions among Muslims on the Caliphate and Islamic state, outlined in the preceding two chapters, have in many ways been the continuation of Islamic political thought as known in history. They have involved issues which are immanent in Islamic culture, however much the rhythm and the accent of each phase of the discussions may have been determined by developments in the contacts between Muslims and the outside world. Despite the occasional venturings of some Muslim thinkers into unfamiliar grounds, such as the question of separation of powers or the theory of revolution, the basic questions they reviewed – the canonical foundations of the Caliphate, the deviations of the Caliph from the *Sharī'ah*, the functions of the 'people who loose and bind', and the attributes of an Islamic state – remained close to the original sources of Islamic law and ethics.

Evidently these have not been the only political questions engaging the Muslim mind over the last two and a half centuries. There have also been others, of which we intend to survey some in this chapter. But in contrast to the issues debated so far, the ones we are going to examine have been forced upon the Muslim mind from outside – from the Western challenge to the credibility and integrity of Islam as a total ideology. We shall concentrate only on three themes which stand out in the politics of the Muslim world today: nationalism, democracy and socialism. These do not represent homogeneous challenges, since each requires a different set of values, attitudes and institutions. Nor have they all been thrown at Muslims at the same time. But they have all formed the multiple dimensions of a single urge for material welfare and technological progress. In them mesh some of the major strands of Muslim thinking on the most important cultural and political problems of the Muslim peoples.

I Nationalism

We start with nationalism, because, taking the eighteenth century as our point of departure, the Muslims' first consequential encounter with the West was through its physical (military, commercial, colonial) expansionism. This soon awakened in them that collective emotional response which is the very essence of a nationalistic movement. In the history of political thought, the term *nationalism* sometimes refers to a movement for guarding a nation's independence and freedom in the face of an external aggressor, and at others to an intellectual assertion of a nation's separateness and identity – or, in its extreme form, of superiority over other nations. It can have other meanings as well, but they do not concern us at this juncture. Muslim writers in the nineteenth century, such as Ṭahṭāwī,[1] Nadīm,[2] Marṣafī,[3] and 'Abduh,[4] understood the term primarily in the first sense, identifying it with the term *patriotism* (in Arabic, *waṭaniyyah*, from *waṭan*, abode, and later, by extension, homeland) which although signifying a different concept, is related to the territorial aspect of the national identity.[5] Since the Prophet is said to have praised the 'love of abode' (*ḥubb al-waṭan*) as a mark of faith, these authors easily managed to combine their demands for reforms with an appeal to the patriotic feelings of Muslims in Egypt, Syria, Iran and Afghanistan.

In the twentieth century, with the collapse of the Ottoman Empire and the gradual withering of the colonial system, Muslim peoples achieved the status of nationhood one after another. The result was that, in the new phase of Muslim self-assertion, concern with the criteria of nationhood began to prevail over the notion of patriotism, especially in the minds of Arab writers. This marked the beginning of an ideological controversy among the Muslim intellectuals which is still continuing. It centred round the basic contradiction between nationalism as a time-bound set of principles related to the qualities and needs of a particular group of human beings, and Islam as an eternal, universalist message, drawing no distinction between its adherents except on the criterion of their piety. The problem was particularly acute in the case of Arab nationalism after the First World War, when it appeared on the political scene as a distinct ideology – for two reasons. First, the goal of Arab unity, embracing as it did large numbers of people of diverse characteristics and inhabiting a vast expanse of territories, represented a larger vision than that of the movements with more limited scope, such as Turkish, Egyptian or Syrian nationalism. Hence it could not be easily stigmatised as being divisive. Second, there is the intimate, subliminal association between Arabism (*'urūbah*) and Islam. The Arabs cannot promote their identity without at the same time exalting Islam, which is the most abiding source of their pride, and the most potent stimulant of that identity down the ages; conversely, the fact that Islam was first revealed to the Arabs, and in their language, emboldens some Arab nationalists to try to pre-empt Islam as a primordially Arab religion. Some Arab writers try at first to prove that there is no contradiction between Islam and Arab nationalism. But they often end up confirming the Arabic identity of Islam. A typical illustration of this attitude can be found in the views of 'Abd ar-Raḥmān al-Bazzāz (d. 1972), an outstanding exponent of Arab nationalism, and Iraq's Prime Minister in 1965–6. He starts off by criticising the misrepresentation of the notion of religion among Arabs under the impact of 'cultural imperialism', and the Western usage of the term. Islam, he says, does not admit a narrow view of religion by restricting it within the limits of 'worship, specific rituals and spiritual beliefs'. Contrary to Christianity and Buddhism, and 'in its precise meaning, Islam is also a social order, a philosophy of life, (a system) of economic rules, and of government'.[6] After quoting Bertrand Russell's definition of Islam as a 'political religion, namely, a socially-orientated religion', Bazzāz concludes that 'Islam does not necessarily contradict Arab nationalism unless their political aims differ, but this is unthinkable'[7] precisely in view of the substantive links between the two. He then proceeds to correct another misunderstanding – this time connected with Arab nationalism. Some people believe that Arab nationalism can only be built upon racial appeal or racial prejudice, and would therefore be contrary to the 'all-pervasive nature' of Islam. He concedes that the exaggerations or excesses of some Arab nationalists have been responsible for this misconception, and that no doubt what some Umayyad governors, princes and rulers committed in consequence of their tribal prejudice and racial propaganda collided with the nature of Islam. 'But,' he assures the religious-minded critics, 'the Arab nationalism in which we believe, and for which we call, is based, as has been stipulated in our [Iraqi] National Covenant, not on racial appeal, but on linguistic, historical, cultural and spiritual ties and fundamental interests in life.'[8] Notwithstanding these arguments, and as if sensing that no amount of reasoning along these lines would convince his incredulous detractors, he resorts to his final argument that Islam, although being 'a universal religion, fitting for all peoples, and having been disseminated among numerous nations and races, was revealed primarily, and essentially (*b'idh-dhāt*) for the Arabs'. In this sense, it is their particular religion. The Qur'ān is in their language, and the Prophet from them.' He provides some detailed evidence to substantiate his claim:

> The actions of early Muslims confirm the Arabic nature of Islam. 'Umar greatly hesitated to conquer lands outside the Arabian Peninsula and the Fertile Crescent. He consented to receive a double alms-tax (*zakāt*) from the well-known Arab tribe of Banū Taghlib when the latter found the payment of poll-tax (*jizyah*) to be humiliating. Many Christian Arab tribes participated in the conquest of foreign lands. The Muslims accepted the poll-tax from the adherents of other religions outside the Peninsula, but in the interior, they offered [to non-Muslim Arabs] the choice between conversion to Islam and emigration. All this proves that the Arabs and their land occupy a special status in Islam. That a group of the *fuqahā'*, in discussing the problem of the equality [of husband and wife in social status, *kafā'ah*, as a condition of sound marriage] maintained that a non-Arab is not equal to an Arab, even if they were equals in other respects, is proof of the privileged status [*mumtāz*] of the Arabs in Islam and Islamic civilisation. I can emphasise that many of the

principles that Islam has asserted, and have become part of it, are ancient Arab traditions which were refined by Islam, and invested with a fresh character. The veneration of, and paying pilgrimage to, the Ka'bah, are an ancient Arab tradition, and so are many of the rituals of the pilgrimage itself. The respect for Friday, which the Arabs used to call 'the Day of Arabism' [*yawm al-'urūbah*], and its adoption as a day of 'festivity and adornment', as has been mentioned in the tradition, is another proof of the Arabic character of Islam. Arabic viewpoints abound in the rules of inheritance and statutory shares [*farā'iḍ*], especially in granting the right of inheritance to paternal relatives, and concern for relatives of the first degree.[9]

In defining its relationship with Islam, Arab nationalism thus often ends where it started: with the glorification of Arabism as a commanding value in Islam. On this point, most theoreticians of Arab nationalism seem to be in agreement – whether they are Muslims or non-Muslims, religionists or secularists. Some of them are, of course, at pains to underscore their recognition of Islam as a religion for the whole of humanity and not just for one particular branch of it. Nevertheless, their works impart an unmistakable impression that the Prophet Muḥammad almost acted as the first hero of Arab nationalism by uniting all Arab-speaking inhabitants of the Peninsula under his banner.[10] This view certainly sounds blasphemous to many devout Muslims,[11] Arab or non-Arab, but it bespeaks a sentiment deeply ingrained in the Arab consciousness, however well camouflaged, or hedged in with the kind of qualifications that would make it palatable to dogmatically severe Muslims. A logical extension of the same attitude is the nationalists' favourable verdict on those periods of Arab–Islamic history which do not normally pass muster with pious Muslims. For instance, while the Iranian Muslims condemn the Umayyad dynasty (41–132/661–750) for violating the Islamic norms of equality by virtue of its discriminatory policies against non-Arab Muslims (not to speak of its antipathy towards the members of the Prophet's family), and while such fundamentalists as Rashīd Riḍā also hold Mu'āwiyah, the founder of the dynasty, responsible for the degeneration of the Caliphate because of his role in turning it into hereditary rule (*mulk*) in the 'tradition of Caesars and Khusraws', Arab nationalists praise the Umayyad era as one of the 'glory of the Arab consciousness' (*'izzat al-wa'y al-'Arabī*).[12]

Obviously, this attitude towards Islam is something unique to Arab nationalists, or more precisely, to those Arabs, whether Muslim or Christian, who regard themselves first and foremost as members of a single and as yet unfulfilled entity called the 'Arab nation'. But for an Arab who owes his primary allegiance to an entity smaller, and for that reason more immediate and more real, than the 'Arab nation', as do vast numbers of ordinary citizens of Arab states today, then the status of Islam can become problematical, and its relevance to their tangible territorial, ethnic or parochial interests considerably diminished. Here the particularistic and often conflicting demands of individual Arab states can take precedence over the unifying ideals of Islam. However, it is to the non-Arab varieties of nationalism among Muslims that this statement applies with particular force, because in the case of the Turks, for instance, and as will be further explained below, Iranians, nationalism has no intrinsic link with Islam, and even sometimes implies its total negation. The cultural campaigns of Atatürk in Turkey and Riḍā Shāh in Iran were aimed at eliminating or weakening the Islamic components of the Turkish and Iranian personalities. Even the liberal brands of nationalism in these countries have often found themselves at odds with the religionists because of promoting the pre-Islamic legacies of their nations.

We now have to leave the nationalist attitude towards Islam, and resume our study of the reverse side of this picture – namely, the religious attitude towards nationalism. In the nineteenth and earlier decades of the twentieth centuries, this attitude was easily definable because most of the pioneers of Islamic modernism unhesitatingly tended to oppose nationalism in so far as it was incompatible with Islamic universalism. Sometimes their opposition had political motives: so long as the Ottoman Empire lasted, many Muslims supported it as a bastion against Western expansionism and in the name of an illusory consensus called 'Pan-Islamism', which only served to perpetuate the Ottoman despotism. But by the time the modernists like 'Abd ar-Rāziq were denouncing the nationalistic exploitation of Islam, the emergence of separate Muslim states, each jealously guarding its independence, had relegated the designs of Muslim unity to the realm of visionary politics. This caused important frictions inside the religious camp. Of those who adhered to the previous, orthodox malediction of nationalism the most outspoken were the fundamentalists both inside and outside the Arab world. Unmoved by changing political realities, men like Bannā', Navvāb Ṣafavī, Sayyid Quṭb, Ghazzālī and Maudūdī have taken an unequivocal stand against all varieties of nationalism: linguistic, ethnic and liberal. For them, resistance against foreign domination, which can be the only legitimate ground for such particularistic creeds, does not have to be formulated in the language of nationalism: Islam possesses enough ideological and emotional resources to galvanise the masses in the cause of independence. Even patriotism of the vaunted nineteenth-century type is discarded from the lexicon of these leaders, because the only homeland they recognise is not the familiar one associated with specific ethnic groups, but the global 'abode of Islam' – though this time called, not by the traditional term *dār al-Islām* (the 'abode of Islam'), but by the newly-coined *al-waṭan al-Islāmī* (the Islamic homeland).

Other religious factions have been less consistent, because they have been forced to take account of new political circumstances. In our particular area of study there have been two groups of the 'Ulamā' whose attitudes indicate a mentality which is not only different from that of the fundamentalists, but is also ready to contradict itself in response to the changing political scene. The first are the 'Ulamā' of al-Azhar who, on several occasions in Egypt's recent history, openly supported the nationalist ideology, and the second, the Shī'ī leaders and writers in Iran. Before surveying the position of each of these two groups separately, we have to make a caveat on the way in which the divergence between the nationalists and their Muslim detractors has found expression in, or (as Marxian authors would put it) has been caused by, a clear division in the social structure of their countries. Nationalism has rarely been the conscious credo of the Muslim masses, whether urban or rural, except in its vaguest and most general anti-imperialist or anti-Zionist slogans. As in the West, the most articulate spokesmen and heroes of nationalism in Muslim countries have arisen from the ranks of the bourgeoisie and the aristocratic establishment. Accordingly their constituency has normally been found among civil servants, teachers, middle-rank army officers, and relatively well-to-do tradesmen and shopkeepers. The bazaar merchants have often played an ambiguous role, with affiliations in both camps, maintaining family and business ties with both the 'Ulamā' and liberal nationalists. But whenever the lower strata of urban people have rallied in great numbers to the nationalist platforms it has been, first of all on issues of extreme national concern, giving rise to an unusual degree of harmony between social classes – such as the oil nationalisation movement in Iran in 1951–3, the Suez crisis in Egypt in 1956, and the Bangladesh war in 1971; and second, their support for the nationalist cause has been on sufferance of the 'Ulamā' – by virtue of either their explicit approval or their equanimity. This pattern of the alignment of social forces has had another consequence not exclusively related to the nationalist movement: whereas an orderly, gradual increase in political liberties, such as in Egypt from 1923 to 1939, or in Iran from 1945 to 1949, created favourable conditions for more or less all political groups alike, a sudden relaxation of official controls, allowing the release of long-suppressed, popular frustrations, benefited the religionists more than other factions (examples are: Iran after 1941, 1949, 1961 and 1978; Pakistan after 1971, Egypt after 1967 and 1971, and – with essential qualifications – Turkey after 1950). This has been particularly true of the urban areas, where the means of political communication, organisation and activity have been more available. That is why economic development and urbanisation have often paradoxically contributed in the long run to Islamic revivalist movements. This state of affairs is by no means eternal, or endowed with any sacrosanct character: there is no doubt that the spread of literacy and political education, accompanied by the responsible enjoyment of guaranteed rights of expression and assembly, would eventually reverse the situation, assuring the liberal nationalists of greater influence among the 'disinherited', urban masses, leaving only the traditional-minded, illiterate strata as the preserve of the religionists. This is precisely what differentiates the case of Turkey from that of other Muslim countries, despite the relative failure of her attempt at complete secularisation, and the uneven record of her democratic experience: a higher rate of literacy, and the existence of certain institutionalised liberties in that country since 1950 have visibly strengthened the position of secular political groupings, enabling them to make inroads into the same social classes which, in a country like Iran or Pakistan, would normally be considered as the breeding ground of Muslim fundamentalism – the unskilled workers, and the 'lumpen' proletariat.

The combination of the factors underlying these issues – the doctrinal irreconcilability between Islam and nationalism, the simplicity of Islamic tenets for the masses, versus the relative sophistication of the nationalist ideals (in contradistinction to the facile appeal of anti-imperialist, anti-Israeli slogans), the rough correspondence between the nationalist–religionist rift, and the 'patrician–plebian' dichotomy in the social structure, has had one definite result: in any real trial of strength between the nationalists and the religionists, the latter enjoy a *potential* tactical advantage in terms of popular support, which can be turned into *actual* superiority through shrewd leadership and manipulation of the masses.

* * *

The Azharites' initial attitude towards both Egyptian and Arab nationalisms after the First World War was, in concert with that of fundamentalists, one of outright condemnation. No less an authority than the Rector of al-Azhar, Muḥammad Abu'l-Faḍl al-Jizāwī, and the Muftī of Egypt, 'Abd ar-Raḥmān Qurrah, led the attack on the nationalist 'heresy' as late as 1928, when Arab nationalists were only starting their campaign across national borders,[13] and the earlier amorphous movements were evolving into more determinate political ideologies and trends such as Wafdism and Kemalism. Arabs and non-Arabs, they declared, are unified in a single brotherhood under Islam, in which nationality can only rest on the bonds of faith. Later, in 1938, another eminent religious figure, Shaykh Muḥammad Ghunaymī, stressed Islam's opposition to all forms of geographic or ethnic particularism (*iqlīmiyyah*). Even by 1938, namely at the height of the Arab revolt against Jewish immigration into Palestine, when nationalism had clearly become the most powerful creed in the East as much as in the West, the new Rector of Al-Azhar, Shaykh Muṣṭafā al-Marāghī, reiterated Islam's hostility to racialism, and called upon Arab Muslims to strive 'towards Islamic unity, rather than allowing themselves to be preoccupied with Arab unity.'[14]

The watershed in the transformation of al-Azhar from a champion of Islamic internationalism into one of the spiritual citadel of Arab nationalism came several years after the Second World War, in 1952, when the Egyptian monarchy was overthrown by the Free Officers' *coup* – the 'July Revolution'. Ignoring decades of condemnation of nationalism, the Azharites threw their full weight behind its newest and most ardent protagonist in the whole region. How could this change of heart be explained? The easy answer would be that al-Azhar was simply cowed into submission. Although this explanation would apply particularly to the period after Jamāl 'Abd an-Nāṣir's accession to power in 1954, its general validity does not detract from the importance of other, less apparent, reasons for the Egyptian 'Ulamā's conversion to nationalism. One such reason is that if they had any illusions about their own ability to compete with secular nationalists of the Wafdist type before, and for some time after, the Second World War, such illusions evaporated in the face of the Officers' regime, whose record was unsullied by any corruption or association with the West, and was therefore a more formidable rival. Moreover, what was formerly a creeping Zionist threat – one of the essential promoters of Arab nationalism – had now crystallised in the state of Israel after inflicting a most grievous blow to Arab pride, and this plainly called for the kind of militant response that could not possibly be provided by al-Azhar's hitherto sober catholicity. Although during the first Arab–Israeli war of 1948–9 al-Azhar had appropriately adoped a vociferously patriotic attitude, it had now been forced to carry that posture to its logical conclusion by taking a conspicuous stand in favour of Arab unity. Its own expedient calculation also pointed in the same direction: by joining the Arab nationalist movement, it would not only immunise itself against charges of disloyalty, but also gain a leverage over a leadership which, if abandoned to its own devices, might degenerate, at best into a secular Kemalist, and at worst into an atheistic, Communist state. This was necessitated all the more by a phenomenon which had existed since the twenties, in Egypt as well as in many other Muslim countries, but had now assumed alarming proportions: Islam's diminishing prestige with the rising generation of 'progressive', Westernised youth whose main characteristic was a readiness to identify Arab backwardness with adherence to Islam, and, in general, to regard religion as an ally of reaction. It was indeed from this same generation that the new rulers had emerged. Hence it was essential for the Azharites to take advantage of the change of regime, and demonstrate Islam's real revolutionary spirit by supporting the policies of the new regime, including its campaign for Arab unity. What lightened the Azharites' heart-searchings was that it was not, of course, they alone who needed the Free Officers' goodwill to enhance their own, and Islam's, image among the people; the Free Officers themselves also needed the 'Ulamā's blessings to consolidate their power, and – as we shall soon see – to thwart their left-wing challengers. Be that as it may, al-Azhar welcomed the Revolution of July 1952 with an effusiveness that served, among other things, to suggest its own vulnerability in the new political climate. Its ostensible justification at the outset for doing so was the Revolution's role in liberating the 'Ulamā' from a deadening and un-Islamic quietism. It poured scorn on the overthrown monarchy for having done its best to 'confine Islam to the mosque, so that its principles may not extend to the social field, popular institutions, and cultural organisations', while in the same breath giving generous praise to the new regime: 'God has blessed humanity with this Revolution,' wrote Muḥibb ud-Dīn al-Khaṭīb, Editor-in-Chief of the review of al-Azhar, '[an event] which has united the "heirs of the Prophet" [i.e. the 'Ulamā'] in their stand on Islam. The Revolution has refuted all the excuses to which some of the 'Ulamā' resorted in the past to justify their [passive] attitude to the implementation of the Islamic mission, whenever their conscience reminded them of the obligations with which God has entrusted them.'[15] This was at one and the same time a reaffirmation of their status as the 'heirs of the Prophet' and arbiters of all areas of national life – moral, cultural and social – a dutiful acknowledgement of the blissful turn of events, and a warning to the Free Officers against any secularising intentions. As it happened, the regime went ahead with its wide-ranging reforms without much heeding such pious enunciations. Nevertheless, the Azharites continued to display their trust in the Officers as 'the followers in the footsteps of 'Umar and 'Amr ibn al-Āṣ', i.e. the earlier heroes of Islamic militarism, and put an Islamic construction on all their social and economic schemes for the new Egypt – including the controversial land reform. But, more relevant to the topic at hand, they were drawn ever more deeply into the rising chorus of Arabism under Nāṣir's conductorship. This could not be done lightly, not only in view of the contradiction between Islam and nationalism, but also because of al-Azhar's past record.

However, the solution that the Azharites eventually found to their dilemma was none other than the one we noticed in the case of Bazzāz: the complete identification of Islam with Arab nationalism. This could be observed in many of their statements from 1956 onwards: that is from the time that Nāṣirism began to overshadow all other ideological trends in the Arab world. In an editorial entitled 'Has the Giant Woken up?', marking the breakthrough in al-Azhar's search for an identifiable political stance, Khaṭīb depicted the many vicissitudes of Islam and Arabism in history to prove that they have always stood and fallen together. By 'Giant' (*'imlāq*) was meant the Arab nation, and even more specifically, the corporate personality of the inhabitants of the Arabian Peninsula, who, under the Rightly-Guided Caliphs, had carried the 'banner of justice' to the three known continents of that age – Asia (North), Africa and Europe – simultaneously establishing the existence of Arabism (*kiyān al-'urūbah*) and humane Islam (*al-Islām al-insānī*). Khaṭīb's diagnosis of the decline of Islam, though merely repeating 'Abduh's and Riḍā's analysis, underlined his nationalistic approach to history. Islam started to decline, he said, when its system of government was Persianised, and when the 'Giant' was benumbed, among other things, by the 'absurdities of Greek philosophy, and the hallucinations of Brahmanist Ṣūfism'. Consequently, the 'Giant' went into a slumber that lasted many centuries, during which time foreigners, from Mongols and Crusaders to the Portuguese, Dutch, British and French colonialists, occupied many territories in the eastern and western parts of the Muslim world. 'But has the Giant now woken up?', asked the author, 'Are we now passing through a new phase in the history of Arabism and Islam, in which the *history of Mankind* expects us to resume our mission so as to perform on the arena of life another chapter in the story of justice and good deeds?' His answer was that the 'Giant' was now in a state midway between sleep and awakening. It had just recovered from 'the benumbing effect of colonialism in its military and political aspects'. Although there were still many other soporifics keeping it from resuming its mission, the Egyptian Revolution had firmly set the trend in the direction of a full renaissance of the entire Islamic community.[16]

As was noted, the significance of Khaṭīb's article is that it typifies the official, religious rhetoric of the time, in support of Arab nationalism. Such rhetoric, by postulating a complete equation between Islam and Arabism on the one hand, and between Arabism and humanity on the other, left no room for any doctrinal contradiction to mar the case for an alliance between Islam and Arab nationalism. But the whole situation contained an irony which made itself felt outside the realm of speculative politics: the Azharites were making these sanguine statements about the revival of Islam under Nāṣir's leadership at a time when his regime was launching a devastating campaign against an organisation in Egypt which laid claim to representing the real Islam – the Muslim Brothers, who, as we mentioned in the previous chapter, after their unsuccessful attempt on Nāṣir's life, had become the butt of a fierce repression, occasioning strident protests from their sympathisers in Syria, Jordan, Iran and Indonesia.

* * *

The case of the Iranian Shī'ī 'Ulamā' is more complex. This is primarily because of the different significance of nationalism both as an idea and a movement in Iran's modern history. Arab nationalism is a quest for the unity of all Arabic-speaking peoples who lost their independence and identity as a political force after the overthrow of the 'Abbāsīd dynasty by the Mongols in 1258. The prime concern of the political leaders and theoreticians of Arab nationalism during the last two centuries has, therefore, been to vindicate the essential unity of Arabic-speaking peoples despite their geographic, ethnic, confessional, social and economic differences, and to arouse them to a sustained struggle for recovering this unity. Their task has been rendered particularly onerous because of the divisive effects of Arab subjugation by a variety of foreign rulers – Ottoman, British, French and Italian. Polemical discussions on the concept of nationhood, attempts at an exact definition of the Arab nation, romanticisation of early history and appraisal of the role of religion and language in promoting Arabism have been some of the more important themes of modern Arab political literature. By contrast, what is called Iranian nationalism has been concerned less with the problem of *nationhood* than with that of *freedom*. We find scant or only marginal references in the relevant writings of nineteenth-century Iranian intellectuals to such questions as the oneness of the Iranian nation, the constituents of its identity, and the conflict between Iran's pre-Islamic culture and her Islamisation.[17] In their place we find persistent demands for democracy, parliamentarism, and the rule of law; criticism of the existing state of affairs; and wistful comparisons of modernisation with backwardness. This is simply because, since at least 1502, Iran had been an independent state, and the unity and identity of her people had been an accomplished fact. True, the loss of some territories to the Ottomans, Russians and Afghans prompted calls for national vigilance in the face of foreign predators, and even occasional spells of xenophobia; so did the growing rivalries between the Russians and the British to secure financial and commercial concessions in the country. But these never developed into intellectual arguments over the distinct place of the Iranians in history, or into efforts to reach for the past in search of the antecedents of Iranian culture and personality. Hence the Shīʻī religious writers scarcely felt the necessity to pronounce their views on nationalism. Whenever they did, they had no hesitation in denouncing it as an imported heresy undermining Muslim unity. This fact has often been obscured by the objective or practical association between the ʻUlamā' and Iranian nationalism, whether it be against the Ottomans in the Ṣafavīd period, or against the Russians after the wars of 1813 and 1828, or against the British in the Tobacco Rebellion in 1890–2, or perhaps most important of all, against internal despotism in the Constitutional Revolution of 1906. It has been this association, plus the Iranian historical contributions to the flowering of Shīʻī theology, jurisprudence and philosophy, which accounts for a widely held notion in the West about an inherent, mutual dependence between Shīʻīsm and Iranian nationalism. But the truth is that there is nothing in the theoretical principles of Shīʻīsm to make it more amenable to ethnic or racial particularism than Sunnīsm. In point of fact, so far as Arab particularism is concerned, Shīʻīsm may be considered to be, if anything, more Arabist than Sunnīsm, because of insisting on the existence of a set of virtues in one particular group of the Arabs, the House of the Prophet Muḥammad, to the exclusion of all other human groups. There are indeed some Shīʻī traditions which ascribe certain superiority to the Iranians over Arabs in terms of their allegiance to the members of the Prophet's family, but even these make the virtue of being an Iranian seem to be relative to Arab excellence: Iranians are praiseworthy only to the extent that they are loyal to the family of the Prophet. And in any case, such traditions have never been allowed to attain the status of even an implicit article of faith for the Shīʿīs. No wonder then that those few Iranian Shīʿī writers who have discussed nationalism within a deliberate religious framework have condemned it or expressed their preference for Pan-Islamic trends. Even in the nineteenth century when Pan-Islamism was a transparent Ottoman policy of rallying support from Muslims outside the empire, as well as inside, there were authors like the Qājār Prince, Abu'l Ḥasan Mīrzā, known as Shaykh ar-Ra'īs, who, in a tract entitled *Ittiḥād-i Islām* ('Islamic Unity, 1894), felt no qualms in arguing that the best hope for Muslims to save themselves from decline was for them to submit to the leadership of Abdulhamīd, 'this enlightened, wise Sulṭān, intent on unifying the Muslim world.[18] Shaykh ar-Ra'īs had certainly unorthodox views on many subjects, but his position on nationalism was shared by the 'Ulamā', as was shown later, about ten years after the publication of his tract, during the Constitutional Revolution, when one of the main worries of the religious opponents of constitutionalism was its deleterious effects on the purity of Islamic beliefs. But it was in the twentieth century, after Riḍā Shāh embarked on his systematic policy of cultural nationalism, glorifying Iran's pre-Islamic civilisation at the expense of Islamic values and symbols, that opposition to nationalism became a criterion of doctrinal rectitude. Naturally this opposition could not be made public so long as official suppression continued. Even the removal of the suppressive machinery after Riḍā Shāh's abdication in 1941 did not lead to an immediate expression of Islamic internationalism, since it coincided with a swelling tide of revulsion against the Allies' occupation of Iran, culminating in the short-lived, nationalist–religious coalition during the oil nationalisation movement of 1951. The bitter memories left by the collapse of that coalition made a lasting impact on the political stance of religious groups in the course of following decades. The collapse was caused both by personal rivalries between the two principal leaders of the popular movement against the British, Muḥammad Muṣaddiq and the Āyatullāh Sayyid Abu'l-Qāsim Kāshānī, and certain fundamental differences between them over the methods of reorganising Iranian society after the immediate aim of the movement, namely nationalising the oil industry and expelling the British, had been achieved. The two leaders' outlooks mirrored their class and cultural backgrounds: Muṣaddiq opted for a Western-type democracy, while Kāshānī, although being equally a champion of political liberties, naturally showed more concern for the observance of Islamic precepts. The nationalists, deeply hurt by what they saw as a cynical co-operation between their religious opponents and the royalist or pro-British elements, launched a campaign during the closing months of the Muṣaddiq era, making full use of all the familiar clichés common to the Westernised political élites of most Muslim countries, portraying the religionists as the natural allies of British imperialism. The mutual recriminations continued after the overthrow of Muṣaddiq, even when most of his religious foes, including Kāshānī himself, became victims of royalist suppression. But the religionists now enjoyed a clear advantage: they could still substantially influence public opinion through the mosques at a time when the nationalist parties and press had no such possibility. The urge to eliminate the vestiges of the nationalist campaign of 1952–3 was later compounded by another necessity: the royalists, having weathered the popular upheavals of the fifties and the early sixties, slowly resumed the promotion of Iran's pre-Islamic culture in an attempt to secure the historical legitimacy of the prerogatives of kingship. It was against this backdrop that religious writers, from the mid-sixties onwards, resorted for the first time in Iran's modern history to an explicit condemnation of her pre-Islamic civilisation. The earliest example of a similar campaign which comes to mind is the reaction of some of the Iranian Muslim grammarians and historians, such as Tha'ālibī (d. 429/1038) and Zamakhsharī (d. 538/1144) against the protagonists of the Shū'ubiyyah movement, which claimed racial superiority for the Iranians over the Arabs.

Among modern religious polemists against Iranian cultural nationalism, the most influential has been Murtaḍā Muṭahharī (d. 1979), Professor of Islamic Philosophy at Tehran University, and one of the leaders of the Islamic Revolution in Iran. Together with that most popular exponent of Shī'ī modernism, 'Alī Sharī'atī, and a number of religious teachers and preachers, he founded the *Ḥusayniyyah-i Irshād* in Tehran, a centre of religious education and propagation dedicated to disseminate 'true Islam' among the youth. Eventually the Centre was closed down because of both the government fear of the oppositional implications of its activities, and the hostility it aroused among the more traditionalist 'Ulamā'. The first major publication of the *Ḥusayniyyah* was a scholarly volume on the Prophet Muḥammad which purported, among other things, to oppose the current official and intellectual belief about the virtues of Iran's pre-Islamic civilisation by demonstrating the social injustice and moral depravity of the Sassanian state. Muṭahharī follows the same line in many of his writings. It consists essentially of two arguments against those nationalist writers as well as Western Iranologists who claim that the Islamisation of Iran was never genuine because Islam was imposed on her by force, and that it has always been an alien culture for the majority of Iranians. First, he says, 'those who speak of the military conquest of Iran by the Arab armies as being synonymous with the Islamisation of the country can perhaps present in support of their thesis arguments claiming that the newly-converted Persian performed public prayer because of what might be termed 'public pressure'. But they find it difficult to explain why the Persians produced so many great Islamic scholars. It might be thought that a people, if forced, could submit outwardly to another pattern of life, but not that a people could be forced to contribute creatively and profoundly to this pattern unless it were transformed inwardly by the new way of life.'[19] Second, he argues that if Islam is alien to the Iranians because of having originated outside their geographic borders, then so should Christianity be to the Europeans, Buddhism to the Chinese, and Communism to the Russians. But none of these people have ever expressed a sense of specifically cultural alienation towards their religion or ideology.[20] The fact is that Islam, contrary to the contention of Arab nationalists, is not bound by any ethnic predilection; it treats all human individuals as equally capable of grasping its truths. The Islamisation of Iran, concludes Muṭahharī, took place not at once but gradually.[21] In the meantime, the Iranians were free under the Muslim rule to practise their pre-Islamic beliefs, and had therefore no need to fabricate Shī'īsm to camouflage their ancient traditions. They converted to Islam because they were discontented with the Sassanian autocracy and corruption, and thirsty for a new message of justice and equality. They developed a deep affection for the members of the Prophet's family because they found them the most sincere and most fearless champions of Islamic ideals.[22] There are indeed some Shī'ī traditions which give weight to the contention that the Iranian admiration for the Imāms is connected with the marriage between the third Imām, Ḥusayn, and Shahrbānū, the daughter of Yazdigird, the last Sassanian king. These traditions should be treated with the greatest caution, because, according to Muṭahharī, some of their narrators have been proved, by the standards of the 'science of tradition', to be unreliable. He indulges in further polemics against European and Iranian exponents of the family link between Shī'īsm and Iranian nationalism, and says that if inter-marriage were to give rise to sectarian preferences, the Iranians had an equally valid reason for loving the Umayyads, because the Caliph Walīd Ibn 'Abd al-Malik is also reported to have married Shāh-āfarīd, another descendant of Yazdigird.[23]

We are not concerned here with the historical accuracy of some of Muṭahharī's arguments. He himself tends to be cautious in the best scholarly tradition whenever dealing with specific historical details. What should be of greater interest to us is his attitude towards the whole phenomenon of cultural nationalism in modern Iran, an attitude which is shared by all those thinkers who insist on the authenticity and primacy of the Islamic components of her historical conscience, and so willy-nilly collides with the nationalists. Any upsurge of nationalism inevitably leads to a renewal of this conflict, as long as Iran does not, or cannot, part with her pre-Islamic heritage, a heritage which is to a considerable extent embedded in her language and culture. There are other Muslim nations which have had varying degrees of attachment to their pre-Islamic legacies – the Egyptians to the Pharaonic, the Lebanese to the Phoenician, the Tunisians to the Carthagian, and the Iraqis to the Babylonian. But the temptations of these pristine glories have so far been offset by the countervailing pull of the Arabic language and culture, which, in their turn, can secure some kind of symbiosis between Arab nationalism and Islam. Many Arab nationalists have managed to profess to be good Muslims at the same time by putting an Islamic construction on their pride in Arabism. Iranian nationalists, by contrast, have often found themselves driven to underlining the purely Iranian elements of their culture, mostly reminiscent of pre-Islamic times, or of the resistance to the Arab invasion during the first two centuries of Islam. In their eyes, the real renaissance of the national self-consciousness starts with the great epic poet Firdawsī (d. 411/1020), whose account of the Arab conquest remains to this day the most poignant epitaph on the destruction of the Sassanian state.[24] Some 'Pan-Iranist' enthusiasts have even joined the campaign for 'pure Persian', eliminating foreign, mostly Arabic, words, from the national language, something which deeply offends not only the guardians of the Islamic heritage, but also many classicists. Hence, although any nationalism is fundamentally irreconcilable with Islam, Iranian nationalism is more so than its Arab counterpart, and by the same token its conflict with Islam is much more difficult to resolve.

* * *

Although since the Second World War Muslim peoples have gained their independence from Western powers, and have even, in some cases, succeeded in achieving some degree of national integration, few of their political or intellectual leaders can honestly claim that this by itself has solved any of their major political, social and economic problems. In many cases, independence has been vitiated by economic backwardness and continuing dependence on Western powers. National unity has also been placed under severe strain as cultural self-consciousness and political separatism have gained in strength among infinitely diverse ethnic groups, often artificially under external pressures. Nourishing the sense of frustration have been the persistence of autocratic forms of government, and the apathy of vast masses after brief periods of outbreak of nationalistic fervour. The struggle for democracy has been one way of overcoming this frustration.

II Democracy

Historically speaking, democratic ideals of free opinion, free speech, free assembly and representative government impressed themselves on the Muslim mind as corollaries to the goals of national independence and unity. When large sections of a population are aroused and mobilised in the name of a common aim, it is only natural that wider popular participation in determining the affairs of the state should be either demanded or promised as necessary instruments or rewards in the national struggle. The problems raised by this development for Muslim thinkers were far more complicated than those posed by nationalism. It is fairly simple to shelve or play down the theoretical and doctrinal issues which are likely to divide a nation when it faces a foreign aggressor or usurper. It is far more difficult, especially in times of sober stock-taking and decision-making, to agree on a set of principles and mechanisms to ensure equal possibilities of self-expression and access to the levers of power for the citizens of a state which needs strong, centralised leadership in the solution of its urgent problems.

The irreconcilability between Islam and nationalism is due to the former's *specific* quality as a religion opposed to all ethnic and racial differentia which would justify the superiority of one group over others. Not every religion by itself, and necessarily, contradicts nationalism. On the contrary, there are religions like Judaism, Zoroastrianism and Hinduism which, apposite as they are to ethnic division, have been smoothly integrated into the nationalist ethos of the Israelis, Iranians and Indians. To say the least, the use of these religions for cultivating nationalistic symbols and values among their followers has not aroused the same degree of doctrinal squabbles and moral indignation as has the use of Islam by some Arab or Pakistani nationalists among advocates of Islamic universalism.

The case of democracy is different. If Islam comes into conflict with certain postulates of democracy, it is because of its *general* character as a religion. Every and any religion is bound to come into a similar conflict by virtue of being a religion – that is to say, a system of beliefs based on a minimum of immutable and unquestionable tenets, or held on the strength of received conventions and traditional authority. But an intrinsic concomitant of democracy, whatever its definition, is ceaseless debate and questioning, which unavoidably involves a challenge to many a sacred axiom.

But since there is no consensus on the exact meaning of democracy as a political system, we cannot adopt a single definition as our reference point, although we shall later have the opportunity to delve into some of the current Muslim perceptions of the term. However, what we should note at this point is that no form of government, whatever its ideological underpinning or its social and economic configuration, can be entitled to the epithet *democratic*, as the term is generally understood in our times, without being predicated on a number of principles which would be either implicit in the attitudes and social values of its subjects, or explicitly formalised in its laws. The most important of these principles are a recognition of the worth of every human being, irrespective of any of his or her qualities, the acceptance of the necessity of law, that is a set of definite or rational norms, to regulate all social relationships, the equality of all citizens before the law, regardless of their racial, ethnic and class distinctions, the justifiability of state decisions on the basis of popular consent, and a high degree of tolerance of unconventional and unorthodox opinions.

Islam contains many basic principles which would make it highly responsive towards some of these moral and legal, as distinct from sociological, prerequisites of democracy. To start with, any Muslim intellectual seeking to construct a modern theory of Islamic democracy is particularly heartened by a comparison of the concepts of equality in Islam and classical Western political thought. The equality recognised by Islam, contrary to that among the Greeks, for instance, is not subordinate to any prior condition. Equality for the Greeks had meaning only within the range of law. Their isonomy guaranteed equality, in the words of Hannah Arendt, 'not because all men were born equal, but, on the contrary, because men by nature were not equal, and needed an artificial institution, the polis, which by virtue of its *nomos* would make them equal. Equality existed only in this specifically political realm, where men met one another as citizens and not as private persons. The difference between this ancient concept of equality and our notion that men are born and created equal and become unequal by virtue of social and political, that is man-made institutions, can hardly be over-emphasised. The equality of the Greek polis, its isonomy, was an attribute of the polis and not of men, who received their equality by virtue of citizenship, not by virtue of birth.'[25] It may be argued that the equality envisaged in Islam also depends on a political pre-condition, which is the membership of the *Ummah*, the community of the faithful. But while this pre-condition could be achieved by any person through the simple act of conversion to Islam, for the Greeks the access to the political realm, which was the precondition of equality, was possible only to those who owned property and slaves – a privilege which could not certainly be enjoyed by the majority of the people. Medieval Muslim thinkers, such as Khājah Naṣīr Ṭūsī (d. 672/1273), who were obviously aware of the explosive consequences of the Islamic concept of equality, took care to emphasise the basic inequality of men. 'If men were equals, they would have all perished,'[26] he said, quoting an Arabic aphorism of unknown origin in support of his thesis. And Ṭūsī was an Aristotelian *par excellence*.

The difference between the Islamic and classical Western concepts of equality is reflected partly in the political terminology of the two cultures. The Qur'ān recognises Man (*insān*), irrespective of his beliefs and political standing, but has no word for *citizen*. That is why Muslims in modern times have had to invent new terms for the concept: *muwāṭin* in Arabic, *shahr-vand* in Persian, and *vatandàş* in Turkish, are all neologisms. However much the political rights of the individual may be considered to be undefined or ill-defined in the traditional sources of Islamic political thought, the position of Man himself, in his pre-social state, is ennobled in the Qur'ān as God's 'vicegerent on the earth' (2 : 30). Conversely for the Romans, the Latin word *homo*, the equivalent of Man, 'suggested originally somebody who was nothing but a man, a rightless person, therefore, and a slave'.[27]

To go back to the doctrine of equality, if Islam is antithetical to nationalism, it is because of its negation of all racial, ethnic and hereditary criteria of distinction among human beings, and of its belief that all of them form one community. The only valid Islamic ground on which an individual may be superior to another is his fear of God, or piety (*taqwā*). It might be objected that what Islam grants with one hand by positing the basic equality of all human beings, it takes away with another by ruling that non-Muslims living in an Islamic state should be inferior to Muslims by incurring heavier financial liabilities and civic deprivations. The answer to this objection is that no egalitarian school of political thought provides for absolute equality – unless it is hopelessly utopian, or has no intention of achieving political power. In our times, any democratic system of government inevitably imposes certain implicit or explicit discriminations in favour of all those who pay allegiance to a set of ideals, norms and symbols, forming the subject of a presumed consensus, whether it be the 'American way of life', or 'scientific socialism', or a liberal–monarchical democracy. Moreover, the exercise of all civic liberties is limited by that commonplace and oft-abused proviso that freedom of any individual should end whenever it interferes with the freedom of another individual. But none of these limitations *per se* disqualifies any of these political systems from being called democratic by its beneficiaries. Islam's treatment of the 'People of the Book', or its denial of political rights to atheists, can be similarly justified in terms of the constrictions necessitated by the nature of any political regime. But what ultimately decides whether a regime is or is not genuinely dedicated to the principle of equality despite these limitations should be whether the ostensible factor giving rise to them is permanent and unremovable, such as the membership of a race or caste, or conversely accidental and temporary, such as the membership of a party, or the status of foreign residents of a state. And the decisive fact is that the limitations placed by the *Sharī'ah* on the rights of non-Muslims are not permanent and unremovable, because non-Muslims always have the option to convert to Islam, and thereby overcome their political incapacity.

Likewise, if by democracy is meant a system of government which is the opposite of dictatorship, Islam can be compatible with democracy because there is no place in it for arbitrary rule by one man or a group of men. The basis of all the decisions and actions of an Islamic state should be, not individual whim and caprice, but the *Sharī'ah*, which is a body of regulations drawn from the Qur'ān and the Tradition. The *Sharī'ah* is but one of the several manifestations of the divine wisdom, regulating all phenomena in the universe, material or spiritual, natural or social. The use of multiple words in the Qur'ān to define this normative character of God's wisdom – *sunnat allāh* (the way or tradition of God), *mīzān* (scale), *shir'ah* (another term for the *sharī'ah*), *qisṭ* and *'adl* (both meaning justice) – is perhaps one way by which Islam has tried to impress its significance on the minds of the faithful. Again, at a purely abstract level, all this satisfies another pre-requisite of democracy which is the rule of law. Some authors maintain for the same reason that a proper Islamic state should be called, not a theocracy, but a nomocracy. The distinction may not be of much value when one considers that what is sacred and binding in Islam is not law in general, but only the Law, which is of divine inspiration. But what is pertinent to our discussion is that by upholding the *Sharī'ah* Islam affirms the necessity of government on the basis of norms and well-defined guidelines, rather than personal preferences. This alone should establish considerable common ground with all the opponents of personal rule, so that the dispute as to whether the norms and principles should be determined by reason or revelation, or both, or what kind of authority is to decide whether a particular policy or attitude is sanctioned by the *Sharī'ah* or not, and how controversies over the correct interpretations of the Qur'ān and Tradition can be settled to the satisfaction of all those concerned, may be put off until a later stage. The derivation of the concept of man-made law from the notion of the *Sharī'ah* may seem to any Westerner and Westernised Muslims to be an unsatisfactory way of deducing so vital an element of social engineering. But remaining within the frame of reference of the same critics, one cannot in all fairness find much fault with this method, except in its being rather archaic, because in the history of Western political thought also the modern concept of law was a by-product of the development of the medieval debates on the divine wisdom. The idea of law as 'a rational ordering of things which concern the common good; promulgated by whoever is charged with care of the community' was extracted by men like St Thomas Aquinas[28] from the perception of the reason of God as the source from which all the levels of the cosmic order emanate.

Islam can pass yet another moral test of democracy, which although being of a formal nature is indispensable to its functioning, namely, the requirement that a government should not only rule by law, but also reckon in all its decisions with the wishes of the ruled. This requirement is met by the principles of *shūrā* (consultation) and *ijmā'* (consensus), which are drawn from both the Qur'ān and the Tadition. In enumerating the qualities of a good Muslim, the Qur'ān mentions consultation on the same footing as compliance with God's order, saying the prayers and payment of the alms-tax. The Prophet and the first four Rightly-Guided Caliphs (*Rāshidūn*) are known to have accordingly made consultation with, and in some cases deference to, the opinions of their critics, an abiding characteristic of their rule. According to Maudūdī, they took counsel not from a bunch of 'hand-picked men', but only from those who enjoyed the confidence of the masses. These practices were admittedly discontinued after the assassination of 'Alī, except for brief, exceptional periods of the rule of just and pious rulers. But Muslims were henceforth generally less tolerant of disaffection within their own ranks, than of non-Muslim groups, or the 'People of the Book'. The Muslims' record, over the whole span of history, on this rare civic virtue in inter-cultural relationships is decidedly superior to that of Westerners. Anti-Semitism, in the form prevalent in European history, was unknown among Muslims, and in any case there were no Islamic equivalents of the mass expulsions of the Jews such as those which took place in Germany, Spain, France, England, Rumania and Poland. The Muslim tolerance of other great religions may not be directly connected with the moral prerequisites of democracy, but as a concrete historical precedent, especially when added to the practices of the Prophet and the Rightly-Guided Caliphs, it provides a persuasive subsidiary argument in favour of Muslim democrats against advocates of intolerance.

To the extent that there are such theoretical affinities between Islam and democracy, the exertions of some Muslim writers either in devising a theory of Islamic democracy or in demonstrating the democratic temper of Islam cannot be dismissed as an unfounded and desperate presentation of Islam in a form palatable to the rising generation of unbelieving, politicised youth. Some of these writers adopt a philosophical standpoint, concerning themselves not with the social and political history of Muslims, nor even with the formal principles of the faith, but rather with its underlying concepts. Thus the Indian Muslim Humāyūn Ẓahīruddīn Kabīr tries to show the common grounds between Islam, democracy and science. He starts off by describing the three basic concepts governing the growth of science in human history.[29] These are, according to him, the uniformity of the universe, the universality of the laws of nature, and the value of the individual instance. He then goes on to prove that democracy is but the application of these three concepts to the social life of human beings. 'From the homogeneity and unity of the world,' he says, 'follows the universal application of moral and political laws. From the uniformity of the laws of nature follows the equality of all before the law. From the emphasis on the particular instance follows the recognition of the dignity of the individual human being.'[30] After explaining these principles, he observes 'the remarkable similarity'[31] between them and the fundamental teachings of Islam. The first presupposition of both science and democracy is the existence of a unitary world, in which Islam declares its belief by emphasising the unity of Godhead in a 'manner which has been rarely equalled by any other religion.' Islam accedes to the second principle of science and democracy, namely, the universality of the law, by holding that 'as a religion valid for all times, it must reveal the eternal nature of truth', and that 'since God is one, and reason seeks to express his nature, the Laws of reason cannot but be the same for all'. Finally, Kabīr deduces the third principle, the reverence for the individual, from Islam's denial of any distinction between the phenomenal and the transcendent, and its appreciation of nature not as a symbol of something hidden, but for its own sake. 'When the reality of the empirical is recognised, the particular comes to its own, for the empirical is always revealed in the particular as the human personality. On this basis, many theosophical schools in Islam, including the *wujūdī* (existential) and the *shuhūdī* (intuitive) have emphasised that the individual cannot be regarded as a mere element in a universal system, because it has an independent status of its own. 'The overriding unity of God,' concludes Kabīr,' seems to be challenged (in Islam) by the uniqueness of the individual.'[32]

The question as to why the very reverse has happened in Islamic history, with the personality of the individual crushed under the weight of an overawing collectivity, lies outside the scope of Kabīr's philosophical discourse. Living in independent India, a country where at least elementary political rights and liberties have been ensured, despite the tragic history of communal strife, to a degree unequalled by any Muslim state, Kabīr could afford to indulge in abstract thinking on democracy. But Muslim writers living in more difficult times, and under much harsher regimes, have had to pay attention to more tangible issues bearing on the concrete safeguards against unscrupulous tyrannies. Hence one favourite exercise of successive generations of Muslim proponents of democracy since the middle of the nineteenth century has been to scour religious literature in search of prescriptions for the rights of the individual, and checks on state power. Their writings, from the Iranian Mīrzā Yūsuf Mustashār ud-Dawlah's *Yak kalimah* ('One Word', ?1870) to the Egyptian 'Abbās Maḥmūd al-'Aqqād's *Ad-dimuqrāṭiyah fi'l Islām* ('Democracy in Islam', 1952) are certainly impressive examples of ingenious political pamphleteering. The Qur'ān admittedly contains few specifically political verses, and the Tradition, although richer in this respect, can be the subject of violent disagreements. Historical precedents are even less helpful because again, except for the period of the Prophetic mission and of the Rightly-Guided Caliphs, they indeed give more weight to the cynics' taunting that, for the better part of their history, Muslims have known no political system other than the most arbitrary. As regards the *Sharī'ah*, it was never implemented as an integral system, and the bulk of its provisions remained as legal fictions. Nevertheless, it is neither inordinately difficult nor illegitimate to derive a list of democratic rights and liberties from all these sources, given a fair degree of exegetical talent.

The Egyptian writer Aḥmad Shawqī al-Fanjarī has compiled perhaps the most comprehensive catalogue. He allows himself considerable latitude by following the example of Ṭahṭāwī, the famous pioneer of cultural Westernisation in Egypt, who maintained that 'what is called freedom in Europe, is exactly what is defined in our religion as justice (*'adl*), right (*ḥaqq*), consultation (*shūrā*), and equality (*musāwāt*).... This is because the rule of freedom and democracy consists of imparting justice and right to the people, and the nation's participation in determining its destiny.'[33] Pursuing the same point, Fanjarī says that every age adopts a different terminology to convey the concept of democracy and freedom. In his opinion 'the equivalent of freedom in Islam is kindness or mercy (*raḥmah*), and that of democracy is mutual kindness (*tarāḥum*)'. In the Qur'ān, he reminds us, Muḥammad is instructed to show leniency and forgiveness in the same verse as he is ordered to consult the believers in the affairs of the community. Muḥammad is reported to have said that God 'has laid down consultation as a mercy for His community.' 'Alī is also quoted as having prescribed to Mālik Ashtar, whom he appointed as Governor of Egypt, to adopt as his motto kindness towards the people under his rule.[34] Thanks to these terminological and conceptual idiosyncracies, Fanjarī is able, on a much larger scale than that of his predecessors, to deduce every conceivable democratic right and liberty from the Qur'ān, the Tradition and the practice of the first four Caliphs. A few examples will suffice to show his method as well as the scriptual basis of the whole *genre* of theoretical expositions of Islamic democracy.

The sanctity of human life, as the most fundamental principle of any civilised community, is inferred from the verse: '...he who slayeth any one, unless it be a person guilty of manslaughter, or of spreading disorders in the land, shall be as though he had slain all mankind; but that he who saveth a life, shall be as though he had saved all mankind alive' (5:32), and from the Prophetic saying: '[Three things of] a Muslim are prohibited for another Muslim: his blood, his property, and his reputation', which is the most concise textual authority for respecting the triple individual rights of life, ownership and freedom.[35] In the same category, the inviolability of domicile is expressly declared in the verse: 'Enter not into other houses than yours, until you have asked leave, and have saluted the inmates. This will be best for you.... And if ye find no one therein, then enter it not till leave be given you' (24:27–8).[36]

Equal rights for women are said to be ensured by two verses in particular: 'And it is for the women to act as they [the husbands] act by them in all fairness' (2:228), 'And their Lord answereth them, "I will not suffer the work of him among you that worketh, whether of male or female, to be lost"' (3:195), as well as by the Prophet's encouragement to his favourite wife 'Ā'ishah, to take an active part in the political, legal and scholastic activities of the young Muslim community.[37] The right to elect rulers is easily found in the institution of *bay'ah*, or the contract of the appointment of Caliph – but no reference is made to the endless theoretical and practical problems that Muslims have faced in history to make it work. Apparently the practice of the first four Caliphs is considered to be convincing proof of its practicability.[38] As regards freedom of opinion, the matter cannot be settled simply by quoting any particular Qur'ānic verse or Prophetic saying. So the concept is subtly examined in its negative sense – namely, in the sense of the absence of restrictions on the freedom of expression, and then this is deduced from such provisions as the necessity of removing all barriers between the rulers and the ruled (*suhūlat 'al-ḥijab*), the absence of the practice of imprisonment, the prohibition on presuming the bad faith of others, and the obligation of every Muslim to 'adjudicate justly' (4:58).[39] The right to criticise rulers is inferred from two Qur'ānic verses – 'Clothe not the truth with falsehood, and hide not the truth when ye know it' (2:42), and 'God loveth not that evil be matter of public talk, unless any one hath been wronged' (4:148) – and from the general obligation of the believers to 'enjoin the good and forbid the evil'.[40] The licence to form political parties is thought to be granted by the verse (9:122), declaring that the believers should not all go out to the wars, but of every band of them only a party should go forth, so that those who are left behind may gain sound knowledge in religion, and warn the other people when they come back from the battlefields to beware.[41] (Incidentally, it is the same verse which is cited by some commentators, particularly the Shī'īs, to prove the legitimacy of the function of the 'Ulamā' and the *mujtahids* in the social structure of Islam.) Personal immunity against intimidation and torture is asserted on the basis of the Prophetic saying: 'My community is exonerated in three matters: error, forgetfulness, and that into which it has been coerced', and a saying by the Caliph 'Umar: 'A man is not secure in his person when he is starved, or degraded, or imprisoned to make a confession against himself.'[42]

It may be easy to find fault with such deductions on both methodological and substantive grounds. They may well prove to be questionable on the touchstone of traditional exegetics, since they sometimes treat the Qur'ānic verses out of context, with no regard for their 'cause of revelation' (*sha'n nuzūl*) or context. The citation on the equal rights for women also fails to mention the remainder of the verse: '... and men are a step above them' (2:228). More seriously, such quotations may be censured in terms of an integral theory of democracy. Safran rebukes 'Aqqād for tending 'to view democracy, which he understood to mean as essentially the right to vote, as a primary natural right rather than as a system expressing and applying certain fundamental ideals', and for his intention 'to interpret the general *bay 'ah* of Islam as the equivalent of the right to vote, and hence as evidence that Islam is democratic'.[43] Since in all the accepted Islamic definitions of the term sovereignty belongs only to God, and without sovereignty the popular vote is but a hollow shell, Safran's objection is hard to refute. He also disagrees that *ijmā'* can be made – as it has been made by 'Aqqād and many exponents of Islamic democracy – a political as well as a judicial concept, and that its validity can be extended to 'the thing which comes nearest to it (that is, majority)', because Safran rightly regards *ijmā'* as 'the traditional *ex-post-facto* sanction of change already established, resting on the divine assurance that the community would never agree on what is wrong.'[44] Similarly, when he attacks 'Aqqād for his disdain of 'questions of expediency and practicality',[45] he is referring to a flaw in the political thinking of numerous modern Muslim writers whose total attachment to lofty ideals has prevented them from making due allowance for practical matters – although we tried to show in the previous chapter how men like Rashīd Riḍā and Maudūdī are free of this flaw by reason of their honest concern for the feasibility of most of their suggestions.

But strictures on the modern theories of Islamic democracy have not come only from non-Muslim scholars. An Iranian Muslim political scientist, ʻAbdul-Hādī Ḥāiri, has similarly criticised Muḥammad Ḥusayn Nā'īnī, an eminent Iranian Shī'ī theologian of the era of the Constitutional Revolution of 1906, and the author of the only known systematic treatise in defence of parliamentary democracy by a religious figure at the time. He finds Nā'īnī's understanding of freedom to be 'completely traditional', not going beyond the Islamic interpretation of the freedom of expression. This is because, says Ḥāiri, Nā'īnī 'did not know the meaning of freedom as it was interpreted in the West. Being misled by the Muslim modernists, Iranian or otherwise, Nā'īnī had simply learnt that the principles of democracy were similar to those of Islam without paying much attention to the sharp distinctions found in their meanings.'[46]

But these criticisms risk missing the main point about most of the contemporary Muslim writings on democracy. First of all, what is conspicuously omitted or not sufficiently conceded by the critics is that there is no universally accepted definition either of democracy in general, or of its Western version in particular. Any formulation of democracy, therefore, stressing one or the other of the known attributes of a democratic system – whether it be the right to vote, or of self-expression, or of assembly – can be valid, provided it enjoys a reasonable degree of internal coherence. ʻAqqād may be wrong in equating democracy with the right to vote, but by doing so he is expressing a view over which controversy is still raging among Western scholars themselves. Hence his opinion cannot be summarily rejected by asserting that voting is not what democracy is all about. There is a respectable school of thought in the West, acknowledging its debt to Rousseau and Mill, which holds a high conception of voting, not as act by itself, but, in the words of Stephen Lukes, as 'the culminator of long, thoughtful, and fair consideration of the relevant issues.'[47] In Schumpeter's theory also, of the two strands of the 'democratic method', one is voting. He has defined the 'democratic method' as 'that institutional arrangement for arriving at political decisions in which individuals acquire the power to decide by means of a competitive struggle for the people's vote.'[48] Comparative politics apart, in most 'Third World' countries, where despotism has always been the dominant norm of rulership, often revered as part of a divinely sanctioned, pre-destined scheme of things, and where the majority of people are illiterate and apathetic, appeals for the right to choose the rulers, or to participate in political decision-making through voting, is the shrewdest, the most direct and popularly the most comprehensible method of creating an urge for democracy. Second, even if there existed a single definition of democracy in Western political theory, Muslim writers are not rationally bound to adhere to it rigidly, especially if their primary concern is not to devise a theory of Islamic democracy, but to explain democracy in Islamic terms. At best, their writings should be treated – and this brings us back to what we held to be the main point about them – as nothing more than an attempt to live down the legacy of generations of intellectual inertia by trying to show that submission to stultifying political practices and institutions has no sanction in religious dogma. This is demonstrably the case in the ideas of earlier Muslim modernists. Asad-ābādī (Afghānī) and 'Abduh, for instance, both coupled their enumeration of the virtues of government by popular consent with persistent and vigorous attacks on the popular belief in divine predestination, arguing that Islam is a religion of free will.[49] But it would be patently wrong to conclude from this that in their definition of popular participation the doctrine of free will figures as the central element. To mention another example, many of them attach great importance to the necessity of reviving the practice of *ijtihād* as a *sine qua non* of breaking the spell of all irrational forms of authority, whether political or religious. However, although the actualisation of democratic ideals is thus made dependent on the permissibility of *ijtihād*, there is no suggestion of an inherent, necessary link between the two. For this reason, scholarly fault-finding with the innovations in the nomenclature of Islamic institutions similarly fall wide of the mark. Redefinition of terms like *ijmā'* and *bay'ah* as equivalents of 'public opinion' and 'social contract', by a whole generation of Muslims, from 'Abduh, through the authors of the resolution of the Turkish National Assembly on the Caliphate in 1924, to 'Aqqād and recent Azharites, do indeed deviate from their traditional usage, but they are no more removed from their original meanings than modern European models of democracy are from the ancient Greek *demes*.

What is blatantly missing from contemporary Muslim writings on democracy, in spite of all the claims to the contrary, is an adaptation of either the ethical and legal precepts of Islam, or the attitudes and institutions of traditional society, to democracy. This is obviously a much more complex and challenging task than the mere reformulation of democratic principles in Islamic idioms. It is because of this neglect that the hopes of evolving a coherent theory of democracy appropriate to an Islamic context have remained largely unfulfilled. Perhaps the neglect is deliberate or unavoidable, because – as we mentioned at the beginning of our discussion – all efforts to synthesise Islam and democracy are bound to founder on the bedrock of that body of eternal and unchangeable doctrines which form the quintessence of every religion. Those Muslim thinkers who face this issue boldly, and free of any compulsion to keep their faith abreast of ephemeral political fashions, normally come up with the open admission that Islam and democracy are irreconcilable. The contemporary Iranian Shī'ī philosopher Sayyid Muḥammad Ḥusayn Ṭabāṭabā'ī, author of an authoritative, multi-volume commentary on the Qur'ān, *Al-mīzān*, makes the same point. After arguing that no other great religion, or even worldly ideology, can rival Islam in its concern for social problems, he takes issue with those Westernised intellectuals in the Muslim countries who claim that the social norms of Islam are no longer applicable to the conditions of the modern world, in which it is the will of majorities which is expected to determine the nature of social laws and relations. He rejects this claim by recalling that in history usually the reverse has been the case: at their inception, all great religions conflicted with, rather than pandered to, the wishes of the majority. Human beings often dislike what is right and just. The Qur'ān confirms this repeatedly: 'Or do they not recognise their apostle; and therefore disavow him? Or they say, "A Djinn is in him?"; but the truth most of them abhor. But if the truth had followed in the train of their desires, the heavens and the earth, and all that therein is, had surely come to ruin' (23:70–1). It is therefore wrong, says he, to treat the demands of the majority *always* as just and binding.[50] Elaboration of the hazards of acceding to popular wishes leads Ṭabāṭabā'ī to a critique of libertarian interpretations of the Qur'ān.[51] He finds such interpretations to be false so far as they give the impression that Islam subscribes to freedom in the same sense that is cherished by the modern, materialistic civilisation – that is, abolition of all manner of moral restrictions on human behaviour, and total subordination of matters lying outside the penumbra of law to unfettered individual will. He takes particular exception to the claim that Islam sanctions the freedom of opinion. He admits that Islam has granted the Man the licence to enjoy all pleasant and beautiful things in life, provided that He does this in moderation (Qur'ān, 7:32, 2:29, 45:13). But it would be absurd to conclude from such verses, especially the one on the absence of 'compulsion in religion' (2:256), that opinions are free in Islam. How can Islam lay down the freedom of opinion while belief in the unity of God, the prophecy of Muḥammad, and the certainty of Hereafter, constitutes its unquestionable premises? However, this should not deter Muslims from collective reflection and debate on religion,[52] in order to become profoundly convinced of the truth of its injunctions, and avoid disagreement and disunity among themselves – an enterprise to which they are expressly instructed by the Qur'ān (4:59, 82, 83; 16:43–4; 29:43; 39:18).[53] Under no circumstances should force or coercive measures be used to impose an opinion. This is the meaning of the 'absence of compulsion in religion', and not the permissibility of adhering to any idea at will. Ṭabāṭabā'ī expatiates on the same point from a more general, philosophical standpoint as well, when he tries to answer the criticism of 'some dialectical materialists' that, by attempting to eliminate all contrariness in ideas, Islam aims to contravene the 'principle of contradiction', which is the driving force of all evolution in human history, thus dooming the community of its followers to be static, and insulated against the invigorating effects of conflicting opinions. Ṭabāṭābā'ī could have retorted simply by saying that dialectical materialism also seeks the same aim since in the ideal society of Communism too all contradictions are dissolved or 'sublimated'. But instead he prefers to answer the charge through an excursus into epistemology. All valid propositions, he says, are of two categories: some are relative, capable of infinite permutations, others are absolute and eternal, needless of any adaptation. Science and technology belong to the former category, and the more frequent their change the greater their contribution to human welfare. Universal religious truths are of the latter kind, but, in Ṭabāṭabā'ī's view, their constancy cannot arrest, or accelerate, social change for the simple reason that they cannot affect social life. Indeed, how can doctrines such as 'the universe has a creator', or 'God has transmitted his laws for the happiness of Mankind through his prophets', or 'God will one day bring together all human beings in one place to give them full recompense of their actions' be held responsible for the stagnancy of a society? So the democrats have nothing to fear from the eternal truths of Islam which are concerned with matters unrelated to their political convictions. When all such arguments in the direction of assuaging the fears of 'progressive' Muslims are exhausted, Ṭabāṭabā'ī appropriately resorts to the final reasoning of all those conservative schools, whether in Western or Islamic political philosophy, whose ancestry can be traced back to that arch-critic of democracy – Plato. Why should right-minded people, he asks, be infatuated with change, which is after all the hallmark of imperfect societies? A proper Islamic state does not need change because it is perfect.[54]

Inasmuch as Ṭabāṭabā'ī meets the problematic of freedom of opinion in Islam head-on, his stand is much more sincere and courageous than that of all the theoreticians bent on an artificial integration of democracy in Islam. But the problematic is not so simple as he describes it, and his reluctance, as a philosopher, to spell it out in more concrete examples, makes his theses appear much more opposed to democracy than they actually are, and likewise of much value to all the not-so-philosophical factions who try to suppress their rivals in the struggle for political supremacy. Certainly reconciliation between Islam and democracy would have been much easier if the topics on which free opinion is not allowed in Islam were confined to the three basic principles that he mentions (unity of God, prophecy of Muḥammad, and certainty of Hereafter). But the fact is that, as all experiments in the Islamic state have shown in our time, the taboo subjects do not remain limited to these sublime axioms, but involve much lower, pedestrian problems whose number and nature are both determined by the rulers. In these conditions even minor disagreements with the state, let alone the right to criticise major policies and resist injustice, can be alleged to ultimately impinge on any of those principles, or run counter to a holy consensus.

Ṭabāṭabā'ī stands for a tradition in Islamic thought which thrives on philosophical speculation. But the type of objections he raises against democracy can be found in the pronouncements of many writers, some of whom have an outlook diametrically opposed to his. 'Abd al-'Azīz al-Badrī, for instance, has set forth some of the same ideas, although from the austere perspective of the jurists, in a little book, *Ḥukm al-Islām fi'l ishtirākiyyah* ('The Ruling of Islam on Socialism', 1965), which has been endorsed by Shaykh Amjad az-Zahāwī (d. 1967), one of the most respected Sunnī scholars of Iraq, and the Muftī of Baghdad. The book has an added interest for us, because it is one of the few publications from Saudi Arabia on a topical ideological theme. Badrī is not only opposed to democracy, but also strongly disapproves of even the use of such modern political terms. He admits that in the history of Islamic sciences there has never been any interdiction on newly coined terms (*la mushāḥḥah fi'l iṣṭilāh*, 'there should be no dispute over terminology', says an old scholarly maxim). But, warns Badrī, when the concept behind a term is un-Islamic the term itself also becomes exceptionable. This is evident, according to him, from that Qur'ānic verse (2:104) which forbids the Muslims to use the verb *rā'inā* (look at us), instead of *unẓurnā* (regard us), because the Jews used *rā'inā* in Hebrew, by a slight mispronounciation, as an insult, meaning 'our bad one'.[55] Even the epithet *Islamic* cannot expurgate the term *democracy*, because in his opinion Islam recognises only rights (*ḥuqūq*) and limitations on them (*ḥudūd*), or penalties, but never liberties (*ḥurriyyāt*).[56] He is semantically right when he says that in Islam *ḥurr* can mean free only as the opposite of slave (*'abd*), but what he fails to mention is that since the early days of Islam some Muslims, not all of them heterdox, also advocated the doctrine of *ikhtīyār* (literally, to choose the good, hence option or free will), which is at least a substantive precondition for the acceptance of the concept of freedom as understood in Western political philosophy.

* * *

If the periods of liberalism, mainly in the form of parliamentary rule (in Egypt from 1923 to 1952, with some interruptions; in Iran from 1941 to 1953; in Turkey from 1950 to 1960; in Pakistan, between 1959 and 1976), ended in failure, it was not, of course, solely because of the flaws in some of the Muslim ideas of democracy as studied in this section. In fact, with all their protestation of loyalty to national cultures, the protagonists of liberalism in these countries (the Wafd in Egypt, the National Front in Iran, the Democrats in Turkey, and so on) often espoused a totally Western notion of democracy, thus avoiding the problems faced by those who wanted to incorporate democracy into Islam. But this still did not save them from failure.[57]

The failure has certainly been caused not so much by conceptual incoherence as by the absence of specific social and economic formations, including an autonomous, conscious, and articulate middle class. Aggravating the effects of all these factors have been phenomena of a more general character, such as educational backwardness, widespread illiteracy, and the prevalence of servile habits of thinking and blind submission to authority. Perhaps no less important are the periodic crises of Western democracies themselves – in the thirties, with the rise of Nazism and Fascism, and in the sixties, with the reluctance of the United States and some West European powers to adjust themselves to the realities of the post-colonial era. The result in each case has been the further discrediting of liberal trends in the Muslim countries, and the commensurate strengthening of the groups seeking radical, violent, sweeping and élitist solutions to their political and economic problems – a process which gained further impetus with the growing world-wide prestige of the Soviet Union, the People's Republic of China and other socialist states, particularly their popularity among Muslim peoples because of their anti-imperialist posture, as well as with the rise of the Third World as the embodiment of new hopes and visions in international politics. It was in deference to this complex situation that some Muslim thinkers turned their faculties to a new ideological enterprise – Islamic socialism.

III Socialism

Of all the ideological challenges to Islam in the twentieth century, Socialism has been the most congenial to its overriding temper. It comes closer than nationalism and democracy to Islam's central summons for brotherhood, social harmony and egalitarianism. On a more specific plane, as two systems of socio-political engineering, Islam and socialism are united in their high regard for collectivism, or a balance between corporate and individual interests, state control, and an equitable distribution of wealth. So while Islam is at variance with nationalism over the latter's basic belief in ethnic specificity as the only valid criterion of group interests, and with democracy over the permissibility of absolute freedom of opinion, it finds itself in no contradiction with the broad principles of socialism. Tension no doubt arises between the two either when socialism is intertwined with the Hegelian promotion of European ethnocentricity and Marxian atheism, or when Islam is presented as the guardian of the sanctity of private ownership. But then again neither are Hegelianism and Marxism integral constituents of socialism, nor is private ownership a cardinal tenet of Islam.

In modern Islamic political thought, socialism has been conceived as a set of fairly coherent ideas in essentially one of two forms: either as an officially sponsored ideology justifying state policies of social and economic reforms, or as a popularly inspired system of critical thought in protest against prevailing conditions. The most influential example of the former during the sixties was the Egyptian version of Islamic socialism as expounded under Nāṣir, and of the latter the work of the Egyptian fundamentalist Sayyid Quṭb (who was executed by Nāṣir's regime in 1966), and the current 'radical' Muslin literature in Iran. So there are three varieties of Islamic socialism that we should study: (a) official, (b) fundamentalist, and (c) radical.

a The official version

As a theory, Islamic socialism was for the first time formulated in Egypt as part of the 'Ulamā's' response to the demotion of Islam in the official ideology from a position of centrality to that of only one element of a complex synthesis. The circumstances of its inception may induce some critics to dismiss it as yet another piece of casuistry, and one which has been concocted not voluntarily but through blatant official intimidation. However, the imprint of official approval does not seem to have debased this brand of socialism at least as a conceptual model for many Muslims elsewhere – rulers and intellectuals alike. Its birth dates back to the dissolution of Egypt's union with Syria (the United Arab Republic) in 1961, and President Nāṣir's decision to shift the emphasis in his policies from the ideal of Arab unity to internal problems and to socialism as the most effective means of turning Egypt into a modern industrialised state ensuring justice and equality for all its citizens. Such a strongly doctrinaire posture stood in sharp contrast with his previous attitude.[58] From the time of Nāṣir's accession to power in 1954 up to 1961, Egypt's idea of social revolution, as one of the aims of the regime that had replaced monarchy, was based on the assumption that the interests of all classes of the Egyptian (and later Syrian) people were reconcilable within the framework of broad national goals. This assumption found its institutional expression in the National Union, a political mass organisation, charged with materialising the revolutionary aims, embracing 'both the reactionary elements of capitalism and feudalism, as well as the progressive working powers of the people'. With the collapse of the union with Syria, which Egyptian leaders put down to the machinations of the 'exploiting classes' in Syria, this illusion of 'class alliance' was thrown overboard, and national unity, in the sense of an overarching consensus eradicating all class differences, was admitted to be an impossibility. Class alliance was then considered to be feasible only among 'the working forces of the people', who according to the 1964 Constitution, consisted of 'the farmers, workers, soldiers, intellectuals and national capital'. But it was stressed that there could be no 'peaceful coexistence' between 'the working forces of the people' and the exploitative classes whose affiliations with imperialism as well as inherited privileges were to be liquidated. In conformity with these ideas, the National Union was replaced by the Socialist Union, a tighter organisation which was closed to the 'reactionary elements'.[59] One could say, in view of this onset of class mentality, that the most salient doctrinal feature which differentiated the statements of the Egyptian rulers on their internal policies after 1961 from those uttered before that year was some notion of social determinism, i.e. a belief in the decisive influence of class interests and status on the socio-political outlook of individuals, whereas all the other declared principles of their socialism, such as planning, justice and freedom, figured in one way or another in their pre-1961 blueprints too.

Nevertheless, the new socialism in the official ideology was decidedly Fabian: the rulers always accompanied their statements of the belief in the primacy of class interests with a firm denial of the inevitability of class struggle or warfare, or the necessity of proletarian dictatorship. They claimed that the aim of their socialism was merely to remove class distinctions, emancipate the exploited, and safeguard their rights without 'inflicting retribution on former exploiters or taking revenge on past oppressors'. The purpose was to create, not a classless society, but 'conditions in which diverse classes, each performing a valid function, and all free from domination and exploitation' could peacefully live together. Stemming directly from this evolutionist, conciliatory view of social life was respect for religion – not Islam alone, but all great religions. It is here that we can locate the point of both tension and fusion between the Nāṣirite school of Arab socialism and Islam. On the one hand, the intention to emancipate the exploited masses necessitated extensive acts of sequestration, nationalisation and other forms of encroachment on the right of private ownership – acts which are held by a considerable body of orthodox opinion to be against Islamic sanctions of private property. On the other hand, the reverse side of this task, namely avoidance of class hatred and warfare, which was held to be an equally important pillar of Arab socialism, stood in need of appeals to the moral precepts of Islam. In between the two sets of issues lay the broad desiderata shared by Islam and socialism *tout court*: securing social justice by fostering the spirit of fellowship and mutual help among individuals, discouraging or prohibiting the accumulation of wealth, and an idealised respect for the poor and disinherited.

While it was thus conceivably possible to weld together some Islamic and socialistic concepts into a wholly new synthesis, matters were further complicated by the ambivalent attitude of the Egyptian leaders and their intellectual sympathisers towards Islam in their new ideological orientation. This ambivalence was epitomised by Nāṣir himself: while in private life he was a staunch practising Muslim – a fact which must have been decisive in bringing the Free Officers close to the Muslim Brothers before 1952 – in public he often acknowledged the role of Islam only as a subsidiary or contributory element of Arab nationalism – just as before him that other great Egyptian patriot, Muṣṭafā Kāmil (d. 1908), also prized Islam only in so far as it buttressed the Egyptian sense of self-identity. On many occasions Nāṣir certainly did pay tribute to Islam on account of its predominant share in Arab glory, particularly whenever he faced the challenge of an alien ideology. When, for instance, the relations between Egypt and the Soviet Union became strained in 1959 as a result of the Soviet support for a new claimant to the leadership of Arab nationalism, Iraq's President 'Abd al-Karīm al-Qāsim (d. 1963), Nāṣir launched a fierce, though short-lived campaign against his Communist critics in which he invoked manifestly religious terms and themes in denunciation of Communism.[60] But more typical of his assessment of Islam was the oft-quoted statement in his manifesto *The Philosophy of Revolution* identifying Islam as only one of the three circles centred on Egypt (the other two being Africanism and Arabism).[61] This stance received further emphasis after

1961, when the uplifting of socialism, added to the already highly cherished symbols of Arab nationalism, left little room for even lip-service to Islam. All the authoritative Egyptian sources for the study of Arab socialism in the sixties testified to this diminished stature of Islam in the official thinking. The maximum compliment that their authors were ready to pay to Islam was to acknowledge its contribution to Egypt's greatness in the past, and its continuing relevance as merely *one* of the numerous bases of her foreign policy. They also declared respect for all the 'divine missions in the world and their moral teachings'.[62]

Such casual treatment of Islam must have aroused grave fears in religious circles regarding the place of Islam in the future scheme of things. Even if such fears were allayed occasionally by the pious assurances of officials on its continuing role as the state religion, they were undoubtedly strengthened by the declarations of many Egyptian theorists of Arab socialism who, in conditions of strict censorship, freely published their views. Some of these theorists openly remarked that attachment to Islam, although potentially a motive for political dynamism, and an indispensable element in the fabric of the Arab national life, had now become incapable on its own of tackling the problems of the 'Arab homeland' – the ultimate focus of the loyalty and concern of the Arab progressives. In the opinion of one of them,[63] Islam had proved a failure, together with the other two solutions to the 'problems of the Arab destiny' suggested by some intellectuals, i.e. pragmatism ('trial and error') or negation of ideological commitment, and its opposite, Marxism, because Islam is a universal religion, unbounded by time and space, and not intended to meet the particular requirements of different ethnic groups. To make Islam an effective solution, it was imperative to derive from the comprehensive body of its doctrinal and legal precepts 'a system or programme (*minhaj*), consonant with the living conditions of the Arab homeland in the Twentieth Century'. But, lamented the writer, the religionists did not meet this challenge and tried 'to identify Islam with either capitalism or socialism, instead of substituting it for both of them; consequently, the problem remained unsolved.... The Arabs had therefore to start their search for a solution from the most difficult point – from scratch.'[64] Elsewhere the same author identified the causes of Islam's incapacity to solve this problem, not only in such well-known causes as the multi-religious character of the Arab peoples, but also in the vanishing role of religion as a valid denominator of divisions within the human community: 'The religious associateships have dissolved, and it is incumbent on the Arab progressives to break free from religious prejudice.'[65] What was then to be done? The official reply to this question was a philosophical blend of materialism and idealism: the evolution of human society is governed by not only spiritual and intellectual values, but also Man's material and economic needs,[66] a point which the religious leaders often ignore until they find their message rendered obsolete by the onrush of materially superior cultures. Two Egyptian authors, in a joint book devoted to a defence of the ideas of the young Marx, as the epistemological foundation of the ruling ideology, tried to show, rather over-confidently, that of all the existing systems of thought only Arab socialism attained the Excellent Mean between capitalism and Communism: 'Arab socialism', they wrote, 'is based on a completely new balance [of thought]. If we describe its position as the Excellent Mean between two extremes, this should not be understood to mean that our socialism stands midway between Capitalism and Marxism [sic], because we are not talking of an arithmetic or geometrical average. What we mean is that while Arab socialism stands midway between Capitalism and Marxism, it represents a jump forward with regard to these opposite poles.... This balance between the two poles has asserted itself as a result of the development of universal thought which, according to dialectical logic, has proceeded from thesis to anti-thesis, and then to state [the synthesis], in which the opposites are reconciled. Thus Capitalism gave rise to Marxism, and then these opposites gave rise to Arab socialism.'[67]

It was one thing to downgrade Islam to the position of a secondary source of official thinking; quite another thing was to legitimise the thoughts of Marx, whether young or old, as an ingredient of Arab socialism. And from 1961 onwards, while official publications took good care not to mention Marx except in dissociating Arab socialism from his atheism, officially sponsored political literature showed a distinct drift in the direction of Marxism. A number of Egyptian intellectuals openly acknowledged their debt to Marxism, and even indulged in an 'historical' criticism of Islam (a criticism, that is, which concerned itself, not with the theological or metaphysical principles of Islam, but rather with the false representations of its ideals in conventional literature).[68] Others, taking advantage of the recognition and respectability enjoyed by the New Left as a result of the de-Stalinising campaign throughout the European parts of the 'Socialist Camp', unabashedly preached the ideas of Sartre, Gurevitch, Brecht and others. True, the vast majority of these intellectuals, no less than the official pamphleteers, favoured a *modus vivendi* with Islam; but the net result of all their efforts, official and unofficial, was an unintegrated conglomerate of doctrines to which Islam contributed only a crust of moral values and a belief in God, while at the bottom the bulk of the epistemological and ideological propositions were borrowed from a cohort of Western thinkers ranging from Marx to the most *avant-garde*, 'committed' writers and poets. A situation had thus arisen by the mid-sixties in which, while Egypt was constitutionally regarded as a Muslim state, and the regime assiduously respected all the observances and symbols of Islam, the emerging socialist mentality considered Islam to be, at best, providing only half of the solution to the problem of the country or the Arab homeland.

The response of the 'Ulamā' to the combination of these challenges was inspired partly by the government pressure on al-Azhar to reform itself, and partly by the realism (or opportunism?) of a number of astute shaykhs and Western-educated professors, such as Muḥammad Ḥasan al-Bahī, who were anxious to prove that Islam by itself contained all the provisions of socialism, thus rendering any resort to an alien ideology unnecessary. An Egyptian academic summarised the situation at the time to this author in these terms: 'While the crypto-secularists [in the Government and the intelligentsia] strive to vindicate socialism through Islam, the Shaykhs are trying to prove Islam through socialism.'

The spokesmen of Islamic socialism in Egypt during the early sixties mostly acknowledged their debt to the pioneering work of a Syrian, Muṣṭafā as-Sibā'ī, sometime the Dean of the Faculty of Islamic Jurisprudence and School of Law in the University of Damascus. His book entitled *Ishtirākiyyat 'al-Islām* ('The Socialism of Islam') was for a long time recommended to any inquirer both inside and outside al-Azhar as the most acceptable exposition of the congeniality of Egyptian socialism with Islam. The fact that it had been produced by the official publishing house was also evidence of the government approval of its contents. All this was rather ironical, since Sibā'ī was also the leader of the Syrian organisation of the Muslim Brothers (called the Islamic Socialist Front). So while, as we saw before, their comrades were being persecuted in Egypt, the work of their leader was promoted in the same country as an authentic Islamic confirmation of the state ideology.

A number of reasons can be adduced in partial explanation of this apparent paradox. First of all, that a leader of the Muslim Brothers should commit himself to a socialism of sorts should by no means be surprising, since the ideas of social justice and reform, which are identified by some Brothers with the whole of socialism, have always constituted one of their cardinal principles. Since the Brothers have always contended that Islam itself contains all the elements of a socialistic regeneration, it is also natural that they should translate socialism as they understand it into a purely Islamic body of dogmas. The second reason should be sought in the tactical divergence between the Egyptian and Syrian Brothers in the late fifties.[69] At that time – contrary to what is happening at the moment this book is being written, when they are locked in a deadly struggle against the Ba'thist regime of Ḥāfiẓ Asad, and contrary to their Egyptian comrades, who have often adhered to militant if not terroristic activities – the Syrian Brothers preferred peaceful struggle under the leadership of their 'mild and devout shaykhs'.[70] It was presumably because of this difference in attitude that the Brothers and their sympathisers in Syria, who until 1955 had actively taken part in, and in fact fostered, an anti-Nāṣir campaign, were gradually divided after the revelation of the terroristic activities of their Egyptian counterparts, and particularly following Nāṣir's successive exploits on the international scene. The 'idealists' stuck to their previous ideas and categorically opposed the union of their country with Egypt; the 'realists' either chose to be silent, or were won over to the Free Officers' cause. The fact that Sibāʻī's book was written in 1959, i.e. when the union between Syria and Egypt was still in existence, and that its few references to the United Arab Republic are innocuous, shows that its author must have belonged to the 'realist' wing, although one could not assess how much this weakened his leadership of the Brothers' movement as a whole. The year 1959 also marked the height of the Nāṣirite–Communist conflict which had started with the Iraqi coup of July 1958. A side-effect of that conflict was the spontaneous rallying of all the traditionalist forces, including the Brothers', on the side of Nāṣir. This can account for the pronounced anti-Communism of Sibāʻī's book, which manifests itself through his frequent contrasting of Communism with Islam.[71]

One may not find anything particularly novel or original in Sibāʻī's arguments. Most of these could be found, in one form or another, in numerous books and publications which appeared before 1959 in various Muslim countries. But the main value of his book lies in its comprehensive collection and lucid presentation of all these arguments, although throughout the book Sibāʻī relies unfailingly on firsthand sources.

Sibāʻī is basically concerned in his book with the anticipations, or elements, of socialism in Islam. He sets out to adumbrate all the Islamic rules of 'state control over the social uses of wealth', realisation of state provision for all members of society, and state assurance to them of a life of dignity. Nowhere in his book does he attempt a serious discussion of the principles and ideas of socialism in any of its known versions. In the introduction of his book he admits that socialism has multiple varieties, resembling 'a creature with twenty heads', but he says that all these varieties share 'a belief in the necessity of state control over the use of wealth in the society and in the realisation of "mutual social responsibility" (to be defined later) for all its members, so that they can partake of a life in which human dignity and human confidence in his present as well as future are guaranteed'.[72] Elsewhere, he also offers, as we just said, a series of contradistinctions between Islam and Communism. These are focused on such specific points as 'freedom of constructive competition [which, according to him, is promoted by Islam, but destroyed by Communism], class conflict [which Islam denounces but Communism fosters], and religious and moral values [which, he emphasises, form the cornerstone of Islam, but have no place in Communism]'. He also contrasts Islam with capitalism in an endeavour to underline the independence of Islamic socialism of Eastern and Western extremes.

But Sibāʻī's major concern in writing his book, as stated in its introduction, is to refute 'the misconception of some people that Islam is alien to socialism because it has asserted [the right of] private ownership and approved of the institution of inheritance, and of big landlordism, giving the rich absolute freedom in disposing of their wealth'.[73]

In Sibāʻī's view 'the socialism of Islam' is composed of four elements: (1) natural rights for all citizens (*muwāṭin – sic*), (2) laws for guaranteeing these rights and regulating them, (3) laws of mutual social responsibility (*at-takāful al-ijtimā'ī*), and, finally, what Sibā'ī terms as (4) 'supports' or sanctions (*mu'ayyidāt*) for ensuring the implementation of the previous three sets of laws.

Of these, the first and the third elements are particularly relevant to Sibā'ī's purpose and therefore claim his greater attention. The right of ownership, among the natural rights of individuals, repeatedly comes up for discussion in the various chapters of the books, and is studied in some detail. The author's overwhelming concern for this right is shared by nearly all those Egyptian exponents of socialism, whether Islamic or secular, who try to establish the compatibility of socialism with Islam. This has been in response to the attitude of the majority of the orthodox detractors who, in castigating socialism, identify it, next to materialistic heresy, with the expropriation of individuals.

Under the heading 'The Origins of Ownership', the author opens his discussion by saying that in Islam the real owner of things is God (Qur'ān 2:284). This fundamental belief, says the author, has two benefits: first, it dispels vanity and arrogance from the heart of the property-owning mortals; second, it obliges him to abide by the *Sharī'ah* rules on ownership. But God, though being the original and ultimate owner, has liberally and freely put all his worldly possessions at the disposal of human beings (Qur'ān 22:65). Sibā'ī derives two conclusions from this Qur'ānic statement: first, there is nothing in the material world which cannot be possessed by Man given determination, intelligence and effort. Second, all groups of people are equally entitled *to make use* of 'the good things of the earth'. Once a person has taken possession of a thing *through honest means*, he is recognised by Islam as its rightful owner. And no means is more honest in attaining ownership than work. Consequently ownership based on begging, injustice, deceit and harm is forbidden. But possession of a thing is not an end in itself: just as its origin should be honest work, its aim should also be honest and useful, both individually and socially: in Islam individual ownership is a social duty.[74]

The most interesting and important part in Sibā'ī's discussion on ownership is his justification of the nationalisation (*ta'mīm*) of certain categories of property. He recognises multiple rules and institutions in Islam which make nationalisation an essential feature of its socialism. Foremost among these is a prophetic tradition, reported by Aḥmad and Abu Dawūd, to the effect that 'People own three things in common: water, grass and fire'; another tradition mentions salt too. Sibā'ī says that since these things were the basic necessities of desert life at the time of the Prophet their enumeration should on no account be regarded as exhaustive or exclusive. Thus, in a modern context, 'water' can be taken to stand for the entire installations of water-supply, 'fire' for electricity, and 'grass' and 'salt' for all the indispensable requirements of contemporary life. In a word, the Prophet's saying should be interpreted as warranting the communisation of any resource and material which, if allowed to remain in private hands, might lead to monopolised exploitation of public need. This tradition, together with its interpretation as suggested by Sibāʻī, figures prominently in the apologetics of Egyptian socialists at the time against orthodox attacks.[75] On the institutional side, the writer mentions *waqf* and *ḥimā*. 'According to the legists', he says, '*waqf* consists of removing the object of an endowment from the possession of its owner, so that it ceases to be the property of only one person, and its unsufruct becomes confined to those for whom the endowment is intended – *and this is nationalisation*'. *Ḥimā* is to reserve a piece of land as a grazing ground for public use. The Prophet Muḥammad and the Caliph 'Umar are known to have appropriated land for creating *ḥimā*. Underlying this institution is a regard for the needs of the poorer classes, and the necessity of assigning them priority in enjoying the protection of the State. Sibāʻī therefore feels justified in widening its scope to include the principle of land nationalisation in cases of necessity. The provisions for nationalisation are supplemented by three other Islamic rules: the first deprives the foolish (*sufahā*') of the right of ownership, requiring that their properties should be given over to the community (Qur'ān 4:5); the second prescribes that the properties of persons dying without heirs should also revert to the public treasury, and the third disapproves of (*yakruh*) concentration of property in a few hands. This last principle is borne out, according to the author, by both the Qur'ānic injunctions on the division of the spoils of war (*inter alia*, 59:7), and by the famous ruling of the second Caliph 'Umar (13–23/634–44) that the Muslim conquerors of Iraq and Syria should leave the occupied lands in the possession of their previous owners in return for land tax (*kharāj*) because he feared that this division among Muslim conquerors should lead, through inheritance, to concentration in the hands of one or two owners.

The state can thus interfere in numerous ways with the right of ownership – not to speak of its authority to collect *zakāt* and other taxes from property-owners. All this proves that in Islam the right of ownership – as indeed the rest of the natural rights – is subordinate to the collective interests of the Muslim community.[76]

As regards the laws of 'mutual social responsibility' (*at-takāful al-ijtimāʻī*), although this responsibility is to be shared by all the members of the Muslim community, yet it appears from Sibāʻī's analysis that here also it is the state which should carry the heaviest responsibility of all. He enumerates twenty-nine laws, all deduced from the Qur'ān, Tradition and authoritative books of jurisprudence, which are aimed at protecting the individual as well as the society against poverty and injustice, but at the same time underline the great scope allowed in Islam for state interference in the affairs of the community.[77] The application of the term 'law' (*qānūn*) for all the arrangements connected with 'mutual social responsibility' is Sibāʻī's own invention, and the question is whether all of them possess enough obligatory character to qualify for this designation. An obvious example is the institution of *ḍīyāfah* (hospitality) according to which every Muslim is expected to provide accommodation for his guest at least for one night. As Sibā'ī himself admits, this is regarded by the majority of jurisconsults to be merely a *sunnah* or tradition. But this example illustrates his ubiquitous method of placing every act of altruism in the category of *wājib* (obligatory) when sometimes *mustaḥabb* (recommended) seems to be the correct classification. The Qur'ānic prescription of these acts is based on the condition that they should emanate from their author's true love for God (2:177), otherwise they may be followed by his 'taunt and injury' towards his beneficiary, and this will completely nullify the merits of his acts (2:264).

Finally, Sibā'ī analyses the 'supports' or sanctions which Islam has provided for materialising its socialist aims. These are divided into the credal, moral, material and legal sanctions. His account of the material sanctions purports to substantiate further the case for state control, especially his description of *ḥisbah*, or the office of *muḥtasib* (censor) whose business it is to see that the religious and moral instructions of Islam are obeyed. Because of the all-pervading character of the Islamic state, the functions of *muḥtasib* cover a wide range of financial, administrative, political, social and moral matters.

Sibā'ī's discussion of the legal sanctions is also significant because of the emphasis it lays on the built-in mechanism in the Islamic legal system for its adaptation to social changes. This adaptation is mainly ensured by the permissibility of discretionary treatment of new social problems. The necessity of *ijtihād* is thus demonstrated. He recognises three sources of Islamic legislation to be particularly germane to Islamic socialism:

1 *istiḥsān* (literally, 'to consider something good') which was initiated by Imām Abū Ḥanīfah, and aims at settling the problems of legislation in conformity with the requirements of everyday life. It consists of disregarding the results of *qīyās* (analogy) when it is considered harmful or undesirable to meet the strict demands of theory.
2 *istiṣlāḥ* (literally 'to consider something appropriate or expedient') which is devised to ensure the interests of the Muslim community. These interests are of three kinds: those recognised by the *Sharī'ah*, those not recognised by the *Sharī'ah*, and those which are new, without any precedents at the time of the Prophet. According to the consensus of 'Ulamā', interests of the first kind, such as the protection of the beliefs, lives, intellect, properties and honour of Muslims, as well as the guarantees of their five natural rights, should be respected and upheld. The interests of the second kind, such as those of a profiteering wine-seller, or of a usurer, and the other harmful groups should in no way receive recognition. But the interests of the third category, which are unprecedented, should be recognised and protected in so far as they can be justified on grounds of expediency (*maṣlaḥah*); and the simplest

definition of expediency is given by Ghazālī: 'the aim of the *shar'*', he says, 'is to protect the religion, the life, the intellect, the generation and the properties of the people; whatever involves the protection of these five principles is *maṣlaḥah*, and whatever destroys them is *mafsadah* [opposite of *maṣlaḥah*, inexpediency]'.

3 *'urf*, which is the general practice or usage governing the three above-mentioned categories of human interests. Accordingly, it can be of three kinds: practices created by the Islamic lawgiver, those rejected by him, and those without precedent. The rules concerning these practices are exactly like those relating to the corresponding interests involved in them. Thus all practices based on the third kind of interests which do not contradict the stipulations of the Islamic law are valid and can form a basis of legislation. The tendency of the people to recognise only those social practices which would contribute to their welfare, facilitate their transactions and protect their legitimate rights and interests, is the best safeguard against possible abuses of this dispensation.

In addition to these legal sources, Sibā'ī claims his Islamic socialism to be also vindicated by what he calls the 'legal formulae'. These are in fact a set of both common-sense axioms and jural postulates either taken from the Qur'ān and Tradition, or inferred from the whole body of Muslim law, which have gained currency among the legists, and can serve as further justification for any new measure of socialisation. Below are given some of these rules by way of example:

'And nothing shall be reckoned to a man but that for which he hath made efforts' (Qur'ān 53:39). 'God will not burden any soul beyond its power' (Qur'ān 2:286). 'Repelling the harmful should be prior to obtaining the useful' (legal formula). 'Necessities remove prohibitions' (legal formula). 'Individual losses should be borne for the sake of preventing collective losses' (legal formula). '[State] interference in the affairs of individuals should depend on expediency' (legal formula).[78]

As it was said before, the apologetics of the 'progressive 'Ulamā'' in Egypt in defence of their pro-Revolution stance were mostly either a repetition of, or an elaboration on the above disquisition. Evidence of this can be found in the report of the proceedings of the First Congress of the Association for Islamic Research which was convened in Cairo, under the auspices of al-Azhar, in March 1964. The primary aim of the Congress, which represented the Muslims of forty-one countries of the world, was avowedly to call the attention of Muslim scholars to the most urgent legal, social and political problems of our age, and to help find enlightened solutions to them within the framework of Islamic doctrine. The report of the proceedings, as published by al-Azhar, contains a score of papers, all from the Egyptian participants, dealing with such topics as the limits of private ownership in Islam, the share of the poor in the properties of the rich, and the institution of *ḥisbah*.[79] The common denominator of all the papers is an attempt, along the lines of Sibāʿī's thoughts, to find Islamic regulatives and precedents for state control over the individual in the interest of Muslim community.[80]

The final Declaration and Resolution of the Congress, however, indicates that their 'progressive' sponsors have had to make certain concessions to the demands of the conservative opposition, whether inside or outside Egypt. Contrary to the expectation raised by a perusal of the papers read at the Congress, the Declaration and Resolution make no reference to any topic connected with socialism, except a new recommendation that the subject of *zakāt* and other sources of state income in Islam should be carefully studied by the next Congress. Besides, the sponsors seem to have gone out of their way to stress in article 3 of the Resolution the basic sanctity of the right of ownership, and to restrict the sphere of state interference with this right to extreme cases of necessity.[81] The sole revolutionary feature of the Resolution – apart from its familiar denunciation of imperialism and Zionism – is a blunt assertion of the right of *ijtihād*. The documents of the Second Congress pay greater attention to the problems raised by the expansion of state activities; for instance, they declare the permissibility of measures of social security, re-emphasise the prohibition of usury, fix the minimum value for the liability of commercial goods, cash money and other assets to *zakāt*, and stress the necessity of payment of *zakāt* in addition to official taxes of recent origin.[82] But like those of the First Congress they also carefully avoid any issue connected with the socialistic blueprint or achievement of the Egyptian Government, and even indicate intensified restiveness on the part of the orthodox participants by calling upon all Muslim states to adopt the Islamic jurisprudence as the basis of their legislations, and by openly condemning any state legislation for birth control. In spite of the declarations of some of the Azharites in support of the Government policy on birth control, the religious opposition on this score remained strong, even in the mosques controlled by the Ministry of Endowments, under the Nāṣirite regime.

b *The fundamentalist version*

Such opposition to official socialism, and indeed to all imported ideologies that existed inside al-Azhar did not find any outlet to express itself openly until after the Arab defeat in the 1967 war with Israel, when the regime allowed the release of pent-up frustrations. But there was another form of religious opposition which did manage to express itself, because its authors felt under no obligation to avoid giving offence to the rulers at any price. This came chiefly from Sayyid Quṭb, the chief spokesman of the Egyptian Muslim Brothers after the dissolution of their Society in 1954. Basically his teachings were no different from those of Sibāʿī. He also professed to be striving towards a transformation of Islam from 'a religion seeking an irrelevant, static, purely transcendent ideal' to 'an operative force actively at work on modern problems'.[83] In Sayyid Qutb's works too 'mutual social responsibility' (*at-takāful al-ijtamāʿī*) was offered as Islam's solution to the problems of social injustice and poverty. Contrary to the conservative 'Ulamā', nowhere did he regard the individual right of ownership to be absolute and sacrosanct, and therefore an obstacle to the communisation of the basic necessities of life (he, too, mentions the *ḥadīth* on the collective ownership of 'water, grass and fire' to substantiate his point). Where he parted company with Sibāʿī is in refusing to use the alien symbols which the latter employs to describe Islamic ideals. He did not approve of such terms as *Islamic socialism* and *Islamic democracy* which as he said could only result from the confusion of a divine order with man-made systems.[84] Perhaps for the same reason he did not even use such novel Arabic words as *ta'mīm* (nationalisation) in describing the Islamic provision for state ownership.

But his fundamentalism revealed greater differences from Sibāʿī. The most outstanding points in this fundamentalism which were obliquely tantamount to an implicit criticism of Egyptian socialism, can be summarised as follows:

1 Islam and socialism are two separate, comprehensive, and indivisible systems of thought and living. No reconciliation, or synthesis, is therefore possible between them. If there are occasional similarities between them, this does not warrant their identification with each other, just as the similarities between Islam and Communism cannot be taken as proof that they are congenial or based on the same principles.[85]
2 Genuine belief in Islam starts with absolute submission to the will and sovereignty of God alone. The reader was left to draw two conclusions from this: first, the cult of personality which had developed under Egyptian socialism was un-Islamic. Second, if the Egyptian leaders were genuine in their professions of faith in Islam they should have rejected mundane creeds such as socialism.
3 In the realm of ideas, the real choice today lies between Islam and *jāhiliyyah*[86] (i.e., pre-Islamic ignorance). The latter now pervades the whole human community, including the societies which call themselves Muslim but in practice violate the *Sharīʿah*.[87]
4 Socialism, like Communism and capitalism, is an excrescence of *jāhilī* thought, and therefore carries all the vestiges of its corrupt origin. It stresses such notions as social welfare and material prosperity at the expense of moral salvation.[88] Islam never neglects the material aspect of human life, and this can be particularly demonstrated by its detailed scheme of 'social justice'. But Islam considers the first step towards the realisation of this scheme to be the liberation and purification of the soul. Without this moral catharsis no attempt at improving human life can be successful.[89]

5 Egyptian socialism is closely bound up with nationalism – another *jāhilī* creed which is repugnant to the spirit of Islam.[90]

6 Although because of the interruption in the growth of Islamic jurisprudence, some of the Islamic tenets stand in need of reinterpretation, the means of achieving this aim is not in having recourse to any of the brands of Western political philosophy, or to materialistic ideas. Islamic jurisprudence itself possesses adequate resources for adaptation to unforeseen circumstances.[91] The Islamic socialists admit this, but in their casuistical arguments succumb to foreign ideological influences.

c *The radical version*

The crisis of Nāṣirism from the mid-sixties onwards resulted, among other things, in weakening the appeal of Arab socialism in Egypt and of its Islamic encrustment to baffled Arab–Muslim masses. The frustrations bred of the Arab defeat in the Six Day War of 1967 had naturally created a fresh hankering among the militant youth in the Arab countries as well as elsewhere in the Muslim world, for a more vigorous political doctrine. This was the background to the appearance of a new variant of Islamic socialism. It differed from the model presented by Sibāʿī and his Egyptian or Syrian imitators by virtue not only of its independence of the political exigencies of officialdom, but also of an innovation hitherto unthinkable in an Islamic context – reconciliation with Marxism. This was, as mentioned before, undoubtedly the result of the growing popularity and influence of the Soviet Union and other countries of the 'Socialist Camp' in the Third World as a whole, a process which had started with the death of Stalin in 1953, and had momentous implications at both theoretical and practical levels. A by-product of the campaign of de-Stalinisation was to rehabilitate the 'independent roads to socialism' and the '*Third Worldist*' ideologies in general, and this in its turn had enabled the Soviet leaders to overcome some of their old doubts about the nature of national bourgeois movements in the Third World. It was such doubts that had caused a paralysing ambiguity in the Soviet policy towards the nationalist regime of Muḥammad Muṣaddiq in Iran between 1951 and 1953. By contrast, the Soviet policy towards Nāṣir from 1954 onwards was one of active support and involvement in neutralising the Western challenges to his status as the hero of Arab nationalism. In particular, the attitude of the Soviet Union during the Suez crisis of 1956 greatly enhanced its prestige with the masses throughout the Muslim world. This trend was later strengthened by the Iraqi Revolution of 1958, the heightening of the Algerian War of Independence, and the prevalence of a general mood of anti-Westernism everywhere in the Middle East. So by the time the humiliation of the Six-Day War was inflicted on the Muslim conscience, the ground had been prepared for an ideological synthesis which would satisfy both the urge for a more tightly knit plan of political action, and the requirement of apparent loyalty to Islamic tenets. The blossoming-out of an assortment of Marxist or Marxian schools of thought – revisionism, the New Left, and the motley streams arising from the critique of Marxism–Leninism by Sartre, Lefebvre and others – meant that in the post-Stalin thaw such a synthesis belonged no longer to the realm of intellectual day-dreaming.

Roughly the same process repeated itself in Iran, although it started at least a decade earlier, with the Anglo-American-engineered overthrow of Muḥammad Muṣaddiq's government in 1953. Whereas during the oil nationalisation movement of 1951 nationalism of liberal orientation commanded immense loyalty among the middle classes, even those attached to religious leaders, this was not the case in the period after 1953. As the Iranian national consciousness gradually absorbed the traumatic effects of the failure of Muṣaddiq's 'middle-of-the-road' experience in democratic politics, a conviction gained ground among politicised youth that his fiasco was caused as much by liberalism as by the CIA conspiracies. It was the dispute over this interpretation of the events of 1951–3 that caused deep divisions inside the nationalist groups in the early sixties, and prevented them from taking advantage of the respite gained by them as a result of the internal crisis of the Shāh's regime in 1962–4, and the resultant popular uprisings which were ruthlessly suppressed. Symptomatic of the radically changed political atmosphere of the times was the attitude towards the United States: if in the period prior to 1953 there were many nationalist liberals, and even socialists, who regarded the United States as a 'friendly' or 'harmless' power which could at least be played off against British imperialism, or Soviet threat, there were extremely few leaders who nursed such illusions in the aftermath of Muṣaddiq's fall. Thus by the mid-sixties one could already detect a marked leftward tendency among oppositional, and some religious groups, and this was mirrored in their updated political rhetoric, which could not now be easily differentiated, especially in its anti-imperialistic, anti-capitalistic propositions, from that of the left. But the impact of this gradual conversion had again been somewhat impaired by the newly won recognition and respectability of the 'independent left' in a de-Stalinised world.

Exercises in reconciling Islam with Marxism have never been explicit: their initiators have been wiser than that, making sure that the synthesis they seek always takes an implicit, piecemeal and abstruse form. The label 'Islamic Marxism' which is sometimes used in designating this synthesis is in fact a ploy used by its adversaries to discredit it in the eyes of traditionist Muslims. One could say that the outcome of this reconciliation is, if anything, potentially a serious challenge to orthodox Marxist–Leninist parties in the Muslim countries, since it can act as an alternative carrier of their ideals of social and economic justice without incurring the blemish of irreligiosity or atheism. Its most forceful representative in the Muslim countries to the east of Egypt has been perhaps *Sāzmān-i Mujāhidīn-i Khalq* (the Organisation of the Fighters of the People), a guerrilla organisation created in the early seventies in Iran. In addition to the denunciation of imperialism and despotism – an invariable plank of the platform of all revolutionary groupings – the most outstanding features of the Mujāhidīn's outlook are indeed persistent attacks on the institution of private ownership as the root cause of all social evils, and an unfailing emphasis on class struggle as an ever-present process in history. Both result predictably in a plea for public ownership of all means of production. But their ingenuity in ideological synthesising suggests itself most strongly in their application of 'dialectical materialism' to the Qur'ānic exegesis and some of the most memorable vicissitudes of the lives of Prophet Muḥammad, 'Alī and Ḥusayn. Again what they do is to use this concept and its subsidiary categories as an analytical tool, without actually naming it. Thus they employ the notion of *sunnat allāh* (the tradition or path of God) interchangeably with the idea of the 'law of evolution' as 'one of the substantial and basic (*'umdah va asāsī*) laws of the world of creation'.[92] Any phenomenon, they aver, which is incapable of adjusting itself to this *sunnah* is doomed to vanish, 'for instance, the capitalistic system and the world of imperialism, being no longer in harmony with the vital and historical realities of [human] society, nurture in their side their own enemy and antithesis, namely the working and toiling class, which adopts a novel and progressive posture. The contradiction between the means of production and relations of production intensifies daily with the increase in production, and the advancement of technology, placing the capitalistic system under the pressure of the toiling class. At the end, with the revolution of the oppressed masses, the gigantic power of capitalism will be destroyed, and the working class will inherit the power, and the means of production, and above all, will become God's successors on the earth.'[93] As the illustration, as well as divine testimony, of this vision of history, a Qur'ānic verse is quoted: 'And we were minded to shew favour to those who were brought low in the land, and to make them spiritual chiefs, and to make them heirs' (28:5). In Shī'ī theology, this verse is usually invoked as evidence of the certainty of the return of the Mahdī; but radical Muslim opinion of whatever denomination now interprets it more in the direction of a historicist conviction that human life moves inexorably towards the final triumph of the 'disinherited' and the weak (*mustaḍ'afūn*) over their exploiters. Similarly, metaphysical concepts such as 'divine assistance' (*naṣr min allāh*) and revelation (*waḥy*), and the function of angels are perceived as a manifestation of the same 'tradition of evolution' in the universe: what is called God's help is nothing but conformity with this tradition, which always assists all those who pursue its direction; revelation is but the exertion of the power that is an essential characteristic of every object, whether animate or inanimate (such as honey-producing for the bee, magnetism for the lodestone, etc.); and, finally, angels are merely a metaphor for the 'natural forces' which operate generally on the basis of the laws of causality.

This kind of desacralisation of Qur'ānic terms is certainly not exclusive to latter-day Muslim radicals. One could find examples of it in, for instance, some of the modernistic interpretations of the Qur'ān by Indian and Pakistani Muslims of an entirely different outlook.[94] What is new in the radical literature is, however, the subordination of such a 'scientific' understanding of the scripture to the demands of an activist political ideology. One should also point out that every instance of desacralisation is accompanied by strong affirmation of the supremacy of God and His will to dispel any accusation of blasphemy or heresy against its authors. The indispensability of human will and struggle is also stressed to underline the essential difference between this new philosophy of Islamic socialism and all the fatalistic but secularist ideologies which preach faith in a blind historical necessity, in a determinism guaranteeing the ultimate victory of the oppressed. But the overall impression is one of a syncretism of religion and politics, with a visible slant towards the latter, and predicated on a set of principles which are no different from those of dialectical or historical materialism except on account of the religious idioms and scriptural citations used in their embellishment.

Most of the adherents of this outlook have been profoundly inspired by the idealism of 'Alī Sharī'atī (1933–77), the most popular mentor of Islamic radicalism in modern Iran. As a teacher, orator and theorist, Sharī'atī has exercised an influence which is rarely matched by any other contemporary Muslim thinker anywhere in the Muslim world, not only in the development of the conceptual foundations of Islamic socialism as espoused by the educated youth, but also in the dissemination of the characteristics of militant Islam. His writings may be open to criticism by the scholastic criteria of traditional religionists, and they do indeed fall outside the penumbra of strictly religious literature because of their inclusion of alien terms or concepts, as well as reinterpretation of orthodox doctrines. His heavily sociological understanding of Islam is also bound to be bitterly resented by spirits akin to Henri Corbin's mystical perception of Islam, and especially Shī'ism. True, Sharī'atī too perceives religion as idealism, but an idealism which constantly calls for struggle. The ubiquitous motto in his writings is the saying attributed to the third Imām, Ḥusayn: 'Life is verily faith (*'aqīdah*) and fight (*jihād*)', or its variations. All facets of Islamic culture (mythology, history, theology and even some elements of jurisprudence) are subordinated in his teachings to the compelling necessity of this fusion between 'theory' and 'praxis', which is but one manifestation of the principle of *tawḥīd* (oneness of God). He is the first Iranian writer on religion to have turned this hitherto theological doctrine into a 'world-view' (*jahān-bīnī*), a term coined originally by Iranian Marxists in the early forties as an equivalent for a secular, political system of beliefs, or *Weltanschauung*, since in classical Persian the compound is more suggestive of a mind which is preoccupied with the material world (*jahān*) rather than spirit or soul (*jān*). In this sense, *tawḥīd* means something much more than the 'oneness of God', which is, of course, accepted by all monotheists. 'But', says Sharī'atī, 'what I have in mind (when I use this term) is a world-view. So what I intend by "the world-view of *tawḥīd*" is perceiving the entire universe as a unity, instead of dividing it into this world and the thereafter, the physical and metaphysical, substance and meaning, matter and spirit. It means perceiving the whole of existence as a single form, a single, living and conscious organism, possessing one will, intelligence, feeling and aim.... There are many people who believe in *tawḥīd*, but only as a "religious–philosophical" theory: God is one, not more than one – that is all! But I understand *tawḥīd* as a world-view, just as I see *shirk* (polytheism) also from the same standpoint, that is, a world-view that regards the universe as an incoherent combination, full of division, contradiction and incongruity, possessing conflicting and independent poles, diverging movements, and disparate and disconnected essences, desires, calculations, criteria, aims and wills. *Tawḥīd* sees the world as an empire; *shirk* as a feudal system.'[95] The social and political implications of *tawḥīd* are further spelled out by declaring that such a unitarian outlook involves the negation of all contradictions hampering the development of Man, whether these are 'legal, class, social, political, racial, ethnic, territorial, cognatic, genetic, intrinsic and even economic'. Such a world-view, accompanied as it is by the rejection of materialism and empiricism, by no means reflects on Sharī'atī's standing as a deeply religious thinker, although his strong emphasis on the essential compatibility of matter and spirit does clash with the Qur'ānic denigration of the worldly life (6:32; 47:36; 57:20). But it goes a long way towards disarming, or gratifying, the partisans of dialectical materialism by showing Islam to be also preaching that human salvation, whether material or spiritual, is but the summation of a dialectic – an inner, ceaseless struggle which goes on at all levels of individual and social life until the final triumph of the principle of *tawḥīd*, which reunites the conflicting, separated parts of Man's existence, brings nature and society within an integrating sketch of the universe, and restores absolute equality as the primeval state of social life. Sharī'atī uses the term dialectic freely; contrary to some of his Arab counterparts, he does not deem it necessary even to find an Islamic (Persian or Arabic) equivalent for the term (such as *jadalī*, or *jidālī*, or *jidāliyyah*, which are of medieval origin). For him, the two crucial applications of the principle of dialectic are the philosophy of history, and sociology. Using the story of Abel and Cain as a metaphorical framework, he depicts history as a conflict between two opposing forces represented by these two characters. The Qur'ān refers to the story in a most laconic manner, without mentioning Abel and Cain. It is only in the commentaries that their names appear. This enables Sharī'atī to interpret the story in terms which have never figured in classical exegetics, without appearing to advance any heterodox position. The story has an obvious moral import, and has always been treated as such by religious commentators, Muslim or otherwise, who have seen in it nothing other than a condemnation of greed and murder, especially fratricide. Sharī'atī too takes cognisance of this moral dimension, laying stress on the contradiction between the two types – Abel, 'the man of faith, peaceable and self-sacrificing', and Cain, 'the voluptuous, the transgressor and the fratricide'. But Sharī'atī does not rest content with the moral aspect of the story; he tries to delve into its deeper meaning by means of what he calls 'psychological analysis, and on the basis of a scientific and sociological examination of their environment, their occupations and their class.'[96] The outcome of this examination is that the real cause of the conflict between Abel and Cain lay in their contradictory types of work, infrastructures of production and economic systems – in one word, in their differing class status: Abel being a pastoralist, representing the age of common ownership of the means of production, and Cain being a landowner, representing the age of agriculture and the establishment of the system of private ownership. His reasoning in support of this claim consists mainly of eliminating most of the conceivable factors of the diverging characters of the two brothers. Their difference, he says, could not be put down to their family background or environment, because they both had the same father and mother, belonged to the same race, and were brought up in identical circumstances. Educational and cultural factors could not be held responsible either, because social life at that primitive stage had not yet developed to the extent that differences on this score could be of much consequence. So there remains, in Sharī'atī's examination, only the economic life and class status to account for the cleavage.[97] It is noteworthy that his analysis makes no reference to a factor that in a typically religious explanation would normally rank as the most decisive: the innate nature (*fiṭrah*) of every individual, in the sense of a pattern of behaviour which, either through the divine will or human initiative, or a combination of both, is preordained to lead to perdition or salvation. The same viewpoint is given sharper focus in the survey of the 'dialectic of sociology' and the stages of history. He quotes Marx's classification of history into five stages (primitive communism, slavery and serfdom, feudalism, capitalism, and the 'triumph of the proletariat'), but criticises it on the ground that it confuses the criteria of the form of the ownership, the form of class relations, and the form of the tools of production, whereas Sharī'atī finds the first four stages to share basically the same infrastructure, that is, private ownership of the tools and the resources of production; only the last stage is characterised by common ownership of both. Throughout history, then, 'only two infrastructures have existed, and there cannot be more than two'.[98] What differentiates feudalism, for instance, from capitalism is not infrastructure but the tools of production, the form of production, and consequently the outward form of the relations of production: just as the reverse of this may sometimes take place, namely the tools, form and relations of production can remain the same, but the infrastructure may substantially change; for example, an agrarian society may attain socialism through revolution, or war, or *coup d'état*, without undergoing the capitalistic transformation of the tools of production. The conclusion that Sharīʿatī draws from this exercise in sociological critique is the reaffirmation of his previous thesis: in history, just as in society, there are only two poles: (1) the pole of Abel, consisting of *milk* (ownership), *mālik* (owner) and *mala'* (or *mutraf*, plutocracy), and their ally *rāhib* (priesthood); (2) the pole of Cain, consisting of *Allāh* (God), and *nās* (people), the two terms that the Qur'ān uses interchangeably whenever it speaks of the rights of the society as a whole.[99] In predicting the outcome of the conflict between these two poles. Sharīʿatī replaces Marxian determinism with the Shīʿī millenarian rehabilitation of the universe: the conflict will end, according to him, only with an 'inevitable revolution' which will restore 'the system of Abel' in the world – the system of unitarianism as opposed to that of polytheism; religion of consciousness, movement and revolution, as opposed to the religion of deceit, stupefication and justification of the *status quo*; the system of human justice and unity, as opposed to that of class and racial discrimination.[100]

Such fearless blending of religious lore with modern, alien concepts can by itself be already highly provocative to the religious thinkers and scholars of conventional formation. But when it is compounded by a 'progressive' ideology presented in the name of a reinvigorated Islam, and accompanied by severe strictures on a deviant, hieratic class masquerading as defenders of the faith, then the hostile reaction of large segments of Iranian Shīʿī orthodoxy to Sharīʿatī's views becomes understandable. Some of this hostility evidently correlates with the misgivings of the religious allies of the wealthy classes over the radical implications of his teachings. But some of it also arises from the genuine concern of those religionists who are committed to the safeguarding of the timeless truths of Shīʿī spiritualism against the 'perils of socialisation'. The fact that Sharīʿatī himself was not an *ʿālim* has also made him an easy target for all the authentic or self-appointed advocates of the necessity of immunising the religious leadership against the intrusion of the uninitiated. Much of this variegated hostility was submerged in the wave of pro-Sharīʿatī feelings that swept all over Iran after his death, and particularly during the Islamic Revolution of 1978–9. But it does not lie far below the surface, and re-emerges in periodic campaigns against 'eclectic trends in Islam'.[101] Whatever reservations one might have about the legitimacy of this kind of eclecticism, one can have scant doubt that Sharīʿatī's potent mixture of dialectic and Islamic, especially Shīʿī, ideals of social justice, have done more than any other form of religious indoctrination to make Islam the sole ideology of struggle in contemporary Iran for vast numbers of militant young people, who would have been otherwise attracted to secularist, left-wing doctrines.

Most revivalist movements in the history of great religions have had ramifications in the form of egalitarian and anti-authoritarian doctrines which have sometimes provoked popular uprisings. The peasant revolts of the thirteenth to sixteenth centuries (in France in 1251, in England in 1381, etc.) were no doubt caused primarily by social and economic discontent. But the influence of the teachings of John Wyclif, John Huss, and Martin Luther in precipitating them can by no means be gainsaid. Islamic revivalism has similarly produced its corollary of proletarian ideologies. Nevertheless, the difference with European history lies in the fact that radical Islamic ideas have often been expressed in a vocabulary unfamiliar for the overwhelming majority of the population to which they have been addressed. That is why, although they have sometimes inspired heroic, revolutionary acts on the part of the radical youth in the face of seemingly invincible tyrannies, they have often stopped short of attaining the status of mass movements in the Muslim countries, and have even touched off a popular backlash at the behest of an alarmed orthodoxy.

5 Aspects of Shī'ī modernism

Background

During the last two centuries Twelver Shī'īsm in Iran, Iraq and the Lebanon has displayed a political vitality, both in theory and practice, unprecedented in its long history. Some examples of this vitality, which have been connected with global Islamic trends, were noticed in the previous chapter. In the present chapter, we are going to review three further examples that relate specifically to the development of Shī'īsm in modern times, and are apt to alter its relationship not only with other Islamic trends, but also with the non-Muslim world. One central point which has to be dealt with at the outset is the background to the apparently sudden advent of this phenomenon.

Shī'ī vitality can be explained primarily by some of its potentialities for adaptation to social and political change. The most essential of these are the principle of *ijtihād*, or independent judgement, as a device supplementing the sources of the jurisprudence, and a potentially revolutionary posture in the face of temporal power. A belief-system which thus sanctions the exercise of free opinion even if in matters of secondary importance has manifestly a greater ability for accommodation with circumstances unforeseen in the sources than one which prohibits or severely restricts all forms of doctrinal flexibility, whether on fundamental or secondary matters. Although in contradistinction to the absolute form of *ijtihād* (known by the adjective *muṭlaq*), which was supposedly the exclusive prerogative of the founders of the principal legal schools, the relative and the more accessible form (*muqayyad*) has never in practice been totally abandoned among Muslims of whatever description, there is no doubt that, as was mentioned previously, only in Shī'īsm is *ijtihād* the logical and imperative concomitant of the creed.[1] The fact that the Shī'ī jurisconsults down the ages did not use this device as thoroughly and frequently as they should have done, at least on burning socio-political matters, and the Shī'ī mind was consequently hemmed in with the same unbending dogmas that characterised all other Muslim sects, does not invalidate our observation. In the Shī'ī case, the failure to practise *ijtihād* was not an ordinary lapse, but a serious dereliction of a cardinal duty, and therefore more damaging to the credibility of its authors. To these theoretical pecularities must be added the psychological tensions and heart-searchings of a religious community which, even in societies where it formed the majority or could nominally rely on official support, often found the existing state of affairs falling short of its ideals, either because those ideals were formulated in such a way as to become unattainable until the apocalyptic end of the universe, or because the rulers betrayed their mission. These points will be further elaborated, and we will familiarise ourselves with other theoretical roots of political dynamism, when we discuss its more concrete aspects in the coming pages.

The wider social, political and economic matrix which may have been instrumental in turning these potentialities into doctrinal reformulations and occasional mass movements should certainly not be overlooked. An impressionistic account of this can be obtained from the history of the one country which has been both the birthplace and testing-ground of Shī'ī modernism: Iran. As far as the genesis of new ideas is concerned, her history is not dissimilar from that of the Ottoman Empire or Egypt: increasing contacts with the West since the Ṣafavīd period (1502–1736), disastrous consequences of the wars with Russia (in 1813 and 1828), inconclusive attempts at modernisation by two enlightened statesmen (Mīrzā Taqī Khān Amīr Kabīr and Mīrzā Ḥusayn Khān Mushīr ud-Dawlah known as Sipahsālār), introduction of the printing press, the despatch of students abroad, and, finally, the influence of cultural and intellectual notions from the West, all contributed to a general trend in the direction of questioning the traditional modes of thought. The religious community could not be immune from this trend. The triumph, for instance, of the so-called *Uṣūlī* school of jurisprudence, insisting on the legitimacy of reasoning, and practising *ijtihād* on the basis of *uṣūl* (principles) in the face of the *Akhbārīs* (Traditionists) could not be unrelated to the pervading awareness of the inadequacy of rigidified legal formulae to cope with such changes. There is now a growing appreciation, among both Iranian and Western students of Shī'īsm, of the impact of this triumph on the development of the Shī'ī social and political thought.[2] To the chagrin of partisans of social determinism, one cannot define the exact relationship between specific social and economic processes, on the one hand, and the transformation of the religious mind, on the other. We do not know, for instance, whether the *Uṣūlī–Akhbārī* division corresponded to any particular polarisation of socio-economic forces, although – as will be explained below – the expected alliance of the *Uṣūlī* 'Ulamā' with the 'freedom-seekers' at the time of the Constitutional Revolution of 1906 served the interests of the bourgeoisie. Again, the ever-widening interest of the 'Ulamā' in political matters from the mid-nineteenth century onwards may be accounted for by their reaction to consecutive imperialist ventures: the Reuter Concession of 1872, the opening of the Kārūn River in 1888, the Imperial Bank of Persia, the Tobacco *Régie* of 1890–2, and the manoeuvres of the Russian *Banque des Prêts* from 1900 onwards. (We must add, however, that imperialistic threats in all forms seem to have played a much less important role in the emergence of Shīʻī modernism in the nineteenth century than in the case of its Sunnī equivalent, and this was mainly because of the relative aloofness of Iran, as compared with the Ottoman Empire and Egypt, from the maelstrom of European politics.)

The revival of Shīʻī thought since the Second World War has also been stimulated by social causes. We leave aside the general causes affecting all social groups and classes, and mention only one, which is confined to the leadership of the religious community. Even religious or religious-minded writers have identified one of the principal factors of the immutability of Shīʻī thought to lie in the dependency of the ʻUlamāʼ for their livelihood on the individual donations of the faithful, known as the ʻImām's share' (*sahmi-i Imām*), and hence their inclination to steer clear of any idea that might offend popular predilections.[3] If this diagnosis is correct, then the gradual radicalisation of certain areas of Shīʻī thought since the Second World War must have been brought about at least in part by a converse phenomenon: the rise of a small, but highly influential group of religious intellectuals who were less in need of such donations, because they could earn their living through teaching, preaching, writing and publishing, thanks to the increase in literacy, the growth of student population and the coming of mass media. This category of religionists could thus address some of their 'unorthodox' ideas to large social groups inaccessible to their predecessors, without much fearing the dire consequences of alienating obscurantist circles.

Finally, the power and prestige of the office of *Marjaʻ-i taqlīd* (the 'Source of Imitation', the highest religious authority whose rulings and opinions should supposedly be accepted by all Shīʻīs), presents another example of the working of mundane forces in religious affairs. This office did not exist in Twelver Shīʻīsm until the middle of the nineteenth century, when the peerless jurisprudential genius of Shaykh Murtaḍā Anṣārī (d. 1864) introduced a centralised leadership in the hitherto pluralistic system of Shīʻī scholarship and pastoral guidance. A climate of opinion was thereby reached to acknowledge henceforth the 'most learned' (*aʻlam*) of the ʻUlamāʼ as worthy of being 'imitated' by all Shīʻīs in his pronouncements. Spiritual centralisation soon entailed financial centralisation: a growing proportion of the payments made previously to local and provincial 'clergy' were now redirected towards the *Marjaʻ*. It was certainly the resultant concentration of both spiritual and material powers which made it possible for the *Marjaʻ* at the end of the nineteenth century, Ḥājj Mīrzā Muḥammad Ḥasan Shīrāzī, to lead the first mass movement in Iranian history against European encroachments, in the famous 'Tobacco crisis' of 1890–2. In the same way, the controversy which broke out seventy years later over the wisdom of such concentration had visible political and social reasons. The watershed was the death of the *Marjaʻ*, the Āyatullāh Ḥusayn Burūjirdī in 1961. By then the immense influence of the position had exposed it to the intolerable pressures and expectations of the officialdom, particularly when the latter's authority was in jeopardy. In due course the *Marja's* had come to the conclusion that the safest policy for them was to keep out of active politics. Their quietism manifestly favoured the rulers, as was demonstrated by Burūjirdī's refusal to condemn the *coup* against the Muṣaddiq's government in 1953. The unsavoury memories of that neutrality in the eyes of the militants, against the background of political upheavals accompanying the rise of the Āyatullāh Rūhullāh Khumaynī in the early sixties, fostered grave doubts over the viability of the position of the *Marja'*. Meanwhile the growing complexity of social and economic life threatened to place the 'Ulamā' in the awkward position of having to answer an infinite variety of questions from their followers on issues which required expert, specialised knowledge. In such circumstances, no *'ālim* of upright character could lay claim to being the 'most learned' of his peers. An intriguing debate was thus engaged on the wisdom and feasibility of the institution itself, with most participants expressing preference for decentralising it, or giving it a collegiate form and most importantly, for lessening its paralysing dependency on the populace.[4] This, in its turn, led to a critical examination of other related issues, such as the function of the *'ālim* in the modern world, the relevance of his education to the social and political problems facing the Muslims today, the justification, and limits, of *taqlīd* (imitation), the definition of *ijtihād*, the chasm between ideals and reality in Shī'ism and the attitude towards Sunnī Muslims.[5]

However, no amount of socio-political analysis of facts can account for the subtleties of thought processes. The historical background briefly described here can explain only the timing, but not the nature, of the new phase of Shī'ī dynamism. And it is against this background that we now study three revised notions in modern Shī'ism which are important not only because of their character as determinants of political behaviour, but also owing to their implications in the total system of Shī'ī culture: (1) constitutionalism, (2) *taqiyyah*, and (3) martyrdom. These do not represent three disjointed, random categories of thought. Chronologically, it was constitutionalism which brought the Shī'īs, for the first time in their history, face to face with the democratic demands of the modern age. But the Shī'īs soon realised that they could not rise to this challenge without first overcoming the inertia wrought in the popular conscience by an officially sponsored ideology which exonerated the distance between the political ideals and realities as an inevitable fact, and exalted self-sacrifice for lofty principles as the unique virtue of an infallible and divinely designated élite. A heightened political atmosphere in Iran since the end of the nineteenth century, combined with the pressure of having to answer Sunnī criticisms of Shī'ism–as described in Chapter 1–as well as the rivalry of growing popular secular ideologies, both forced and helped a number of Shī'īs to rethink the traditional attitudes on the second and third themes. The outcome of this rethinking has undoubtedly changed some of the political features of Shī'īsm which we enumerated in Chapter 1 – turning it from an élitist, esoteric and passive sect into a mass movement animated by democratic ideals, and contempt for innate privilege. It is a rethinking which has greatly diminished Shī'ī differences with the Sunnīs, and is as much entitled to the epithet *modernist* as similar stirrings of religio-political thought among the Sunnīs during the last century.

I Constitutionalism

As was mentioned before, the patterns of the development of new political ideas among the Ottomans, Egyptians and Iranians in the nineteenth century and at the beginning of the twentieth display significant similarities, despite many differences in their social and historical backgrounds. National awakening among all these peoples resulted in a more or less uniform critique of the existing political order, and pleas for the establishment of a constitutional system of government and modernisation of the state apparatus, especially its administrative and military institutions.

The similarities could make the comparative study of Ottoman, Egyptian and Iranian intellectual trends in that period rather tedious for the specialists of any of these three countries. But political thought in Iran, during the last three decades of the Qājār period (1779–1925) has one characteristic which is undoubtedly missing, at least on the same scale, in the Ottoman or Egyptian case. This is the strong and unequivocal stand by the Iranian Shī'ī 'Ulamā' in support of the Constitutional movement which led to the Revolution of 1906. Advocacy of constitutionalism was not confined to the so-called 'freedom-seeking' 'Ulamā'–Sayyid Muḥammad Ṭabāṭabā'ī, Sayyid 'Abdullāh Bihbihānī, Mullā Muḥammad Kāẓim Khurāsānī, Muḥammad Ḥusayn Nā'īnī and many others. Even a number of 'reactionary' divines, above all Shaykh Faḍlullāh Nūrī, never doubted the basic virtues of legal restraints on the kingly powers. On the other hand, very few enlightened souls inside the religious communities of Ottoman Turkey or Egypt ever attained the same commanding position in the national struggle for freedom and the rule of law – a point which, as we saw before, has been admitted by even such a fervent critic of Shī'īsm as Muḥammad Rashīd Riḍā.

The special place of the 'Ulamā' in Iran, the power and prestige conferred on them by a combination of spiritual, social, political and financial functions, and their active participation in the Constitutional Revolution, are well-known.[6] What is less widely known and much less appreciated is the way in which the 'Ulamā' conceived the ideas of constitutionalism, and interpreted them in terms compatible with Islamic tenets. This lacuna, which has so far been caused partly by the non-availability of sources and partly by an 'anti-clerical' prejudice, has been responsible for several generalisations, of which only two are mentioned here by way of example:

First is a view whose most aggressive exponent was Aḥmad Kasravī

(d. 1946), one of the most controversial of Iranian historians, and author of the most popular existing account of the Revolution. According to him, the Shī'ī 'Ulamā', by virtue of their belief in the exclusive legitimacy of the rule of the Imāms, have always been opposed to the very notion of state and political order[7] – a view which is curiously at variance with Kasravī's own detailed descriptions of the efforts of many of the 'Ulamā' towards creating the Constitutional regime. It is interesting to note that starting from diametrically opposed premises, Hamid Algar, who is deeply sympathetic to the 'Ulamā', has also arrived at more or less the same conclusion in his study of religion and politics in the Qājār period: 'In the new situation [that is, after the establishment of Qājār rule]', he says, 'a political theory to accommodate the state within the system of belief was still not developed. Such a theory was probably impossible: The 'Ulamā', having established their position as *de facto* regents of the Imām, could not then have allotted the monarchy a similar position. Without such a position, the monarchy was bound to be regarded as illegitimate.'[8]

Second is the opinion of intellectuals who, despite their occasional appreciation of the positive part played by the 'Ulamā', on the whole regard the 'Ulamā' as a negative, retrogressive factor in the national struggle – with at best confused and contradictory ideas about the aims of the Revolution. Typical of this opinion is the statement by the contemporary historian, Firaydun Ādamiyyat, to the effect that 'the only group which had a clear concept of Constitutionalism were the progressive, educated individuals committed to the (Western) type democracy'. He says this in connection with his critical survey of the ideas of two religious exponents of constitutionalism.[9]

Although such statements hold good for the attitudes of many of the 'Ulamā' during the eighteenth and greater part of the nineteenth centuries, they do not reflect the views of all of them certainly not during the Revolution. Ādamiyyat himself refers in another context to a number of 'progressive' 'Ulamā' during the Sipahsālār period who supported reforms; one of them, Mīrzā Ja'far Ḥakīm Ilāhī, even advocated changing the script.[10] In the absence of more specific information, we can only surmise that the political outlook of such men could not be the same as their predecessors'. Whatever the case, the fact that during the Revolution the urban masses, who were surely not less religious-minded then than they are now, responded so enthusiastically to the call for a constitutional government, should be proof enough that the opinion of the 'freedom-seeking' 'Ulamā' held great sway over them. There was one other possible centre for the dissemination of democratic ideals among the people: the writings of such Westernised thinkers of the period as Ākhūndzādih, Mīrzā Ḥusayn Khān Mushīr ud-Dawlah, known as Sipahsālār, Mīrzā Malkam Khān, and Ṭālibov. But what should make us cautious in estimating the influence of such modernists is not only their exotic ideology, but also their style of prose. Containing numerous Persianised forms of

European political terms, as well as newly coined words and phrases belying unassimilated Western notions, their work could not possibly produce the same effect as the tracts of the 'Ulamā', whose style, however equally stilted, was at least familiar to the indigenous bourgeoisie, and comprised many symbols which could not fail to galvanise popular feelings, and many arguments which afforded evidence of greater originality of mind, and powers of synthesis. It is necessary to take a cursory glance at these arguments to see whether Shī'ī political thought at the turn of the century accords with the picture painted of it by its critics.

* * *

The Constitutional Revolution represents the first direct encounter in modern Iran between traditional Islamic culture and the West. All the earlier attempts at modernisation, although involving important changes in the legal, governmental and administrative systems, were conducted in areas tangential to underlying traditional values. None of them openly and radically challenged any of these values. The great modernising minister, Mīrzā Taqī Khān, known as Amīr Kabīr, certainly took vital measures for centralising the judicial system, such as his curbs on the powers of the Imām Jum'ah (leader of the Friday Prayer), or abolition of *bast* (sanctuary from secular oppression offered by mosques, residences of the 'Ulamā', etc.),[11] in the teeth of the 'clerical' prerogatives, but they did not aim at undermining any specific Islamic institution and principle. Such measures, just as the modernising campaign of men such as Mīrzā Malkam Khān, the advocate of the 'total Westernisation of Iran', were individual enterprises whose repercussions never went beyond a small élite. By contrast, Constitutional Revolution was a movement of unprecedented dimension in Iran's modern history which embraced vast groups of people from every social quarter, thus generating a heated debate between diverse ideologies, old and new. The implication of many a constitutionalist idea challenged the very foundation of the religio-political consensus as well as the relative cultural harmony of the traditional order, thereby causing a deep rift amont the élites. Perhaps the significance of this rift can be better understood if a comparison is drawn with the constitutional history of Ottoman Turkey. When similar controversies broke out in Turkey during the famous Meşrutièt period from 1908 to 1918, that country had long passed through the travails of the Tanẓīmāt period (a half-century of reforms from 1826 onwards), and the Young Ottoman movement (formed in the mid-1860s).[12] By that time both sides in the debate had accumulated considerable eristic ability and sharpened their polemical tools, particularly over the thorny issues of the legal codification and judicial reforms, and modernisation of the educational system.

Neither side in the constitutional debate in Iran had such precedents to fall back on. Even the duality of the judicial system (between the religious and non-religious courts) had lasted so long (since the Ṣafavīd times) that it had become part of the traditional structure, and lost its potential for initiating ideas of change. So discussions on the uses and abuses of man-made laws inevitably provoked in its train dissensions over the virtues and vices of modernisation. The novelty of the controversy and the complexity of the issues involved could hardly be helpful to mutual understanding between the two sides of the debate. But there was one precedent which gave the religious proponents of the constitution an edge over all other groups in terms of argumentative skills. This was the development of the science of *Uṣūl-i fiqh*, the 'roots' or theory of jurisprudence, which had achieved great subtlety among the Shī'īs, but reached new peaks in the nineteenth century. Tension between the *Uṣūlīs* and their opponents, the *Akhbārīs* (Traditionists), to which we referred before, had grown sharply since the middle of the eighteenth century. The *Akhbārīs* dominated the centres of religious teachings until the beginning of the Zand period, but with the emergence of Muḥammad Bāqir Waḥīd Bihbihāni (1704–91) they were decisively routed. The ground was then prepared for men like Mīrzā-yi Qumī, Shaykh Murtaḍā Anṣārī, Mullā Muḥammad Kāẓim Khurāsānī and Muḥammad Ḥusayn Nā'īnī to afford philosophical depth and methodological precision to this most stimulating of traditional Islamic sciences. Now there were of course some distinguished *'alims* who opposed constitutionalism: Shaykh Faḍlullāh was a *faqīh* of the highest rank. But it is noteworthy that while the opponents resorted to simple canonical strictures on the Constitution (such as the conflict between the superiority of Islam, and the recognition of all Iranian citizens as equals before the law, irrespective of their religion; the dangers of a free press which could open the way to atheistic foreign ideas; and the unacceptability of compulsory education for girls),[13] the proponents countered by using concepts drawn from the science of *Uṣūl*. The presence of Khurāsānī and Nā'īnī among the foremost champions of constitutionalism, and the fact that Nā'īnī was the author of the only well-known and fairly coherent treatise in defence of its principles can, of course, be no more than circumstantial evidence of the link between their jurisprudential theory and their political outlook. But when one examines the principles of the *Uṣūlī* school, one can hardly escape the conclusion that they were more likely to produce a pre-constitutionalist mentality than its opposite.

The chief doctrine of the *Uṣūlī* school is the competence of reason (after the guidance of the Qur'ān, the Tradition and consensus) to discern the rules of the *Sharī'ah*. This faith in reason brings forth other essential teachings: the necessity of *ijtihād*, the refusal to accept uncritically the contents of the four principal codices of Shī'ī traditions (by Kulaynī, Shaykh Ṣadūq and Shaykh Ṭūsī), adoption of more precise criteria for ascertaining the reliability of sayings attributed to the Prophet and Imāms, and prohibition of the imitation of deceased authorities to ensure the abiding dynamism of *ijtihād*. The *Akhbārīs* contradict the *Uṣūlīs* on all these points: they reject reason and consensus, and find all individuals to be of the same level of mediocrity, and hence worthy of being only *muqallid* (imitators). They forbid *ijtihād*, and believe in the imitation of deceased authorities, saying that the truth of a proposition is not affected by the death of its expositor: the rulings of the past 'Ulamā' should be rejected if they are the products of their own arbitrary, probable knowledge or conjecture (*ẓann*), and accepted if they prove to be based on definite knowledge (*'ilm-i-qat'ī*), but this can only be communicated by the Imām. Instead of *ijtihād*, they regard the collection of sayings or narratives of the Imāms to be an obligatory duty, and reckon that every Muslim, even the uninitiated and the ordinary (*'ammī*), is capable of performing this. Meanwhile, the *Uṣūlīs* allow wide scope for juridical innovations through their belief in the validity of 'probable knowledge' to deduce canonical rules, whenever access to 'definite knowledge' proves impossible. They also maintain that any act should be presumed to be permissible (*aṣālat al-ibāḥah*), except when explicitly forbidden by the *Sharī'ah*. The *Akhbārīs* again disagree with them, saying that all knowledge is untrustworthy, except that conveyed by the Imām, and that whenever an act is not explicitly permitted by the *Sharī'ah* one should refrain from performing it by way of precaution (*iḥtīyāṭ*) against committing a sin.[14]

The political implications of these principles can hardly be overstated. By upholding the authority of reason and the right of *ijtihād*, the *Uṣūlī* doctrines could not fail to render the Shī'ī mind susceptible to social changes, and inspire confidence in the human ability to regulate social affairs. The reassertion of the status of the *mujtahids* and particularly the emphasis on the necessity of following a living authority certainly could help to mitigate the effects of the sclerosis of legal thought, and remove, at least partially, the stigma attached to intellectual dynamism. Moreover, principles such as those of the validity of probable knowledge and the permissibility of actions not specifically forbidden by the sources, encouraged a more flexible approach to the application of jurisprudence to emerging social and political problems. Before elaborating on the political significance of these conclusions, a word of caution is in order. It would be patently simplistic to portray the *Uṣūlīs* as outright 'progressives', and their traditionalist opponents as 'reactionaries'. As can be gathered from the above summary, there were in fact many features in the *Akhbārī* doctrines too which could have made them equally receptive to certain democratic notions, for instance their stance against the *mujtahids* had strong anti-élitist, and consequently populist, implications, just as their distrust of reason could develop into a Lockian belief that ideas come from the senses. Indeed, some recent Shī'ī scholars have hinted at a possible impact of the European school of sensationalism on the genesis of the *Akhbārī* ideas.[15] Nevertheless, by proscribing rationalism, and urging imitation (*taqlīd*) as the only permissible way of learning the canonical rules, the *Akhbārīs* placed an interdiction on all the mental processes which could be turned to integrating new rules and institutions in the traditional political structure.

* * *

Surveying the difference between the Sunnī and Shī'ī concepts of law, and the relationship of the political authority therewith, N. J. Coulson believes that 'politically the difference is between a constitutional and an absolute form of government; legally it is between a system which is basically immutable and represents the attempt by human reason to discern the divine command and one which purports to be the direct and living expression of that command. It follows that consensus (*ijmā'*), whether as a spontaneous source of law or as a criterion regulating the authority of human reasoning, has no place in such a scheme of jurisprudence, where the authority of the Imam supersedes that of agreed practice and his infallibility is diametrically opposed to the concept of probable rules of law (*ẓann*) and equally authoritative variants (*ikhtilāf*).' However, he admits later that despite these restrictions, during the 'protracted interregnum' resulting from the disappearance of the Imām, 'the exposition of the law has been the task of qualified scholars (*mujtahids*), and however much they may have been regarded as the agents of the Imām and working under his influence, their use of human reason (*'aql*), to determine the law has been accepted as necessary and legitimate. Inevitably, therefore, the concept of probable rules of law and the authoritative criterion of consensus have been recognised by the Ithnā-'asharites [Twelvers], and their system is certainly not without its variant scholastic opinions.'[16]

Assuming Coulson's account of the original or earlier form of Shī'īsm to be accurate, the question may well be asked whether the transition from that form to the more flexible version that he describes took place by sheer force of circumstance, or whether the fundamental principles of Twelver Shī'īsm (as outlined in the earlier chapters) should also be given some credit for this change? We believe that the doctrine of the Imāmate is as much a part of the Shī'ī concept of law as the necessity of *ijtihād*. It was thanks to the *Uṣūlīs* that the logical and indefeasible connection between the Imāmate and *ijtihād*, with all that it implies for a much less restricted exercise of human reason, was demonstrated with force and clarity. And if the corollary of the old concept was an 'absolute form of government', the inevitable result of the new one was a system of government which was, if not democratic, then at least accountable to people. The 'Ulamā' of all persuasions already enjoyed great influence among the masses as spiritual leaders, judges, administrators of *awqāf* (endowments), and even land-owners, traders and moneylenders. What they still needed in order to stand up to the despotic monarchy of the Qājārs, without impairing the supremacy of the *Sharī'ah*, was a political theory formulating the principles of representation and government accountability in the categories of Shī'ī jurisprudence. They would not have been able to construct even the rudiments of such a theory without the *Uṣūlī* prelude. We conclude this section by considering some examples of the application of *Uṣūlī* concepts to constitutionalism.

These examples concern the two central issues facing the 'Ulamā' in the Revolution: (a) the novelty of legislation as a deliberate act of the human mind to regulate social relations, and (b) the doctrine of the illegitimacy of the state during the period of occultation of the Imām. In dealing with the first issue, they used specific concepts which were drawn from the theory of jurisprudence, but in dealing with the second they relied on general arguments based on expediency and realism, which they had inherited from the Ṣafavīd period, if not earlier.

(a) The jurisprudential concepts used for the first issue were (1) obligatory preliminary (*muqaddimah-i wājib*), (2) secondary apparent rules (*aḥkām-i thānawiyyah-i ẓāhiriyyah*), (3) miscellaneous formulae relating to the separation of religious (*shar'ī*) from non-religious (*'urfī*) matters. (4) The Tradition of 'Umar Ibn Ḥanẓalah.

1 *The concept of obligatory preliminary*

This forms one of the familiar sub-chapters of the *Uṣūl* treatises, comprising some of the most typically convoluted discussions on the definitions and varieties of the preliminaries of an act. The historian Kasravī denounces the bewildering complexity of such discussions as an exasperating illustration of the futility of some scholastic discourses,[17] and so do many of the more independent-minded Shī'ī jurisconsults.[18] The *Uṣūlīs* define a preliminary as the precondition of an act. They have numerous ways for dividing such preconditions. One is to divide them into internal and external, the internal being the inherent or essential components of an act, and the external being the outside factor causing or facilitating the performance of an act. As always, such divisions are rather abstract, and sometimes extremely difficult to differentiate. But the division which is of interest to us is that between a preliminary which is explicitly required by the *Sharī'ah* (such as ablution for prayer), and one which is not so but can become obligatory if another obligatory act depends on it. For instance, horse-racing and arrow-throwing are normally permissible or recommended practices, but if it becomes necessary for Muslims to wage *jihād* (holy war), the same acts become obligatory by implication. In the same way the adoption of a constitution becomes obligatory for Muslims when it is a precondition of their welfare, security or progress.[19] It is interesting to note that the Sunnīs usually arrive at the same conclusion from a different premise – that of *maṣlaḥah*, literally welfare, which means that public interest should always prevail over the preference of jurisconsults. But since the Shī'īs refute *maṣlaḥah*,[20] the concept of 'obligatory preliminary' is also a device to circumvent any objection to law-making for which there is no specific canonical license.

2 *The concept of secondary apparent rules*
The rules of conduct in the *Sharīʻah* are of two categories: the 'primary, real rules' *aḥkām-i awwaliyyah-i ḥaqīqiyyah*), which explain the eternal and abstract tenets of the religion, and the 'secondary apparent rules' which govern accidental and concrete details concerning their application to worldly affairs. The latter category itself has numerous subdivisions depending on their subject-matter, and the conditions of persons affected by them. Although the 'Ulamā' are the only people qualified to interpret the first category, and even to lay down the general principles concerning the second, deciding the subject-matter of the second kind is only the task of lay experts. Just as if two qualified physicians prescribe wine to a patient, wine-drinking which is otherwise a sin becomes permissible for him, so too if 'doctors of politics', who in this case are none other than the Majlis (Parliament) deputies, deliberate on matters of state interest within their competence, their decisions must be binding even without the approval of the 'Ulamā'.[21]

3 *The* urfī *versus* sharʻī *affairs*
This was the most widely used distinction in the controversy over the Constitution.[22] The concept of *'urf* or non-religious matters was given great prominence to justify law-making as a measure regulating matters outside the purview of the *Sharīʻah*, and therefore not at all detrimental to its paramount position. Since it was originally within the perimeter of the theory of jurisprudence that *'urf* was allowed to operate as a principle of subsidiary value, many notions and maxims taken from its corpus were also invoked in the course of argument. One was the concept of 'deciding the subject matter' (*ta'yīn-i muḍūʻ*) which practically meant applying a general rule to a particular case by allowing it more flexibility. Others were familiar maxims such as 'necessity makes prohibited things permissible', 'actions should be judged by their ends', and so on. Sometimes simple logical terms were used: for instance, the relationship between the Constitutional Revolution and Islam was said to be the same as that between the major premise (*kubrā*) and minor premise (*sughrā*). The major premise stated that Islam must last for ever, and the minor premise merely defined the sciences, instruments and methods which could most effectively bring this about. There was complete agreement among Iranians on the major premise, so it was up to the 'scientists and wise men of the realm' to provide for the means to that end. A simpler dualism, which was used less frequently because of its secular connotations, was that between worldly (*maʻāshī*)and other-worldly (*maʻādī*) affairs, restricting the jurisdiction of the 'Ulamā' to the latter.

4 *The Tradition of 'Umar Ibn Ḥanẓalah*
This Tradition (*maqbūlah*) is usually invoked to justify the authority of the *mujtahids* or the 'Ulamā' to adjudicate the affairs of Muslims in the

absence of the Imāms, and, by extension, to act as their leaders in general. Upon being asked by an inquirer as to whether it is permissible for Muslims to refer their disputes over debts and inheritance right to temporal rulers, the sixth Imām, Ja'far aṣ-Ṣādiq, forbids them to do so, quoting the Qur'ānic verse (4 : 60) which admonishes those who 'go for judgement' to *Ṭāghūt* (illegitimate ruler). Instead, the Imām instructs the Muslims to submit to the verdict of those who base themselves on the *ḥadīth* (saying) and the guidance of the Imāms on permissible and prohibited matters. What if, the inquirer asks, the judges give different verdicts on the basis of different *ḥadīths* ascribed to the Imāms? Then the opinion of the most just and the most learned and the most honest should be given preference over others, the Imām replies. But what if all the judges are equally just, learned and honest? In that case, the Imām answers, one should look into the *ḥadīths* which are attributed to us, accepting that which enjoys the consensus of our followers (*aṣḥāb*), and rejecting the one which is narrated by only a few (*shādhdh*), because 'what is the subject of consensus should not be doubted' (*inna'l mujma' 'alayhi lā rayba fīhi*).[23]

This tradition is still quoted in defence of the juridical authority of the *mujtahids*;[24] indeed Khumaynī refers to it as one reason to vindicate the government by the *faqīh*.[25] But during the Constitutional era, Nā'īnī used it as evidence of the weight given in Shī'īsm to majority opinion – and hence to democracy – against those traditionalists who argued that 'interpreting rules in the fashion of majority is an innovation' (*bid'at būdan-i-ta'wīl bi aktharIyyat*).[26]

Before proceeding to the second issue facing the 'Ulamā' in the Constitutional period, we must point out that, as was mentioned earlier, the majority of the 'Ulamā' were apparently agreed on the necessity of law-making. Even the tracts of the most steadfast opponent of the Revolution, Shaykh Faḍlullālh Nūrī, did not contain any objection to the concept of man-made law as such; on the contrary, the outspoken Shaykh repeatedly agreed with his opponents that the fact that the monarchy, owing to the 'accidents of the world', had deviated from the *Sharī'ah* and degenerated into tyranny, made it necessary to devise special laws for it. Even those who adamantly refused to admit the legitimacy of such laws later on toned down their opposition with the ratification of Article 2 of the Constitution, which required the presence of at least five *mujtahids* in the Majlis to monitor all its enactments so that they would not contravene the *Sharī'ah*. The *'urfī* line of reasoning may have played an important role in making this compromise possible. What both sides to the compromise failed to appreciate at the time was that the social and cultural consequences of the new rules and institutions were going to be far different from those of the politically 'innocent' dispensations on, say, conditions of sale or payment of dower, as demanded by the *'urf*.

(b) Of greater significance for the political theory of Shī'īsm was the attitude towards the state, particularly the legitimacy of the monarchy.

But this was an issue which had already been faced by the ʿUlamāʾ before, not only in the early periods of Islamic history, but also under the Ṣafavīds. The main obstacle to the ʿUlamāʾs acceptance of the necessity of state in its modern form was, of course, the theoretical negation of the legitimacy of all temporal powers. This was not the position of all the ʿUlamāʾ, but nevertheless it was a powerful idea, and one which was always kept in reserve as the most effective weapon against rulers who dared to overrule the will of the men of religion. The way had already been paved for overcoming this obstacle, or at least rendering it less insuperable, by the teachings of such unquestionable authorities as Shaykh Ṭūsī and Ibn Idrīs[27] who recognised not only the permissibility of working for temporal rulers under certain conditions, but also the possibility of the existence of just rulers in the absence of the Imām. This recognition received further refinements during the Ṣafavīd period in the face of fierce opposition from such scholars as Shaykh Ibrāhīm Qaṭīfī who adhered to the fundamental rejection of temporal government.[28] Those religious leaders who supported the Constitutional movement more or less reiterated the arguments of pro-monarchical Ṣafavīd jurisconsults whenever they wanted to show that their antipathy towards despotism did not mean their opposition to all forms of state order. To give an idea of the tenor of such arguments, and thereby of the thinking of religious constitutionalists on rulership, we quote here a typical statement by an influential figure of the Ṣafavīd period, Mullā Muḥammad Bāqir, known as Muḥaqqiq Ṣabzavārī (d. 1090/1679):

> No time is devoid of the existence of the Imām, but in certain periods the Imām is absent from the eyes of human beings for some reasons and expediencies, but even then the world is prospering thanks to the emanation of His existence.... Now in this period, when the Master of the Age... is absent, if there is no just and judicious king to administer and rule this world, the affairs will end in chaos and disintegration, and life will become impossible for everybody. But it is inevitable, and imperative, for people [to be ruled by] a king who will rule with justice and follow the practice and tradition of the Imām.

The author then goes on to enumerate the functions of such a king. These are: (1) to follow the practice and tradition of the Imām; (2) to repel the evil of the oppressors; (3) to protect his subjects who are the trustees of God Almighty; (4) to keep every subject in his deserved status; (5) to safeguard the faithful from the revolt and dominion of the infidel and renegades; (6) to disseminate the word of the *Sharīʿah*; (7) to strengthen the people of piety and religiosity; (8) to refrain from coveting the belongings of his subjects and from making their persons and belongings the instruments of sin and lasciviousness; (9) to enjoin the good and forbid the evil; (10) to maintain the safety of highways and frontiers.[29]

Thus, in return for the justness and integrity of the king, the Ṣafavīd Shīʿīs undertook to recognise his power as legitimate, and obey his commands. But with the monarchs' repeated deviations from the canons of the *Sharī'ah*, the compromise lost its validity, and strict Shī'īs reverted to their pristine stance of total opposition to the state. By the end of the Qājār period, things had come to such a pass that, in the words of Nā'īnī, just kings were regarded to be as rare as the 'philosophers' stone' (*kibrīt-i aḥmar*) and the fabulous bird *'anqā*.[30] But it is an indication of the political maturity of the religious constitutionalists that they combined their demands for justice and legality with a readmission of the necessity of the state. They could not, however, declare their opinion on the state without stating their position towards monarchy. The religio-political tracts of the time denote an attitude which, while returning to the compromise of the Ṣafavīd period, is as anxious to prevent the monarchy from lapsing into despotism and corruption. So on the one hand they accept the necessity of the monarchy, but on the other hand recognise the need for an 'adjusting body' (*hay'at-i musaddidah*), namely the national assembly, to supervise his acts.[31]

What certainly propelled many of the 'Ulamā' to take a conciliatory line on the question of temporal authority was their love of the country rather than monarchy. They felt that the independence and survival of Iran were at stake, and that to safeguard these, the 'illegitimate or irreligious monarchy' (*salṭanat ghayr mashrū'ah*) had to be tolerated, even if temporarily. Some thought that such a course was necessary to protect Islam. The height of this patriotism was reached at the time of the Russian ultimatum to Iran in 1911, when it became almost fashionable for a number of the 'Ulamā' to intersperse their messages of solidarity to the central government with frequent references to the 'Iranian homeland', and their own readiness to defend the state against foreign aggression.

The picture emerging from this survey is indeed different from that painted by Kasravī. Far from indulging in the elaboration of barren jurisprudential schemes or anti-social esoterics, the 'Ulamā' thus appear to have done at least some preliminary work to turn their scholasticism to the service of the political cause of their people. Their realism tempered by a refusal to compromise on points of principle contrasts with their subsequent attitudes, which range from radical puritanism to opportunistic pacification. The reasons for this are manifold, and can only be hinted at. The 'Ulamā' soon came to see that constitutionalism and modernisation lessened their authority and prestige, and that fewer top intellects joined their circle, which until the nineteenth century attracted the best minds. Even many of their sons opted for modern education and Western ways of life. The social upheaval immediately following the Revolution of 1906 resulted in the weakening of all the traditional legitimating factors of authority, a situation which is not normally the right *milieu* for moderation. The bitterness left by the opposition of Shaykh Faḍlullāh to the Constitution, and by his execution, nurtured mutual animosities for a long time. Finally, the absolutism which dominated Iran in the wake of the post-Revolution anarchy naturally stunted the growth of religio-political thought along the course chartered by the Revolution. Conditions did not become propitious for a revival until the years following the Second World War, when the change in the balance of political forces with the collapse of Riḍā Shāh's despotism gave birth to a new phase of religious thinking – this time on some of the crucial themes of Shī'ī culture, of which *taqiyyah* and martyrdom, the subjects of the following two sections, had perhaps the richest potential for political action.

II Taqiyyah

Etymologically, *taqiyyah* comes from the root *waqa, yaqī* in Arabic, which means to shield or to guard oneself, the same root from which the important word *taqwā* (piety, or fear of God) is derived. There is thus nothing in the term itself to justify its standard translation in English either as dissimulation or (expedient) concealment, although both acts may be necessary to guard oneself from physical or mental harm on account of holding a particular belief opposed to that held by the majority. The Shī'ī case for the necessity of *taqiyyah* is based on a commonsense 'counsel of caution' on the part of a persecuted minority. Since for the greater part of their history the Shī'īs have been a minority amidst the global Islamic community and have lived mostly under regimes hostile to their creed, the only wise course for them to follow has been to avoid exposing themselves to the risk of extinction resulting from an open and defiant propagation of their beliefs, although they have not shunned their mission, whenever the opportunity has presented itself, to give a jolt to the Muslim conscience by revolting against impious rulers. This precautionary attitude has not been confined to the Shī'īs alone in Islamic history; other sects and movements have resorted to the same tactic whenever threatened by oppressors. But the practice has come to be almost exclusively associated with Shī'īsm, partly because of the enduring status of the Shī'īs in history as a minority, or 'unorthodox' group, and partly because their opponents have found in it valuable ammunition for their propaganda. Hence the inclusion, in almost every classical work of Shī'ī jurisprudence (*fiqh*), of a chapter which either justifies or outlines the rules of the *taqiyyah*. The justification primarily rests on three Qur'ānic verses. The first is a general warning to the faithful not to associate themselves with infidels: 'Let not believers take infidels for their friends rather than believers; whoso shall do this has nothing from God – unless, indeed, ye fear a fear from them: But God would have you beware of Himself; for to God ye return' (3:28). The second verse exempts from divine punishment those believers who retract their profession of faith under duress: 'Whoso, after he hath believed in God denieth him, if he were forced to it and if his heart remain steadfast in the faith *shall be guiltless*' (16:106). Shī'ī exegetes believe this verse to refer to 'Ammār, the son of Yāsir, who was a prominent pro-'Alī companion of Prophet Muḥammad. Being a frail old man, 'Ammār was tortured by the Quraysh infidels into expressing belief in polytheism, but Muḥammad defended him on the grounds that he was a staunch believer 'from head to toe'. Finally, the third verse is part of the story of Moses: when Pharaoh, Haman and Korah (Qārūn) ordered Moses' followers to be killed, 'a man of the family of Pharaoh who was a believer, but hid faith' questioned the wisdom of killing a man for the sake of his faith (40 : 28). In addition to these verses there are numerous sayings ascribed to the Imāms, particularly the sixth, aṣ-Ṣādiq, confirming the imperative necessity of *taqiyyah*, even to the point of identifying it with the essence of religion itself: 'He who has no *taqiyyah*, has no religion (*dīn*)'; 'The *taqiyyah* is [a mark] of my religion, and that of my forefathers.'[32]

There is another argument in defence of the *taqiyyah* which is mystico-philosophical, and is predicated on the esoteric character of Shī'īs, to which we referred before. If the *raison d'être* and the essential function of the Imāms should be sought in their status as the repository of the truth of the religion, or the 'sacred trust' placed exclusively at their disposal, then their knowledge of that truth cannot be communicable through propagation (*idhā'ah*), otherwise not only will their claim to a privileged position be forfeited, but the knowledge itself will be in danger of being misrepresented and vulgarised. This view of the *taqiyyah* is most elaborately stated by one of the convinced Western exponents of mystico-philosophical schools of Shī'īsm, Henri Corbin, who asserts that the practice was instituted by the Imāms themselves, not only for reasons of personal safety, 'but as an attitude called for by the absolute respect for high doctrines: nobody has strictly the right to listen to them except those who are capable of listening to, and comprehending, the truth. To act otherwise, is to abandon ignominiously the trust which has been confided in you, and to commit lightly a grave spiritual treachery.' On this basis, Corbin tries to explain a number of distinctive features of Shī'ī culture. One cannot, he says, '*ex abrupto*, notebook and questionnaire at hand, ask a Shī'ī about his faith. To do so would be the surest means of making him shut himself off to further questions, and inducing him to get rid of the questioner by giving inoffensive, [but] derisory answers'. This attitude, continues Corbin, may have to do with long periods of fierce persecution, but only in the most ephemeral sense, because the deeper reason is the refusal to allow religious knowledge to be debased through superficial dissemination. As an illustration of this point, he relates how he once heard 'a young *mullā* in his thirties, declaring that while Shī'īsm addresses the whole people, it could not receive the consent of but a spiritual minority'. He explains the absence of 'the missionary spirit, and of proselytisation in Iranian Shī'īsm' in the same terms, and shows *taqiyyah* and Shī'ī esoterics to be mutually dependent. According to a statement by the great Shī'ī theologian Shaykh Ṣadūq (d. 381/991), which he quotes, 'abolition of *taqiyyah* is not allowed until the appearance of the Imām announcing the resurrection [*al-Imām al Qā'im*], by whom the religion will be made integrally manifest.' If, concludes Corbin, 'the teachings of the Imāms concerned only the explanation of the *Sharī'ah*, the Law and the ritual, as some have claimed and still do claim, the imperative of the *taqiyyah* would have been incomprehensible.'[33]

Such sophisticated interpretations of the *taqiyyah* have now come as much under the devastating attacks of the modernists as the more down-to-earth, popular perceptions of the term. For although both the Qur'ānic verses and the sayings attributed to the Imāms, and the glosses by authoritative Shī'ī jurists and theologians, indicate that *taqiyyah* is an exceptional dispensation granted only in cases of emergency and compulsion (*iḍṭirār*), in practice it has become the norm of public behaviour whenever there is a conflict between faith and expediency. Small wonder, then, that it has at times degenerated into an excuse for downright hypocrisy and cowardice. For the same reason, one of the first tasks facing the Shī'ī modernists has been to effect a thorough affirmation of its original meaning with a view to transforming it from a camouflage for political passivity into an instrument of activism. They have realised that unless they overcome this mental barrier among the ordinary Shī'īs to oppositional politics, they have little chance of translating their other militant doctrines into a veritable, sustained mass movement. Hence their efforts to demonstrate how far the current notion of *taqiyyah*, both in Sunnī polemics and in popular Shī'ī usage, has deviated from its real meaning.

The first important point to emerge from the modernist treatment of the subject is that what is commonly assumed to be a simple, monolithic concept is, according to its proper definition, in fact a convenient rubric for a variety of acts, each having a clearly defined purpose. It is, therefore, wrong to think that all acts of *taqiyyah* are either sanctioned or repudiated with unvarying force in religion. Four categories are particularly mentioned: (1) the enforced (*ikrāhiyyah*), (2) precautionary or apprehensive (*khawfiyyah*), (3) arcane (*kitmāniyyah*), and (4) symbiotic (*mudārātī*). The enforced *taqiyyah* consists of acting in accordance with the instructions of an oppressor, and under necessity, in order to save one's life. Although being the simplest of all the four to define, it is also the most controversial kind, because it applies most readily to the political conditions of the Shī'īs in most places – now as much as in the past – and involves the difficulty of reaching consensus as to who an oppressor is. The precautionary or apprehensive *taqiyyah* consists of the performance of acts and rituals according to the *fatwās* (authoritative opinions) of the Sunnī religious leaders, and in the Sunnī countries. Alternatively, it consists of the 'complete precaution of a minority in its way of life, and dealings with the majority, for the sake of protecting oneself and one's co-religionists'. The arcane *taqiyyah* is to conceal one's faith or ideology, as well as the number and strength of one's co-religionists, and to carry out clandestine activity for furthering the religious goals, in times of weakness and lack of preparation for conducting an open propaganda. It is this kind of *taqiyyah* which is the opposite of *idhāʿah* (propaganda). Finally, the symbiotic type is simply a code of coexistence with the Sunnī majority, and of participation in their social and ritual congregations for maintaining Islamic unity, and establishing a powerful state comprising all the Muslims.[34]

The point of this classification is twofold: on the one hand, it attests the Shīʿīs' realistic understanding of the practical problems which arise in reconciling the conflicting demands of a pure faith, and the physical survival of an unlawful minority; on the other, it purports to emphasise that concealing one's faith or ideology is simply a tactical device which should by no means interrupt the efforts towards its triumph, or conceived as a warrant for suspending essential religious duties. But the modernists seem to admit that even the fullest enumeration of the correct forms of the *taqiyyah*, and of their specific purposes, still leaves enough loop-holes for the feeble-minded and the comfort-seekers to use the whole practice as a convenient excuse for neglecting the obligation to speak and fight for the truth, thus acting as silent accomplices in rampant injustice. How can it be otherwise when safeguarding one's life is explicitly recognised as a legitimate aim in the observance of at least two of the four varieties of the practice? A substantial portion of the modernist arguments is allocated, therefore, to a semi-scholarly, semi-ideological debate on the limits of self-protection, on the demarcation line beyond which safeguarding oneself, or one's co-religionists, turns from a legitimate and judicious act of self-defence into a cowardly flight from the unmistakable summons of the religious conscience. The most frequent warning accompanying these arguments is that *taqiyyah* is definitely an illicit act whenever it entails 'a corruption in religion'. What 'corruption in religion' exactly means is never quite clear, but the modernists use one or two vital clues in the sayings attributed to the Imāms, and in the works of distinguished jurists of the past, to elucidate its application. There is, for instance, the statement reportedly made either by the fifth Imām, al-Bāqir, or the sixth, aṣ-Ṣādiq, that they 'never practise *taqiyyah* [although not proscribing it for others] in three things: wine-drinking, wiping over the shoes [instead of bare feet in the ablution for prayer, *masḥ al-khuffayn*], and abandoning the *tamattuʿ* pilgrimage'. Wine-drinking is banned by all Muslims, but the latter two acts are supposed to be Sunnī 'innovations'. The Imām is thus saying that he will never perform these acts for the sake of pleasing the rulers or the majority although he does not prohibit them for others, because his own position as the leader of the Shīʿī community requires absolute avoidance of all offences even those which others may be allowed to commit to escape molestation on the part of the rulers or the majority.[35] Moreover, the Prophet Muḥammad and the Imām aṣ-Ṣādiq are both quoted as having denounced anybody who glorifies the innovators (*dhū bidʿah*); and the Prophet is said to have cursed the *ʿālims* who do not 'proclaim their knowledge' to awaken the public upon the appearance of an innovation.

In another saying attributed to the Imām ʿAlī, the *ʿālims* ʿwho do not proclaim their knowledge in time' have been described as the ʿmost stinking (*antan*) individuals on the Day of Judgement'.[36] Leaving aside the traditions associated with the Imāms, the behaviour of the militant Shīʿīs under the Umayyads and ʿAbbāsīds is also recounted to demonstrate that *taqiyyah* was never used as a means of evading moral responsibility: those militants who were arrested by the authorities never revealed the names or hide-outs of their fellow-fighters even under the severest torture. This attitude is reflected even in the opinion of classical jurists such as Shaykh Ṭūsī and Ibn Idrīs, who unequivocally rule out the permissibility of the *taqiyyah* whenever it results in the killing of people.[37] Having thus established that genuine Shīʿīsm never permits dissimulation if what is at stake is the very essence of religion, the modernists proceed to argue that all the statements ascribed to the Imāms which stress the incumbency of the *taqiyyah*, and identify it as an integral part of the religion, should be understood as a mere pleading for clandestine activity, to create ʿa secret organisation for protecting and propagating the doctrines of a Shīʿī Imām'.[38]

Discussion on *taqiyyah* sometimes involves a more delicate issue which concerns the principle of *al-amr bi'l-maʿrūf wa'n-nahy ʿan al-munkar* (enjoining the good and forbidding the evil), since one possible result of any kind of concealment or dissimulation can be the suspension of this cardinal religious duty. A person who is allowed to hide his real belief or practice to protect himself in a hostile environment should, by the same token, be permitted to abstain from advising others what to do and what not to do. The two attitudes are indeed so interrelated that sometimes *taqiyyah* is thought to be the opposite of, not *idhāʿah*, but *al-amr bi'l maʿrūf*, etc. So if Shīʿīsm is to retrieve its pristine character as a creed of militancy, then it must go on the offensive in all areas of social and political life, and this makes ʿenjoining the good and forbidding the evil' the strongest sanction of its campaign for the total regeneration of the community. Classical authors paid a great deal of attention to the questions of whether ʿenjoining the good and forbidding the evil' is an individual duty (*farḍ ʿayn*, which should be performed by every Muslim, like prayer), or a collective duty (*farḍ kifāyah*, which needs only to be performed by a group of Muslims, like *jihād*, the ʿholy war'); and of whether it is necessitated by reason or the law (*sharʿ*). They also pointed out the different forms in which the duty may be implemented: primarily by speech, and, if this does not produce the desired result, by hand – although the latter is believed to be the exclusive function of the Imāms or their representatives.[39] The modernists mostly refuse to be drawn into discussions of a purely theoretical nature, dismissing them as pedantic digressions.[40] Instead, their debate is focused on the pre-conditions and the forms of the fulfilment of the duty. Most Shīʿī authorities of the past agreed that a Muslim cannot perform the duty unless he meets three requirements: first, he should have the knowledge required to distinguish good from bad; second, he must be fairly certain that his advice will be effective; and third, he must be sure that no harm will come to his or her person as a consequence of performing the duty. The modernists consider the classical treatment of these pre-conditions to be unsatisfactory on two main grounds. First, they believe that even the absence of these pre-conditions does not negate the 'obligatoriness' of the act itself, unlike, for instance, the prerequisite of solvency in the case of paying pilgrimage to Mecca. The latter act ceases to be obligatory for a Muslim who does not have sufficient financial means. But 'enjoining the good and forbidding the evil' remains incumbent on every Muslim even in the absence of its pre-conditions, just as prayer is still obligatory for a person who is not physically clean. The only effect that the absence of these pre-conditions can and must have is to create a further obligation to achieve them. Thus a Muslim who does not have the knowledge of good and evil in Islam should do all in his or her power to obtain it, rather than using his ignorance as a pretext for indifference to problems of public morality. Second, the modernists refute the second and third conditions as absurdly obstructive, and an encouragement to quietism, arguing that if the great heroes of social and political struggle in Islamic history – men like 'Alī, Ḥusayn and Abū Dharr – wanted to observe such conditions, they could have never revolted against the iniquities of their times.[41] The whole debate acquires an all the more disputatious tone against the background of the controversy that has raged in the past among classical Shī'ī jurists on the subject: while men like Shaykh Muḥammad Ḥasan Najafī, author of *Jawāhir al-kalām*, the most widely-used textbook of *fiqh* in centres of religious teaching in Iran, emphasise the essentiality of the preconditions, there are jurists like Shahīd Thānī ('the Second Martyr') and Muḥaqqiq Karakī whose arguments favour the militants' case.[42]

The Shī'ī modernist views on *taqiyyah*, such as those outlined here, present one of the rare examples of genuine critical thinking in present-day Islam. While aiming at a radical reformation of a traditional concept and attitude, they seldom depart, as some quasi-religious modernist works do, from the accepted terms and categories of theology and jurisprudence. The arguments are often 'immanent', remaining always within Islamic idiom and thought, hardly invoking any notion drawn from any of the fashionable ideologies of our time, to substantiate or discredit a viewpoint. Misrepresentation of *taqiyyah* is denounced in the name of upholding religious sincerity, removing a major barrier in the way of unity with Sunnī Muslims, and exhibiting its virtue as a method of clandestine struggle. And the duty of 'enjoining the good and forbidding the evil' is exalted not in order to foster an attitude of inquisitiveness, or to pry into the private life and manners of individuals, but to stress the value of personal example as the most effective way of persuading others to rectify their ways,[43] and stand up to corruption and tyranny. Meanwhile, the fact that the two issues are examined in conjunction with each other signifies an awareness that no traditional or conventional practice, which is likely to have momentous ramifications in the political behaviour of Muslims, can be meaningfully studied without examining the network of supplementary or derivative notions connecting it with the entire system of religious behaviour.

III Martyrdom

In Shī'ī history, the drama of the martyrdom of Ḥusayn, the third Imām, which was fought out on the plains of Karbalā' in the month of Muḥarram in 61/680 ranks next only to the Prophet's investiture of 'Alī as his successor at the Ghadīr of Khumm. From a political standpoint, the drama is significant for two reasons: first, Ḥusayn was the only Shī'ī Imām in the Twelver school who died in consequence of combining his claim to the Caliphate with an armed uprising. The remaining eleven Imāms either attained political positions through regular constitutional procedures (the first and the eighth) or made formal peace with the ruler of the time after hesitant hostilities (the second), or secluded themselves in a quiet life of piety and scholarship; as regards the last Imām, he disappeared before displaying a preference for any of these alternative courses of action. Second, the element of martyrdom in the drama obviously exercises a powerful attraction for all Shī'ī movements challenging the established order. Ḥusayn is thus the only Imām whose tragedy can serve as a positive ingredient of the mythology of any persecuted but militant Shī'ī group of the Twelver school.

The drama can also acquire added significance in the particular context of Iranian culture, not only because of certain nationalistic, anti-Arab or anti-Turkish streaks in its popular versions, but also on account of its merging in the folk culture with the pre-Islamic myth of the Blood of Sīyāvush, as recorded in Firdawsī's *Shāhnāmih*. The religious hymns of the Alawite *Ahl-i ḥaqq* describe how the Supreme Spirit of the Perfect Man transmigrated from Abel, through Jamshīd, Īraj and Sīyāvush, to Ḥusayn.[44] Although containing entirely different features, the myth of Sīyāvush is based on an identical notion of the 'spilled blood of the innocent crying perenially for revenge'. But whereas the legend of Ḥusayn gives rise to an essentially political aspiration of justice, the legend of Sīyāvush inspires faith in a universal nemesis ensuring justice for oppressed souls.

Ever since the Iranian Shī'ī dynasty of the Buyids popularised the Muḥarram ceremonies in the fourth/tenth century the Karbalā' drama has been the object of fervent annual lamentations. In the sixteenth century, the introduction of *ta'zīyah* (passion play) by the Iranian Ṣafavid dynasty strengthened the popular character of the ceremonies, which together with *rawḍah khānī* (recitation of the sufferings of holy martyrs), *zanjīr zanī* (self-flagellation) and other street processions formed a distinct cult despite the opposition of the religious hierarchy, who disapproved of them on account of their 'crude dogma' and irreligious histrionics.[45]

The main purpose of these ceremonies was to perform the lamentations in a form which would cause the greatest amount of weeping. Numerous prophetic sayings recommend or praise weeping, or its affection, during prayer, or recitation of the Qur'ān, or recollecting God, or from fear of God. Wensinck has noted more than forty of them.[46] To this catalogue, the Shī'ī tradition has added the virtue of weeping in memory of the Imāms, particularly Ḥusayn, who is known as the Lord of the Martyrs (*sayyid ash-shuhadā'*). Examples are legion, but here we mention only three, one from an outstanding Shī'ī traditionist, and the other two from conventional collections of stories about the Imāms, both written in the nineteenth century.

First the quotation from the traditionist, Shaykh Ṣadūq. In his *'uyūn akhbār ar-riḍā*, he quotes the eighth Imām, 'Alī 'Ibn Musā ar-Riḍā, to have said to Rayyān Ibn Shabīb, one of his companions: 'O Son of Shabīb! If you want to be with us in the sublime paradise, bear grief for us, and remain stricken with our sorrow.' And elsewhere: 'O Son of Shabīb! If you wept for Ḥusayn until your tears rolled down your cheeks, all your sins, whether major or minor, will be forgiven.'[47]

The same notion of salvation through grief is stated in *Muḥriq al-qulūb* ('Burner of Hearts') by Mullā Muḥammad Mahdī Narāqī, but in an ornate style typical of the more popular literature on the subject: 'Revealed, authoritative *ḥadiths* indicate that had the Prophet willed, he would have averted from Ḥusayn the disaster that was to befall him [at Karbalā']. But the Prophet did not do this for reasons which are partly known to us, but partly known only to God and the Prophet, and of whose perception our minds are incapable. Undoubtedly, the benefits of the martyrdom are countless: among others, it has proved the justness of the cause of the Prophet's family, and the falsity of the way of his adversaries.... Besides, many a wretched sinner is forgiven and attains salvation by weeping for Ḥusayn.'[48]

But the merit attributed to weeping in *Riyād al-quds* ('Gardens of Paradise') by Ṣadr ud-Dīn Vā'iẓ Qazvīnī is of a different kind: here, weeping is said to benefit not the mourners but the cause of the Prophet's house: 'A learned man saw in a dream that the Imām Ḥusayn had recovered from all the wounds [inflicted on him at Karbalā']. He asked the Imām how his wounds had healed up so miraculously. "With the tears of my mourners," replied the Imām.' 'When Za'far the Jinnee, together with thirty-six thousand jinnees, came to help Ḥusayn at Karbalā', the Imām refused him the permission to fight on his side, his reason being: "I am not at all keen on living in this world. I wish to meet my God. Whosoever wants to help me should merely weep for me." '[49]

Thus lamentations for Ḥusayn enable the mourners not only to gain an assurance of divine forgiveness, but also to contribute to the triumph of the

Shī'ī cause. Accordingly, Ḥusayn's martyrdom makes sense on two levels: first, in terms of a soteriology not dissimilar from the one invoked in the case of Christ's crucifixion: just as Christ sacrificed himself on the altar of the cross to redeem humanity, so did Ḥusayn allow himself to be killed on the plains of Karbalā' to purify the Muslim community of sins; and second, as an active factor vindicating the Shī'ī cause, contributing to its ultimate triumph. When one adds to all this the cathartic effect of weeping as a means of releasing pent-up grief over not only personal misfortunes, but also the agonies of a long-suffering minority, then the reasons for the immense popularity of the Muḥarram ceremonies become apparent.

With the increasing tendency of the Shī'īs to a passive form of *taqiyyah*, and acquiescence in the established order, the concept of the martyrdom of Ḥusayn as vicarious atonement prevailed over its interpretation as a militant assertion of the Shī'ī cause. Concomitantly, weeping, and not edification or political indoctrination, came to be recognised as the sole aim of *all* reminiscence of Ḥusayn. This is primarily clear from the very titles of most of the popular histories of the Karbalā' drama: *miftāḥ al-bukā'* ('Key to Weeping'), *ṭūfān-al bukā'* ('Tempest of Weeping'), *muḥīt al-bukā'* ('Ocean of Weeping'), *muthīr al-aḥzān* ('Rouser of Sorrows') and *luhūf* ('Burning Lamentations'). One rarely, if ever, comes across a narrative redolent of combative vengefulness. The dominant trend is an elegiac account of the episodes in the drama, a concern which seems to stem from the conviction that submissive endurance of pain and suffering is the hallmark of all worthy souls. In the *Amālī* ('Discourses') of Shaykh Ṭūsī, 'Alī is quoted as having warned his son Ḥasan that he would always be 'a hostage of death, a target of adversity, and a victim of pain.'[50] 'O brothers!', to quote again from a populariser of the story, Mahdī Narāqī, 'affliction is bestowed (only) on the Friends of God, oppression befalls the Chosen Men, and pain and suffering are proportionate to the degree of dignity and pre-eminence (while conversely) exemption from calamity and hardship is the trait of ill fate and wretchedness.'[51] One could establish a link between this exaltation of suffering, and the asceticism of Islamic Ṣūfī traditions, which preaches the acceptance of pain as a necessary stage in the spiritual development of Man.

Ḥusayn's passive and pietistic behaviour in the drama of Karbalā', as described in orthodox Shī'ī sources, is perhaps best exemplified by the epithet *maẓlūm* which often follows his name in the popular usage. *Maẓlūm* literally means injured, oppressed or sinned against, but in colloquial Persian its connotation goes beyond those associated with incurring injustice; it means a person who is unwilling to act against others, even when he is oppressed, not out of cowardice or diffidence but because of generosity and forbearance. That is why it is normally synonymous with *najīb*, literally meaning noble, but also gentle and modest. Thus being a *maẓlūm*, rather than signifying a negative attribute or a deprivation, counts as a moral virtue.

Hence the paradox of the drama of Karbalā' in Shī'ī literature, whether popular or scholarly. True, outside impassioned scenes, the drama is treated as something more than a simple agent of emotional catharsis, and Ḥusayn is praised for his sacrifice to vindicate the just cause of the Prophet's family, or to revive the religion of his grandfather Muḥammad, and to save it from the Umayyads' deviation. But his predominant image as a saint with an almost masochistic wish for martyrdom defeats any attempt at using the drama as a means of inculcating political activism.

How passive and harmless this image has been, from such a political point of view, can be understood from the fact that the *ta'zīyah* was promoted by the financial and political oligarchs who used it under both Ṣafavīd and Qājār dynasties as a means of consolidating their hold over the populace; and in its golden age, a despot like Nāṣir ud-Dīn Shāh saw no contradiction between his oppressive methods of government and the provision of the most elaborate amenities for the performance of *ta'zīyah*.[52]

During the last ten years or so, the quiescent character of the drama of Karbalā' has started to change at the hands of a number of Shī'ī modernists who could not forego its obvious potential as a rhetorical instrument of political mobilisation. The modernists have tried to develop this potential primarily as part of their general drive for the reformulation of the crucial themes of Islamic history. But there is an ironic coincidence between their reinterpretation of the drama, and the strong interest taken in the drama by a number of Sunnī modernists. It is not unusual to find praise of Ḥusayn, as of any other member of the Prophet's family, in classical Sunnī literature, especially of the Shāfi'ī and Ḥanafī schools. But what is interesting in the new Sunnī literature on the subject is strong rejection of some criticisms of him in classical sources, and his glorification as a rebel and the prototype of all those who challenge false consensus. This provides an important example of that theoretical, inter-sectarian concord of which we spoke in Chapter 1. But the example may be the result of more than a simple coincidence; more probably, the 'revisionist' literature of one side has stimulated fresh thinking by the other.

What should be, however, of greater concern to us is that, however identical their political motives have been, the Sunnī and Shī'ī reinterpretations have been widely different from each other with regard to both the kind of conceptual problems they have had to face, and their consequences. Any latter-day Muslim political activist with a rationalist turn of mind, and anxious to mobilise all the resources of the Muslim historical conscience in the service of a political cause, cannot use the drama for his purpose without first tackling a problem inherent in the drama, relating to Ḥusayn's leadership. The problem is whether Ḥusayn acted responsibly and wisely by launching a revolt without adequate foresight and power, and if his revolt was merely an act of self-sacrifice, whether the long-term results justified its immediate disastrous consequences for the Shī'ī community, or Muslims in general. Now if our political activist is a Sunnī, and finds the answer to be in the positive, all he has to do to exploit the drama for the particular brand of his indoctrination is to refute the Sunnī consensus on the legitimacy of Yazīd's regime, or his personal honesty and integrity.

But for the Shī'īs the problem is more intricate: for they have not only to explain away the numerous supernatural, legendary accretions to the drama, but also deal with the implications of their interpretation in the fields of Shī'ī theology and political theory. Perhaps it was because of the relative ease of their task that the first Muslim writers in recent history to question the traditional accounts of the drama were the Sunnīs. While the Shī'ī literature on Ḥusayn has naturally always consisted of high praise, there have been Sunnī historians who have condemned his uprising either as a sinful disruption of the prevailing consensus, or as an ill-considered move which was bound to end in fiasco.

The first line of criticism was represented by the twelfth-century judge and polemicist Ibn al-'Arabī, the second by the outstanding historian Ibn Khaldūn. Ibn al-'Arabī tries to bring discredit on Ḥusayn's uprising by arguing that Yazīd, contrary to the Shī'ī allegations, was an honest and pious man, and that Ḥusayn revolted against him despite the opposite advice of such distinguished companions of the Prophet as Ibn 'Abbās, Ibn 'Umar and his own brother Ibn Ḥanafiyyah; he wonders how Ḥusayn could have preferred the wishes of the riff-raff (*awbāsh*) of Kūfah to the counsel of these dignitaries. Yazīd's tough reaction against Ḥusayn, concludes Ibn al-'Arabī, was therefore merely an application of the law laid down by Ḥusayn's own grandfather, the Prophet Muḥammad, which provided for the severe punishment of all those subverting the unity and peace of the Muslim community.[53]

Ibn Khaldūn's strictures are of a different kind. As usual, he is fair towards both disputants. He asserts that rebellion against Yazīd was justified because of his wickedness. Ḥusayn was therefore right in regarding a revolt against Yazīd as a duty incumbent on those who had the power to execute it. But he thinks that Ḥusayn was wrong in confusing his qualifications with his power. His qualifications were as good as he thought, and better, but he was mistaken as to his strength. Yazīd, on the other hand, was wrong in trying to justify his actions against Ḥusayn by arguing that he was fighting evildoers, because any such action should be undertaken only by a just ruler, which he was not.[54]

Such criticisms of Ḥusayn's actions have been reproduced by contemporary orthodox Sunnīs, sometimes with even greater emphasis than that of the original, as can be noticed from the footnotes by Muḥibb ad-Dīn al-Khaṭīb, the former editor-in-chief of al-Azhar's review to Ibn al-'Arabī's *Al-'awāṣim min al-qawāṣim*.[55]

Since the turn of the century, when partly as a consequence of the modernism associated with the names of Asad-ābādī (Afghānī) and 'Abduh, many a hallowed stereotype in Islamic history has been revised, the meaning and nature of Ḥusayn's uprising too has gradually come under fresh scrutiny. So far as the present writer could establish, the first Sunnī writer in modern times to challenge the orthodox interpretation of Ḥusayn's uprising was the Egyptian Ibrāhīm 'Abd al-Qādir Māzinī. In an article in the periodical *ar-Risālah* of April 1936 he wrote that after attending for the first time a *rawḍah khānī* at the house of an Iranian shaykh in Cairo, he started to ponder Ḥusayn's intentions in his revolt against Yazīd. He had just read an article in an English review asserting that Ḥusayn deliberately engaged in the enterprise with the full knowledge of his ultimate failure. But why, asked Māzinī, should Ḥusayn endanger his life in such a futile adventure? More important, why did he take the innocent members of his family to such a perilous journey? Māzinī's answers to these questions build up Ḥusayn as a sincere, self-sacrificing, but by no means starry-eyed, visionary. He says that Ḥusayn realised from the outset that the odds were heavily against him, but since he held the Umayyad regime to be immoral, he felt, as an honest revolutionary, compelled to do his utmost, if not to overthrow, then at least to undermine that regime. By provoking Yazīd to adopt a most repressive policy, and commit all those atrocities at Karbalā', Ḥusayn succeeded in creating a deep hatred against him among the masses. Henceforth 'every drop of his blood, every letter of his name, and every invocation of his memory became a mine in the very foundation of the Umayyad state', finally blowing it to pieces.[56]

Almost twenty years after the publication of Māzinī's article, the same theme was picked up and developed by other secular writers in Egypt, the most outstanding of whom is undoubtedly 'Abbās Maḥmūd al-'Aqqād. In his book entitled *Abu'sh shuhadā' Ḥusayn Ibn 'Alī* ('Father of the Martyrs, Ḥusayn b. 'Alī') 'Aqqād first emphasises the profound contradiction between the personalities of Ḥusayn and Yazīd. Their conflict, he says, was basically between two temperaments, magnanimity and meanness, and hence between two concepts, the religious *Imāmah* and the temporal *dawlah* (state, but also worldly fortune). Add to these personal disparities the legacy of internecine animosity among the Quraysh (between the Hāshimids and 'Abd Shamsids) and even the romantic rivalry between Ḥusayn and Yazīd over Zaynab Bint Isḥāq (who married Ḥusayn), and the picture emerges of a most formidable antagonism.[57] 'Aqqād tries not to depart too much from the Sunnīs' overall recognition of the legitimacy of the Umayyad regime by drawing a distinction between the nature of political leadership under Yazīd and that under his father Mu'āwiyah: the latter at least enjoyed the well-meaning advice of such eminent men as 'Amr Ibn 'Āṣ, Mughīrat Ibn Shu'bah and Zīyād Ibn Abih, whereas Yazīd's entourage was entirely composed of worldly, avaricious characters (but 'Aqqād does criticise the 'Abd Shamsīds refusal in pre-Muḥammadan days to take part in the *Ḥilf al-Fuḍūl*, the alliance between the Hashimids and their associates to ensure a degree of social justice in Arabian society by protecting the weak against the strong).[58]

As regards the rightness or wrongness of Ḥusayn's revolt, 'Aqqād insists that the issue should not be judged from the point of view of workaḍay political adventures or commercial bargainings, thus indicating his disagreement with historians like Ibn Khaldūn, who, as we saw, censured Ḥusayn on utilitarian grounds for not having properly assessed his physical or strategic strength before the revolt. Being in essence a conflict between interest (or profit) and martyrdom, Ḥusayn's dispute with Yazīd should be judged by a criterion which cannot be applied to every individual and in every period. With this proviso, he goes on to consider Ḥusayn's revolt from two angles, its motives and its results. On both counts, his verdict is positive: Ḥusayn's motives, all purely moral, were unquestionably noble, determined by his unshakeable faith in religion; and the results he intended were all achieved in due course: Yazīd died, a despondent man, four years after Ḥusayn's death, all the perpetrators of the crimes at Karbalā' were punished, and sixty years later the Umayyad dynasty was overthrown, with the memory of Ḥusayn's martyrdom 'having acted as an insidious disease in its body politic.'[59]

'Aqqād devotes a considerable part of his analysis to the justification of Ḥusayn's conduct of political struggle. Throughout the revolt, he argues, Ḥusayn relied on peaceful means, always preferring persuasion to violence. The very day Muslim Ibn 'Aqīl ascertained a solid popular support for Ḥusayn in Kūfah, he could have proceeded to overtake Yazīd's agents by surprise, and establish an 'Alīd regime; but Ḥusayn had warned him not to resort to deceitful tactics. Ḥusayn knew that what was at stake was the struggle between right and wrong, and trusted that once right became manifest, there was no need to have recourse to violence or stratagem. 'Aqqād even justifies Ḥusayn's decision to take his family to Karbalā' by reminding that this was a custom in Arabian society since pre-Islamic days, whereby warriors took their kith and kin to the battlefield as evidence of their intrepid resolve to suffer all the consequences of their enterprise.[60]

Reference should also be made to two more works by secular Egyptian writers typifying a leftist approach to the drama. In 'Abd ar-Raḥmān ash-Sharqāwī's two-volume poetical play, *al-Ḥusayn thā'iran, al-Ḥusayn shahīdan* ('Ḥusayn the Revolutionary, Ḥusayn the Martyr'), the uprising is portrayed as a class struggle on behalf of the poor masses. Although the limitations inevitably imposed by such a literary genre on a political theme preclude a coherent presentation, the play may succeed in widening the appeal of Ḥusayn's tragedy for a modern audience accustomed to Brechtian radical drama – as urban, sophisticated literates in Tehran and Cairo are.

But apart from his adamant defiance, Sharqāwī's Ḥusayn is poles apart from both Ibn al-'Arabī's seditious adventurer and 'Aqqād's meta-historical visionary. Compared with them, he is a reformist with modest aims: he wants neither to create turmoil and bloodshed, nor to achieve political power, but simply to avert injustice. He often seems to be carried by, rather than lead, the popular effervescence. More significant, he is given to spells of self-doubt and soul-searching, as is apparent from his Hamlet-like soliloquy at the Prophet's grave before fleeing from Medina.[61]

In more radical literature, reformism is replaced by revolutionarism. Here Ḥusayn is decidedly siding with the left – although the meaning of the term *left* in its particular early Islamic context is not clear beyond a general opposition to Meccan capitalism and Damascene extravagance after the Umayyads' take-over. But there is no doubt about the identity of the leaders of the left. These were: first the Caliph 'Umar because of his austere policies, and prohibition against land ownership, then 'Alī, whose regime was based on *shūrā*, or democratic consultation, then his son Ḥasan, who deemed it wise in the interests of the left to adopt a posture of compromise and leniency, and finally Ḥusayn, whose life epitomised the leftist spirit of rejectionism. Aware of the sectarian susceptibilities of some of their readers, such authors argue that if Ḥusayn had connived with Yazīd for the sake of preserving tranquillity, he would have betrayed Islamic ideals of social justice. He could have retired into the safety of isolation from politics the day he heard the news of Muslim's execution, but such escapism was antithetical to his nature which rejected everything around him, and was ready to carry his rejection to critical heights. After the collapse of Muslim's mission, Ḥusayn knew that his revolt would fail, but he also knew that if he wanted to revolutionise the Muslim community, self-sacrifice was necessary. With Ḥusayn's death, the first 'round' of the trial of strength between the right and left came to an end – a process which had started with the right eliminating 'Umar and 'Alī from the political scene (the author does not pause to substantiate this arguable claim, since it has never been proved that 'Umar's assassin, a Persian freed slave, and 'Alī's assassin, a Khārijī, belonged to the same ideological camp). But like previous writers, the radicals too think that the martyrdom was in the long run a triumph for 'progressive forces', for it precipitated the Umayyads' downfall by reinvigorating the Arabs' moribund conscience.[62]

As noted earlier, the Sunnī reinterpretation of the drama of Karbalā' has not been confined to secular, Westernised enclaves, but has also infiltrated the religious circles. The best examples of this can be seen in the issues of the now defunct Egyptian review *Liwā' al-Islām*, which for eighteen years, from 1947 to 1965, rivalled the organ of the University Mosque of Al-Azhar in presenting religious viewpoints, with a fundamentalist flavour, on a wide range of issues relating to Islamic society and history; but it enjoyed the advantage of freedom from the trammels that attach al-Azhar to the officialdom. In an article in the issue of September 1956, Muḥammad Kāmil al-Bannā' is primarily concerned with clearing Ḥusayn of the charge of rashness in opening hostilities against Yazīd. To prove his point, he places special stress on Ḥusayn's precaution in sending Muslim to Kūfah beforehand. Nevertheless, he shares 'Aqqād's judgement that ultimately Ḥusayn could not escape his destiny as a rebel in the face of the worldly Banū 'Abd Shams. So even if Muslim's findings in Kūfah had been negative, Ḥusayn would still have gone ahead with his expedition. But al-Bannā's reason for Ḥusayn's innate tendency to rebellion smacks of the Shī'ī conviction about the inherited moral qualities of 'Alī's descendants: Ḥusayn would have revolted in any case, because he was 'a grandson of the Prophet, the son of 'Alī, the knight of Quraysh and the hero of Badre'. A more interesting feature of his analysis, which again sounds uncanny coming from a Sunnī writer, is his lending credence to the thesis, mostly upheld by the Shī'īs – as we shall see later – that Ḥusayn was aware of his inescapable fate as a martyr right from the beginning, from the time the Prophet had spoken about a dream he had seen in which Ḥusayn's death was foreshadowed.[63]

Another issue of the review carries the report of the proceedings of a symposium attended by such well-known advocates of a fundamentalist or socially committed outlook of Islam as Muḥammad Ghazzālī, 'Abd ar-Raḥīm Fūdah, Muḥammad Abū Zahrah and others. They discuss three specific questions: was Ḥusayn motivated by worldly desires and political ambitions? Second, did he challenge, by his revolt, a qualified and competent ruler? And third, did he employ the right method to attain his goal? The discussants' replies to the first and second questions are negative, and to the third positive, for more or less the same reasons as those adduced by the secular writers. But characteristically, they couch their arguments not in terms of criteria extraneous to their cultural background, but by repeated reference to analogies from Islamic history or Qur'ānic injunctions. Thus Ghazzālī justifies Ḥusayn's seemingly suicidal challenge to the overwhelming forces of Yazīd by likening it to the bravery of Anas Ibn an-Naḍr at the battle of Uḥud who, upon seeing the Muslim troops retreat, sallied forth towards the enemy's lines, shouting 'I smell the paradise from beyond the Uḥud [mountain]'. Such men, concludes Ghazzālī, care more for being consistent with themselves and their God, than for the practical outcome of their actions.[64]

Finally, Khālid Muḥammad Khālid's highly idealistic *Abnā' ar-rasūl fī Karbalā'* ('The Sons of the Prophet at Karbalā''), is distinguished by its elaboration on the background of the drama as a conflict between 'Alī's conception of the Caliphate as an institution which should embody the loftiest virtues of the Prophet's era, and the Umayyads' ruthless determination to reduce it to an instrument of sheer domination. More than a third of the book is taken up by contrasting the honest, straightforward behaviour of the 'Alīds with the artful practices of the first two Umayyad caliphs. So contrary to the fundamentalists, Khālid not only does not absolve Mu'āwiyah, but holds him as ultimately responsible for the bloodshed at Karbalā': by appointing Yazīd as his successor, Mu'āwiyah not only violated his peace treaty with Ḥasan, Ḥusayn's brother, but also offended the collective conscience of the faithful at a time when a number of the capable companions of the Prophet were still alive and could be considered as candidates for the Caliphate. But such historical niceties become irrelevant in the light of Khālid's agreement with the fundamentalists that a bloody conflict between the 'Alīds and the Umayyads was inevitable in any case. In support of this thesis, he quotes a tradition, so dear to Shī'ī hearts, according to which 'Alī had predicted Ḥusayn's martyrdom: on the way to the Ṣiffīn battle. When he saw the plain of Karbalā', he is reported to have said: 'Here is the place of their [his grandchildren's] descent and bloodshed'.[65] Thus the epic of Karbalā' was not a one-act play beginning on the tenth day of Muḥarram and ending on the same day: it was a long story which started many years before 61 A.H., and its results stretched over many years after that.[66] The greatest lesson of Karbalā' is that self-sacrifice should be admired for its own sake, just as right should be prized as a thing in itself. The memory of Ḥusayn's martyrdom should be an occasion for jubilation, not mourning, just as the Great 'Īd of the Muslims (on the tenth day of the month of pilgrimage), equally reminiscent of an act of sacrifice, is celebrated by happy festivities.[67] This, incidentally, is what some Cairenes have been doing for centuries, although not in the militant mood envisaged by Khālid.[68]

We can summarise the foregoing survey by saying that all the Sunnī writers mentioned here are unanimous in their rejection of Ibn al-'Arabī's apologia for Yazīd as an honourable man. They also contest Ibn Khaldūn's verdict that Ḥusayn's adventure was based on his erroneous estimation of his strength, and was therefore a wrong move, because they maintain that the matter should not be judged on pragmatic and utilitarian grounds, otherwise the central meaning of Ḥusayn's martyrdom will be lost. Some writers praise Ḥusayn for moral, others for political, reasons. But in the course of their arguments, they all make a number of significant concessions to the Shī'ī theology or Imāmology, apparently without thinking out their logical conclusions. None of these writers, however, bases his argument on a critical analysis of historical texts with a view to discovering their inconsistencies and inaccuracies. Rather, they all rely on individual speculation, and simply read their present thoughts into conventional sources.

* * *

It is now time to return to the Shī'ī revisionist literature on Ḥusayn. Works under this heading are few and far between, especially when compared with the Sunnī literature. One reason for this, as was hinted before, is the enormity of the doctrinal problems facing the Shī'ī revisionists, with the result that any heterodoxy in Shī'īsm has far greater ideological ramifications than in Sunnīsm. In any event, of the few works that have appeared so far the most daring and the most influential has been *Shahīd-ijāvīd* ('The Immortal Martyr') by Ni'matullāh Ṣāliḥī Najaf-ābādī, a religious scholar from the holy city of Qum. Although the book immediately became the object of a heated controversy among religious circles after its publication in 1968, it went largely unnoticed by the secular intelligentsia, a fact which highlights the dichotomy in Iran's cultural life at the time. But it attracted a great deal of publicity during the uproar provoked in Iran in the spring of 1976 by the murder of a religious figure in Iṣfahān, Shams-Abādī, whose alleged murderers were said to be advocates of the author's thesis. The introduction to the book by the Āyatullāh Ḥusayn 'Alī Muntaẓirī, now designated as Khumaynī's successor, vouches for the militant Shī'ī approval of its contents.

What essentially differentiates 'The Immortal Martyr' from the works we have considered so far, and from other Shī'ī writings on the subject, is its semi-scholarly methodology. True, like the bulk of the committed literature on Islam, the book has been written in a style more apposite to political polemics. But it works out its arguments through a detailed, critical analysis of the orthodox sources. Indeed, the underlying notion of all the author's arguments is that a proper understanding of the Shī'ī history is possible only when all its received dogmas are subjected to a thorough reappraisal. He thus challenges and puts to the test many a familiar anecdote in an attempt to prove the utter unreliability of conventional narratives about Ḥusayn, particularly Ḥusayn Kāshifī's *Rawḍat ash-shuhada'*, Majlisī's account in his *Biḥār al-anwār*, Ibn Ṭāwūs's *Luhuf*, and the Persian translation of *Kitāb al-futūḥ* by the pro-Shī'ī Ibn A'tham. Conversely, he does not shy away from freely seeking evidence, in confirmation of his ideas, from Sunnī authorities such as Ṭabarī, Ibn al-Athīr, Ibn Kathīr and Ibn Asākir, whose statements are otherwise treated with the utmost caution by the orthodox Shī'īs.

Najaf-ābādī's untrammelled approach to historical sources stems from his repeatedly avowed intention of verifying every episode in the drama on the touchstone of what he himself calls 'the ordinary causes, and the natural course of events',[69] which is presumably his chosen term for rational guidelines of research. He follows these guidelines so far as they help him to demystify the drama, to purge it of all the supernatural, romantic and exaggerated versions of events. But he never allows them to impair his vision of Ḥusayn as a hero who combined readiness for self-sacrifice with foresight and political wisdom.

Starting from these premises, he aims at refuting the views of two groups: first those Sunnī critics like al-Khaṭīb, Ṭanṭāwī and Najjār, who, in the footsteps of Ibn al-'Arabī, disparage Ḥusayn's revolt as an improvident act, and a challenge to legitimate authority; second, those Shī'ī writers who believe that Ḥusayn's actions, having been ordained by the divine will, and informed by a knowledge exclusive to the Imāms (*'ilm-i imām*) can be neither fully comprehended, nor imitated as an example of political behaviour by ordinary mortals.

It is, however, to the rejection of the latter view that the greater part of his book is devoted. He says in the preface that ever since his youth he was tormented by a glaring contradiction in the popular narratives of the drama: if Ḥusayn did possess the prescience that all Shī'ī Imāms are believed to possess by virtue of their divinely inspired knowledge, why did he deliberately choose a course of action leading to his and his family's destruction?[70] Such a suicidal venture becomes all the more incomprehensible when one remembers that the Muslim community at the time was in dire need of the leadership of the members of the Prophet's family. Najaf-ābādī's dilemma in his younger days thus seems superficially to have been the same as that faced by Māzinī. But, being the product of a Shī'ī environment, his method of solving the dilemma has been different. Contrary to Māzinī, and indeed to the entire Shī'ī consensus, he starts off by questioning the very belief in Ḥusayn's foreknowledge of his fate. He does this not by openly disputing the Shī'ī theological dogma on the Imāms' prescience, but through exposing the absurdity of some of the popular stories about Ḥusayn's foreknowledge. There are specifically seven such stories that he selects for repudiation, but here we summarise only three of them, and his arguments against them, by way of illustration.

The first story has been related by the tenth-century historian Ibn A'tham: after refusing to pay homage of Yazīd in Medina, Ḥusayn visited the Prophet's grave for two consecutive nights. On the second night, he saw the Prophet in a dream, telling him about his impending martyrdom. When Ḥusayn asked the Prophet to take him to his grave, the Prophet answered: 'You have no choice but to remain in the world to become a martyr.' Other Shī'ī chroniclers of the Karbalā' tragedy, including Kāshifī, have quoted this story either directly from Ibn A'tham, or from unnamed sources. In disproving this story, Najaf-ābādī deems it unnecessary to consider whether dreams, even by the Imāms, can serve as rational proofs of historical claims. Instead, he concentrates on discussing whether the fact of Ḥusayn's dreaming in the way alleged in the story could have taken place at all. His research shows that eleven authoritative Sunnī and Shī'ī historians, including Ṭabarī, Ibn al-Athīr, Dinawarī, Shaykh Mufīd and Ṭabarsī, report that Ḥusayn stayed only one night in Medina after meeting the governor; some historians like Ya'qūbī, Ibn 'Asākir and Ibn Abd al-Barr even say that he left Medina on the same evening. So it is highly doubtful, concludes Najaf-ābādī, that Ḥusayn could have seen the dream in question, which is claimed to have taken place on the second night.[71]

The second story is traced back to 'Ibn Ṭāwūs's *Luhūf*. Here Ḥusayn's brother Muḥammad Ibn Ḥanafiyyah is reported to have heard from Ḥusayn, before the latter's departure from Mecca for Kūfah, that the Prophet had once told him (Ḥusayn) in a dream: 'Go forth [to Kūfah]. God has willed to see you killed.' The author has two objections to this story, one historical or factual, the other rational. The historical objection is that according to Ṭabarī and Ibn Qūlūyah, at the time of Ḥusayn's departure from Mecca for Kūfah, Ibn Ḥanafiyyah was in Medina, not

Mecca. Besides, none of the outstanding Muslim historians and traditionists, whether Sunnī or Shī'ī, mentions this story at all. The rational objection is that why should God want to see Ḥusayn killed in that gruesome manner? The death of Ḥusayn was a mortal blow to Islam, and especially to the young Shī'ī community. It was perfectly logical for Yazīd or Ibn Zīyād to wish such a disaster on Islam and Shī'īsm, but not for God. One conceivably logical purpose of God in decreeing Ḥusayn's martyrdom is—as was suggested by Māzinī—the ultimate demeaning of Yazīd: Ḥusayn allowed himself to be killed, at the behest of God, so that his death would arouse popular resentment against Yazīd. But the author dismisses this supposition in the light of the controversial Qur'ānic verse: 'Do not throw yourselves into death with your own hands.' Just as it is a sin to kill the innocent, it is equally a sin to allow oneself to be killed, particularly in the case of an Imām, who is believed to be impeccable and infallible. Even the Qur'ānic verses on the *jihād* enjoin the Muslims primarily to kill the infidel and not to be killed, although those who get killed are entitled to the same reward as that conferred on those who kill.[72]

Finally, there is the story told by Abū Ja'far Ṭabarī, quoting a Sunnī narrator, Sufyān Ibn Wakī', to the effect that before leaving Medina for Kūfah, Ḥusayn was met by two men who offered him their help. Thereupon the Imām pointed to the sky, whence innumerable angels descended; he then said that he could always call on those angels to help him. But he knew that it was useless, since Karbalā' was to be the place where he, together with the members of his family and his companions, would perish, all except his son 'Ali.[73] But this story is also considered worthless because no less than ten of Ḥusayn's companions did survive the Karbalā' massacre, and it was through them that the Muslims came to know the full account of what had happened.[74]

Although Najaf-ābādī thus succeeds in demolishing much of the authority of secondary Shī'ī traditions about Ḥusayn's foreknowledge of his martyrdom, his position is plainly vulnerable because of his refusal, perhaps deliberate, to come face to face with first-hand Shī'ī sources on the subject, namely the great compendia of Kulaynī, Ṭūsī and Shaykh Ṣadūq, which abound in the *ḥadīths* confirming the Imāms' divinely inspired knowledge 'of the past, present and future affairs'.[75] But the author's main intention in discrediting the secondary traditions is not so much to rebut the dogma on the Imāms' prescience as to pave the way for the presentation of his thesis on the uprising itself. Here his difference with the Sunnī modernists is that he does not see the uprising in idealistic perspectives at all. He maintains that Ḥusayn began his movement neither to fulfil his grandfather's forebodings, nor in a reckless mood of defiance, but as a wholly rational and fairly well-planned attempt at overthrowing Yazīd. Political circumstances at the outset looked promising: Yazīd's regime was very unpopular, and the Kufans had rallied to the 'Alīd cause. He himself was sacredly bound, as an Imām, not to condone an unjust and impious government. Motivated thus by a combination of political and religious considerations to start his rebellion, he took all the precautions that a responsible political leader should take before embarking on a momentous enterprise. The trepidations he felt are shown not only by his decision to send Muslim to Kūfah, but also by the doubts that invaded his mind after he heard the news of Muslim's death. From that moment onwards, his actions were purely in self-defence, and should *a fortifori* be free from any reproach of precipitance. So the collapse of the rebellion was entirely due to objective, rational causes, with no room left for the vagaries of supernatural powers.[76]

As can be readily seen, the principal aim of the 'Immortal Martyr' is the politicisation of an aspect of the Shī'ī Imāmology which until recent times was generally interpreted in mystical, lyrical and emotional terms. The result has been a cautious, but growing tendency among the Shī'ī militants to treat the drama of Karbalā' as an essentially human tragedy, and concurrently, to avoid regarding Ḥusayn's heroism as a unique and inimitable event in history, above the capacity of the common run of human beings. This tendency is epitomised by Khumaynī, who, perhaps more than any other Shī'ī theologian of comparable stature, has used the memory of Karbalā' with an acute sense of political urgency. 'It was', he says in his *Wilāyat-i faqīh* ('The Guardianship of the Jurisconsult'), 'to prevent the establishment of monarchy and hereditary succession that Ḥusayn revolted and became a martyr. It was for refusing to succumb to Yazīd's hereditary succession and to recognise his kingship that Ḥusayn revolted, and called all Muslims to rebellion.' Khumaynī likewise calls upon Iranian Muslims 'to create an 'Āshūrā' in their struggle for launching an Islamic state.'[77]

The orthodox religious hierarchy in Iran, however, received Najafābādī's book in a different spirit. They took particular exception to two features of his work: first, his over-reliance on non-Shī'ī sources, and his failure to abide by the rule of *tawthīq*, namely verifying the accuracy and reliability of historical accounts in accordance with Shī'ī criteria; second, his denial of the Imām's prescience, with its clear threat to the doctrine of the Imāms' divinely inspired knowledge, and indeed to the entire edifice of the Shī'ī theory of the Imāmate. This soon led to an acrimonious debate on a host of issues not directly connected with the drama itself, such as the attributes of the Imāms, the nature of their knowledge, the scope left for human will by divine predestination, and the rational limits of self-sacrifice in the fulfilment of religious duties. But these are issued which should be discussed on another occasion.[78]

References

Introduction: the relevance of the past

1 For a discussion of such sociological issues see Brian Turner, *Marx and the End of Orientalism* (London, 1978) especially pp. 39–80, and Brian Turner, *Weber and Islam* (London, 1974) pp. 39–106, 137–50; Maxime Rodinson, *Islam et Capitalisme* (Paris, 1966) particularly pp. 19–45; Maxime Rodinson, *Marxisme et Monde Musulman* (Paris, 1972) pp. 95–129; Jean-Paul Charnay, *Sociologie Religieuse de l'Islam* (Paris, 1977) pp. 325 ff.

2 For an authoritative, modern Shīʻī exposition of this subject see Muḥammad Ḥusayn Ṭabāṭabāʼī, *Shīʻah dar Islām* (Tehran, 1348/1969) pp. 28–58 (English translation by S. H. Nasr, entitled *Shiʻite Islam* (London, 1975) pp. 63–106). See also Muḥammad Jawād Maghnīyah, *At-tafsīr al-kāshif* (Beirut, 1968) vol. I, pp. 13–15, 88.

3 For recent Sunnī presentations of the theory of government and Caliphate see Muḥammad Abū Zahrah, *Al-mujtamaʻ al-insānī fī ẓill al-Islām* (Beirut, n.d.) pp. 154–206. Abū Zahrah was a distinguished Sunnī Egyptian scholar who, although never abandoning his strongly orthodox vision of Islam, worked for reconciliation between Shīʻīs and Sunnīs.

4 Richard P. Mitchell, *The Society of the Muslim Brothers* (London, 1969) p. 320. Cf. ʻAbd Allāh Al-ʻArawī (Laroui), *Al-īdīyulujiyyat' al-ʻArabiyyat' al-muʻāṣirah* (Beirut, 1974) p. 129. A lucid account of the ideas of Khawārij can be found in Henri Laoust's *Les Schismes dans l'Islam* (Paris, 1965) pp. 36–48.

5 Muḥammad Iqbāl, *Reconstruction of Religious Thought in Islam* (Lahore, 1934) p. 4; see also Muḥammad ʻAbduh, *Risālat' at-tawḥīd*, 10th ed. (Cairo, 1361/1941–2) pp. 17–18.

6 See the present author's 'The Political Philosophy of the Ikhwān aṣ-Ṣafā'' in S. H. Nasr (ed.), *The Isma'ili Contributions to the Islamic Civilization* (Tehran, 1977) pp. 25–49.

7 Abu'l Ḥasan al-Māwardī, *Al-aḥkām as-sulṭāniyyah* (Cairo, 1380/1960) pp. 33–4.

8 H. A. R. Gibb, *Studies in the Civilization of Islam* (London, 1962) (hereafter cited as Gibb, *Studies*) pp. 142–3.

9 Erwin I. J. Rosenthal, *Political Thought in Medieval Islam* (Cambridge, 1958) p. 43.

10 Dominique Sourdel, 'L'Imamisme Vu par Cheik al-Mufid', *Revue des Etudes Islamiques*, XL (1972) pp. 217–96.

11 [Abū ʻAbd Allāh Muḥammad] Ibn Idrīs, *Kitāl as-sarā' ir* (Tehran, 1390/1970) p. 203; [Abū Jaʻfar Muḥammad Ibn Ḥasan Ibn ʻAlī] aṭ-Ṭūsī, *An-nihāyah* (Tehran, 1342/1963) p. 358. On the Shīʻī's view about the 'obligatoriness of rulership' (*wujūb ar-riyāsah*) see Ṭūsī's *Kitāb al-ghaybah* (Tehran, 1385/1965)

pp. 4 ff. For a modern version of the same view in support of 'just, temporal government' see Luṭf Allāh Aṣ-Ṣāfī, *Ma'al-Khaṭīb fī khuṭūṭihi'l-'arīḍah* (Tehran, n.d.) pp. 75–81.

12 [Taqī ad-Dīn Aḥmad] Ibn Taymiyyah, *Minhāj as-sunnat'an-nabawiyyah fī naqd kalām ash-shī'at'al-qadariyyah* (Cairo, 1962) vol. I, p.371. See also his *As-sīyāsat' al-shar'iyyah* (Cairo, 1951) p. 173.

13 Gibb, *Studies,* pp. 148–9.

14 See below, Chapter 2.

15 'Abd al-'Azīz al-Badrī, *Al-Islām bayn al-'ulumā' wa'l ḥukkām* (Mecca, n.d.) pp. 156 ff.; the author also depicts the sufferings of members of the Prophet's family, particularly Ḥusayn, Zayd and the Ja'far aṣ-Ṣādiq, in their resistance against unjust rulers (pp. 129–49).

Chapter *1*

1 Cited in Bernard Lewis's *The Origins of Ismailism* (Cambridge, 1940), p. 24.

2 Henri Corbin, *En Islam Iranien,* 4 vols (Paris, 1971) (hereafter cited as Corbin, *Islam Iranien*) especially vol. I, pp. 12 ff.

3 W. Montgomery Watt, *Islam and the Integration of Society* (London, 1961) pp. 106–10.

4 Cited in Y. Marquet's 'La place du travail dans la hiérarchie isma'lienne d'après l'Encylopedie des Frères de la Pureté' *Arabica,* VIII (1961) p. 236.

5 I. P. Petrushevskii, *Islām dar Irān* (Persian translation by Karīm Kishāvarz) (Tehran, 1350/1971) p. 283.

6 George Makdisi, 'L'Islam Hanbalisant', *Revue des Études Islamiques,* XLII (1973) p. 242.

7 S. Husain M. Jafri. *Origins and Early Development of Shi'a Islam* (London, 1979) p. 312.

8 [Abū Ja'far Muḥammad Ibn Ḥasan Ibn 'Alī] aṭ-Ṭūsī, *al-Amālī* (Najaf, 1384/1964) vol. I, p. 19.

9 Fadl Ibn Shādhān Nayshābūrī, *al-Īḍāḥ* (Tehran, 1351/1971) (hereafter cited as Ibn Shādhān, *al-Īḍāḥ*) pp. 125–6.

10 Sayyid al-Murtaḍā, *Kitāb al-intiṣār* (Najaf, 1391) vol. I, p. 6.

11 Muḥammad Kāẓim al-Khurāsānī, *Kifāyat'al-uṣūl* (Tehran, n.d.) vol. II, pp. 68–70. See also Maḥmūd Shihābī's *Taqrīrāt-i uṣūl*, 7th ed. (Tehran, 1344/1965) (hereafter cited as Shihābī, *Taqrīrāt*) pp. 114–17.

12 Corbin, *Islam Iranien*, vol. I, p. xiv; also pp. 181, 186, 210; vol. III, p. 254.

13 *Rasā'il ikhwān aṣ-ṣafā' wa khillān al-wafā'* (Beirut, 1377/1957) vol. I, pp. 42–7.

14 Muḥammad Ḥusayn Kāshif al-Ghiṭā', *Aṣl ash-shī'ah wa uṣūluhā* (Tehran, 1391/1971) pp. 79–80.

15 *Rasā'il,* vol. III, p. 264, also p. 253.

16 'Ibn Khaldūn, *Muqaddimah,* ed. Quatremère, vol. I, pp. 305–7; see also Muḥsin Mahdī's *Ibn Khaldūn's Philosophy of History* (London, 1957).

17 [Taqī ad-Dīn Abī Muḥammad] Maqrīzī, *An-nizā' wa'at-takhāṣum fīmā bayn banī umayyah wa banī hāshim* (Leiden, 1888) especially pp. 69–71.

18 [Abu'l Qāsim Jār Allāh Maḥmūd Ibn 'Umarl] az-Zamakhsharī, *Al-Kashshāf* (Calcutta, 1856) p. 959; [Nāṣir ad-Dīn Abī Sa'īd 'Abd Allāh Ibn 'Umar Ibn Muḥammad ash-Shīrāzī] al-Bayḍāwī *At-tafsīr* (Cairo, 1330/1911) vol. IV, pp. 48, 85; 'Abd Allāh Ibn Aḥmad an-Nasafī, *Madārik at-tanzīl wa ḥaqā-iq at-ta'wīl* (Cairo, 1343/1924) vol. III, p. 70.

19 [al-Faḍl Ibn al-Ḥasan] aṭ-Ṭabarsī, *Majma' al-bayān* (Cairo, 1354/1935) vol. IV, part 7, pp. 66, 67, 152, 239.
20 Corbin, *Islam Iranien*, vol. I, p. 80, also footnote no. 54 on the same page.
21 W. Ivanow, *Studies in Early Persian Ismailism* (Leiden, 1948) pp. 29–30.
22 [Abū Ja'far Muḥammad Ibn 'Alī] aṣ-Ṣadūq, *'Uyūn akhbār ar-Riḍā* (Najaf, 1384/1964) vol. I, p. 30.
23 [Najm ad-Dīn Ja'far Ibn Ḥusayn] Ḥillī, *Sharāyi 'al-Islām* (Persian translation) (Tehran, 1352/1973) vol. VI, pp. 1623–4.
24 Abu'l Qāsim al-Mūsawī al-Khuī, *Tawḍiḥ al-masā'il* (Tehran, 1382/1962) p. 153.
25 Louis Gardet, *L'Islam* (Paris, 1967) p. 88.
26 Fazlur Rahman, *Islam* (London, 1966) p. 35.
27 T. Izutsu, *Ethico-Religious Concepts in the Qur'ān* (Montreal, 1966) pp. 65 ff.
28 D. M. Donaldson, *The Shi'ite Religion* (London, 1933).
29 F. R. C. Bagley, 'The Azhar and Shi'ism', *Muslim World*, vol. L 2 (1960) p. 129.
30 Mullā Muḥammad Mahdī Narāqī, *Muḥriq al-qulūb* (Tehran, 1247/1831) p. 4.
31 Ṭāhā Ḥusayn, *Min tārīkh al-adab al-'Arabī* (Beirut, 1970) vol. I, pp. 463 ff.; Shawqī Ḍayf, *Tārīkh al-'adab al-'Arabi* (*al 'aṣr al-Islāmī*) (Cairo, 1963) vol. II, p. 42; on the 'Alīds' contribution to the religious elegiac poety, see p. 181.
32 Abu'l Qāsim 'Alī Ibn Musa' Ibn Ja 'far Ibn Muḥammad Ibn Muḥammad aṭṬāwūs al-'Alawī al-Kāẓimī, *Muhaj ad-da'wāt wa manhaj al-'ināyāt*, manuscript no. 284, written in 1099/1687, no pagination; Muḥammad Riḍā Ibn Āmīr Muḥammad (Aāsim al-Ḥusaynī a'-Qazvīnī, *Baḥr al-maghfirat*, manuscript no. 210, no date, no pagination (both manuscripts in the Caro Minasian Collection, Wadham College Library, Oxford).
33 [Jamāl ad-Dīn Ḥasan Ibn Sadīd ad-Dīn Yūsuf Ibn 'Alī] Ibn Muṭahhar Ḥillī, 'Minhāj al-karāmah fī ma'rifat'al-imāmiyyah' (hereafter cited as Ḥillī, 'Minhāj'), text in Ibn Taymiyyah's *Minhāj as-sunnat' an-nabawiyyah fī naqḍ kalām ash-shī'at' al-qadariyyah* (Cairo, 1962) (hereafter cited as 'Ibn Taymiyyah, *Minhāj*) vol. I, p. 132.
34 Muḥammad Bāqir Majlisī, *Biḥār al-anwār* (Tehran, 1301–15/1883–97) vol. VIII, pp. 253/344.
35 Ḥillī, '*Minhāj*', pp. 140–5.
36 [Abū Ja'far Muḥammad Ibn Ya'qūb Ibn Isḥāq] al-Kulaynī, *Uṣūl kāfī*, ed. Ḥajj Sayyid Javād Muṣṭafavī (Tehran, n.d.) (hereafter cited as Kulaynī, *Kāfī*) vol. II, p. 216; Ibn Shādhān, *al-Iḍāḥ*, pp. 281–3.
37 Majlisī, quoted by *Kāfī*'s editor, vol. I, p. 217.
38 Ibn Shādhān, *al-Iḍāḥ*, p. 285. There are also quotations by *Kāfī's* editor from Majlisī's *Biḥār*, al-Muḥaddith al-Qummī's *Safīnat' al-biḥār*, and other sources asserting the equality of Arabs and Iranians, and on 'Alī's equal treatment of both, pp. 284–5 (footnote).
39 Henri Massé, *Croyances et Coutumes Persanes* (Paris, 1938) vol. I, pp. 166–70.
40 'Abd al-Ḥusayn Sharaf ad-Dīn al-Mūsawī, *An-naṣṣ wa'l-ijtihād* (Najaf, 1384/1964) pp. 315 ff.
41 Ibid. pp. 82–4, 103, 156; see also 'Abd al-Jalīl Ibn Abi 'l-Ḥusayn Ibn Abu'l-Faḍl al-Qazvīnī, *Kitāb an-naqḍ, ma'rūf bi ba'ḍ mathālib an-nawāṣib fī naqḍ ba'ḍ faḍā'iḥ ar-rawāfiḍ* (Tehran, 1371/1951) pp. 623–5.
42 Abu'l Ḥasan al-Khunayzī, *Ad-da'wat' al-islāmiyyah ilā wāḥdat' ahl as-sunnah wa 'l-imāmiyyah* (Beirut, 1376/1956) vol. I, pp. 96–107.
43 For further specifications of these works, see above, note 33.
44 Shihābī, *Taqrīrāt*, p. 53.

45 Ibn Taymiyyah, *Minhāj*, vol. I, pp. 6–9, vol. II, p. 360; cf. M. St. Guyard, 'Le fatwā d'Ibn Taymiyyah sur les Nosairis', *Journal Asiatique* XVIII (1871) pp. 162–78.

46 Ibn Taymiyyah, *Minhāj*, vol. I, pp. 56–60, 75.

47 Ibid. vol. I, p. 384.

48 Ibid. vol. II, pp. 361–76.

49 Ibid. vol. I, pp. 379–85.

50 Ibid. vol. II, p. 361.

51 [Abu'l Ḥasan Ibn Muḥammad] 'Abd al-Jabbār [Asadābādī al-Hamadānī], *Al-mughnī fī abwāb at-tawḥīd wa'l-'adl* (Cairo, 1966) vol. XX, pp. 112–97.

52 Qazvīnī, *Kitāb an-naqḍ*, p. 625.

53 Ibn Taymiyyah, *Minhāj*, vol. I, p. 28.

54 Ibid. vol. I, p. 43.

55 Ibid. vol. I, p. 27.

56 M. Molé, 'Les Kubrawīya entre Sunnisme et Shiisme', *Revue des Études Islamiques*, XXIX 1 (1961) (hereafter cited as Molé, 'Les Kubrawīya') pp. 61–142.

57 Ibid. p. 74.

58 Ibid. p. 99.

59 D. S. Margoliouth, 'Nūrbakhshīya', in *Encyclopedia of Islam*, 1st ed.

60 Molé, 'Les Kubrawīya', p. 130.

61 Ibid. p. 129.

62 Z. Thābitīyān, *Asnād va nāmih-hāy-i tārīkhī va ijtimā'ī dawrān-i Ṣafavī* (Tehran, 1343) pp. 231 ff.

63 Hamid Algar, 'Shī'īsm and Iran in the Eighteenth Century', in T. Naff and R. Owen (eds), *Studies in Eighteenth Century Islamic History* (London, 1977) pp. 288 ff.

64 Ibid. p. 292.

65 Ibid. p. 299.

66 Muḥammad 'Abduh, *Risālat' at-tawḥīd*, 10th ed. (Cairo, 1942) pp. 12–19.

67 For a definition of *Salafiyyah* and its political significance see below, Chapter 3, section 1. For Riḍā's views on Shī'īsm see his *As-sunnah wa'sh-shī'iah* (2 vols in 1) (Cairo, 1366/1947) pp. 4–49. For his earlier pro-Shī'ī stance see ibid. pp. 14–25; also below Chapter 3, section 1.

68 Jamāl ad-Dīn al-Ḥusaynī al-Afghānī and Muḥammad 'Abduh, *Al-u'irwat' al-wuthqā wa'th-thawrat' al-kubrā* (Cairo, 1957) p. 242.

69 On the Shī'ī leadership of the Iraqi revolt of 1919–20, see Farīq al-Muẓhir, *Al-ḥaqā' iq an-nāṣi 'ah fi'th thawrat' al-irāqiyyah* (Baghdad, 1371/1952) pp. 192, 243–5; *Abd ar-Raḥmān al-Bazzāz, Muḥāḍarāt 'an al-'Irāq min al-iḥtilāl ḥatta'l-istiqlāl* (Cairo, 1954) pp. 29, 33 n. 4; 'Abd Allāh al-Fayyāḍ, *Ath-thawrat' al-'Irāqiyyat' al-kubrā* (Baghdad, 1963) pp. 81–2: Sayyid 'Abd ar-Razzāq al-Ḥasanī, *Al-'Irāq fī dawray al-iḥtilāl wa'l-intidāb* (?Najaf, 1354/1935) vol. I. pp. 71 ff.; Kāmil Salmān Jubūrī, *Al-Kūfah fī thawrat' al-'ishrīn* (Najaf, 1392/1972) pp. 13–14 and 229–33; and Rajā Ḥusayn Ḥusaynī al-Khaṭṭāb, *Al-'Iraq bayn 1921 wa 1927* (Najaf, 1976) pp. 272 ff.

70 Aḥmad Amīn, *Ḍuḥa 'l-Islām*, 6th ed. (Cairo, 1936) (hereafter cited as Amīn, *Ḍuḥa 'l-Islām*) vol. III, pp. 209, 233, 250, 267; *Fajr al-Islām*, 8th ed. (Cairo, 1933) (hereafter cited as Amīn, *Fajr al-Islām*) p. 112. For a study of Amīn's ideas in general see Detlev Khalid, 'Aḥmad Amīn and the Legacy of Muḥammad 'Abduh', *Islamic Studies*, LX 1 (1970), pp. 1–32. Cf. Aḥmad Amīn, *My Life*, translated from Arabic with an introduction by J. Boullata (Leiden, 1978).

71 Amīn, *Fajr al-Islām*, p. 276.
72 Amīn, *Ḍuḥa 'l-Islām*, vol. III, p. 221; see also pp. 226 ff.
73 Ibid, p. 244.
74 *Fajr al-Islām*, p. 274, footnote 1. Also *Ḍuḥa 'l-Islām*, vol. III, p. 247.
75 Sayyid Muḥammad Ṣādiq aṣ-Ṣadr's introduction to *An-naṣṣ wa 'l-ijtihād* (above, note 40) pp. 6–44.
76 A summary of Kāshif al-Ghiṭā's biography can be found in his *Aṣl ash-Shī'ah* wa *uṣūluha* (above, note 14) p. 20.
77 'Abd al-Ḥusayn Aḥmad al-Amīnī an-Najafī, *Al-ghadīr, fi'l kitāb wa's-sunnah wa'l adab* (Beirut, 1967). For Amīnī's biography and views see Sayyid Ja'far Shahīdī and Muḥammad Riḍā Ḥakīmī, *Yādnāmih-i Amīnī* (Tehran, 1352), and Muḥammad Riḍā Ḥakīmī (ed.), *Ḥamāsih-i ghadīr* (Tehran, 1396).
78 Maghnīyah is a prolific writer, and it is difficult to identify any one of his works as the definitive source for his ideas on the Shī'īs' differences with the Sunnīs. However, some examples of these can be found in his *Min hunā wa hunāk* (Beirut, 1388/1968) pp. 95–8, 158, 160, 163, 188–9, 229–36, 244–59.
79 Some of Muṭahharī's and Sharī'atī's views will be discussed in Chapters 4 and 5.
80 Muḥammad Taqī Sharī'atī, *Khilāfat va valāyat az naẓar-i Qur'ān va sunnat* (Tehran, 1351/1972) pp. 111–14.
81 Maḥmū Shihābī, *Al-Islām wa'sh-Shī'ah (al-imāmiyyah) fī asāsiha'ttārīkhī wa kiyāniha'l-i'tiqādī* (Tehran, 2536/1978) pp. 400–2.
82 Muḥammad aṣ-Ṣādiqī, *'Alī wa'l-ḥākimūn* (Beirut. 1389/1969).
83 Shaykh Rāḍī Āl Yāsīn, *Sulḥ al-Ḥasan* (Kāẓimiyyah, 1384/1965).
84 See Chapter 5, the section 'Martyrdom'.
85 S. Husain M. Jaffri, *Origins and Early Development of Shi'i Islam*, pp. 259–83.
86 Kāshif al-Ghiṭā, *Aṣl ash-Shī'ah*, p. 59; Khunayzī, *Ad-da'wat' al-Islāmiyyah,* pp. 15 ff.
87 See the present author's 'Islam and Socialism in Egypt', *Middle Eastern Studies*, IV 2 (1968) pp. 156 ff.
88 Among the examples of this 'historical revisionism' one should mention Ṭahā Ḥusayn's *Al-fitnat'al-kubrā* (Cairo, 2 vols, 1956, 1959), *Ash-Shaykhān* (Cairo, 1960), *Al-wa'd al-ḥaqq* (Cairo, 1960); for other examples, see notes 57, 61, 62 and 65 to Chapter 5.
89 On modern Sunnī criticisms of the Prophet's Companions see Shaykh Maḥmūd Abū Rayyah, *Aḍwā' 'alā's-sunnat' al-Muḥammadiyyah* (Cairo, 1958).
90 *Majallat' al-Azhar*, XXX 8 (1959) supplement.
91 *Two Historical Documents*, Dār al-Taqreeb (Cairo, 1383) pp. 8–9. See also Muḥammad Taqī al-Qummī, *Qiṣṣat'at-taqrīb* (Cairo, 1960) pp. 6, 9, 11.
92 *Middle East Journal*, XIV (Winter 1960) pp. 452–3, entered under 'August 7'.
93 See, for instance, the collection of statements by the 'Ulamā' of various schools in support of the PLO: *Kibār 'ulama' al-Islām yuṭālibūn al-musli mīn bi da'm mujāhidī ḥarakah 'Fatḥ'* (Dār Abī Dharr, 1396/1976).
94 Algar, *Shī'īsm*, p. 298.
95 See Yaḥyā Hāshim Ḥasan Farghal, *Nash'at'al-ārā' wa'l madhāhib wa'l firaq al-kalāmiyyah* (Cairo, 1972) where he argues that Shī'ī ideas inevitably lead to belief in Divine incarnation, and merge with the theses of the Extremists (*Ghulāt*) (pp. 138 ff.); Muḥammad Abū Zahrah, *Al-madhāhib al-Islāmiyyah* (Cairo, n.d.) especially pp. 54–7; and issues of *Liwā' al-Islām*, particularly XI 5 (1957) pp. 321–9; XIII 6 (1959) pp. 339–40; XVII 3 (1963) pp. 187–201.

96 See the account of a symposium on *ijtihād* in *Liwā' al-Islām*, xv 2 (March 1961) pp. 98–100, also xv 4, pp. 228–30 and xv 5, pp. 293–5, where Zakariyya al-Barrī argues against the individual *ijtihād*, but recommends its collective form.

97 A clear example of this line of thought is Amīnī's *Al-ghadīr* (above, note 77), but see also Ṣayyid Muḥammad Ḥusayn Tabāṭabā'ī, *Shī'ah dar Islām*, op. cit., pp. 7–10.

98 S. Kh. (Salmān al-Khāqānī?), *Ash-shī'ah wa's-sunnah fi'l mīzān* (Beirut, 1397/1977); Muḥammad 'Alī az-Za'bī, *Lā sunnah wa lā shī'ah* (Beirut, 1961).

Chapter 2

1 Halil Inalcik, 'The Rise of the Ottoman Empire' in *The Cambridge History of Islam*, vol. I (London, 1970) pp. 320–2.

2 T. W. Arnold, *The Caliphate*, with a concluding chapter by Sylvia Haim (London, 1965) (hereafter cited as Arnold, *Caliphate*) pp. 164–5.

3 Haim, 'The Abolition of the Caliphate and Its Aftermath' (hereafter cited as Haim, 'Abolition') in Arnold, *Caliphate*, p. 209.

4 Arnold, *Caliphate*, p. 180

5 Quoted in A. Nallino's 'La Fine del Cosi Detto Califfato Ottomano' (hereafter cited as Nallino, 'Califfato Ottomano') in *Oriento Moderno*, vol. IV (1924) pp. 141–2.

6 Bernard Lewis, *The Emergence of Modern Turkey* (London, 1961), pp. 257–8.

7 W. C. Smith, *Islam in India* (London, 1946) (hereafter cited as Smith, *Islam in India*) p. 206.

8 Nallino, 'Califfato Ottomano', pp. 139–41.

9 Haim, 'Abolition', pp. 210–18.

10 'Califat et souveraineté nationale', *Revue de Monde Musulmane*, LIX (1925) especially pp. 3, 10, 18, 50, 53, 64, 67, and 73.

11 'Abd ar-Raḥmān al-Kawākibī, 'Umm al-qurā' in Muḥammad 'Amārah (ed.), *Al a'māl al-kāmilah* (Beirut, 1975) pp. 356–8. See also George Antonius, *The Arab Awakening* (London, 1938) pp. 97–8; Hazem Zaki Nuseibeh, *Ideas of Arab Nationalism* (New York, 1956) p. 48; Ziene N. Zeine, *Arab–Turkish Relations and the Emergence of Arab Nationalism* (Beirut, 1958) p. 70.

12 *Umm al-Qurā*, p. 365.

13 'Dokumente zum Kampf der Araber um ihre Unabhangigkeit', *Die Welt des Islams*, VIII (1923–6) p. 99.

14 Jalāl ad-Dīn as-Suyūṭī, *Ḥusn al-muhāḍarah min akhbār miṣr wa'l qāhirah* (1327) vol. II, p. 24.

15 A's Suyuti, *History of the Caliphs*, translated by H. S. Jarrel (Amsterdam, 1970) p. 500–1.

16 Aziz Ahmad, *Studies in Islamic Culture in the Indian Environment* (Oxford, 1964) (hereafter cited as Ahmad, *Islamic Culture*) pp. 62–3.

17 Smith, *Islam in India*, p. 198. The Khilafatist movement was, in fact, more radical and more militant than the Congress (p. 200).

18 Smith, *Islam in India*, p. 204.

19 Lini S. May, *The Evolution of Indo-Muslim Thought after 1857* (Lahore, 1970) p. 206.

20 Ahmad, *Islamic Culture*, pp. 66–8. See also Ashfaque Husain, *The Quintessence of Islam*, 2nd ed. (London, 1960) p. 16.

21 Muḥammad Iqbāl, *The Reconstruction of Muslim Thought* (London, 1934) p. 150.
22 Ibid. p. 149.
23 Ibid. pp. 150–1.
24 'Qarār al-hay'at' al-'ilmiyyat' al-dīniyyah bi'd-dīyār al-miṣriyyah fī sha'n al-khilāfah', in *Nūr al-Islām* (Sha'bān, 1350/1931) pp. 590–4.
25 For different interpretations of 'Abd ar-Rāziq's ideas see C. C. Adams, *Islam and Modernism in Egypt* (London, 1933) pp. 259–69; G. Kampffmeyer, 'Egypt and Western Asia', in *Whither Islam?* (London, 1932) p. 142; Albert Hourani, *Arabic Thought in the Liberal Age* (hereafter cited as Hourani, *Arabic Thought*) (Oxford, 1962), pp. 183–8; also note 37 below. Here we have concentrated on those elements of 'Abd ar-Rāziq's thought, which, despite his unconventional remarks, could have brought him nearer to religionists.
26 'Alī 'Abd ar-Rāziq, *Al-Islām wa uṣūl al-ḥukm*, with introduction and comments by Mamdūḥ Ḥaqqī (hereafter cited as ar-Rāziq, *Islām*) (Beirut, 1966) p. 40.
27 Ibid. p. 46.
28 See, for instance, his book *Al-ijmā' fi'sh-sharī 'at' al-Islāmiyyah* (Cairo, 1947).
29 ar-Rāziq, *Islām*, p. 79, also p. 74.
30 Ibid. p. 118.
31 Ibid. pp. 143 ff.
32 Ibid. pp. 167–77, also pp. 191 ff.
33 Ibid. pp. 13–17, 199.
34 Ibid. p. 201.
35 Ibid. p. 82.
36 *Ḥukm haya'ah kibār al-'ulamā' fī kitāb al-Islām wa uṣūl al-ḥukm* (Cairo, 1925) pp. 29–30.
37 Shaykh Muḥammad Bakhīt, *Ḥaqīqat' al-Islām wa uṣūl al-ḥukm* (Cairo, 1926) p. 446.
38 See, for instance, the postscript by the Iranian Muslim scholar, Muḥammad Riḍā Ḥakīmī to this author's book *Andīshih-yi sīyāsī-yi 'Arab* ['Arab Political Thought'] (Tehran, 2536/1977) pp. 279–87.
39 E. I. J. Rosenthal, *Islam in the Modern National State* (Cambridge, 1965) p. 89.
40 Ibid. p. 86.

Chapter 3

1 Aḥmad Ṭarabayn, *Al-waḥdat' al-'Arabiyyah bayn* 1945–66, p. 133. Also A. L. Tibawi, *Anglo-Arab Relations and the Question of Palestine* (London, 1977) pp. 152–6.
2 For a study of Rashīd Riḍā's idea of the Caliphate in the context of his modernism see Malcolm Kerr, *Islamic Reform* (Berkeley, 1966) (hereafter cited as Kerr, *Reform*) pp. 153–208; and Albert Hourani, *Arabic Thought* pp. 222–44. Here, our emphasis is on the connection between Riḍā's theses on the Caliphate and his notion of the Islamic state.
3 Riḍā's broad-mindedness, however, broke down when he came to deal with the Shī'ī polemists; see above, Chapter 1, section 2.
4 In his excellent introduction to the French translation of Riḍā's *Al-khilāfah*, Henry Laoust has *mainly* discussed the first two stages of the argument analysed here; see his *Le Califat dans la doctrine de Rashīd Riḍā* (Beirut, 1938) p. 2.
5 Muḥammad Rashīd Riḍā, *Al-khilāfah aw' al-imāmat' al-uẓmā* (Cairo, n.d.)

(hereafter cited as Riḍā, *Al-khilāfah*) comprising the author's articles on the subject published in *al-Manār*, vols XXIII and XXIV, year 1341/1922, p. 37.

6 Ibid. p. 41.
7 Ibid. p. 40.
8 Ibid. pp. 11–13, 57–61.
9 Ibid. p. 18; see also Māwardī, *Al-aḥkām as-sulṭāniyyah*, p. 15.
10 Muḥammad 'Abduh, *Risālat' at-tawḥīd*, pp. 25–6.
11 Riḍā, *Al-khilāfah*, pp. 60, 65.
12 Ibid. pp. 6, 38.
13 See above, Chapter 2.
14 Riḍā, *Al-khilafah*, p. 10.
15 Ibid. pp. 30–3.
16 Ibid. p. 35.
17 Ibid. pp. 67–71.
18 Ibid. pp. 66.
19 Ibid. p. 77.
20 Ibid. p. 78.
21 Ibid. p. 79.
22 Ibid. pp. 76–106.
23 Ibid. p. 79.
24 Ibid. pp. 77, 78, 96.
25 Ibid. pp. 78, 106, 112.
26 Ibid. pp. 94, 142; also pp. 30–3.
27 Ibid. pp. 57–60.
28 Ibid. pp. 90–1: Hourani, *Arabic Thought*, p. 152.
29 E. I. J. Rosenthal, *Islam in the Modern National State* (Cambridge, 1965) (hereafter cited as Rosenthal, *Islam*) p. 72.
30 For Ḥusayn's own interpretation of the criticism against his work see his *Fi'l adab al-jāhilī* (Cairo, 1926) pp. 7–67. On the antecedents of his work see the article by Aḥmad Kamāl Zakīy in *Ṭahā Ḥusayn kamā ya'rifuhu kuttāb 'aṣrih* (Cairo, n.d.) p. 182; also G. E. von Grunebaum, *Islam: Essays in the Nature and Growth of a Cultural Tradition* (London, 1955) p. 209.
31 Riḍā, *Al-khilāfah*, p. 90.
32 Louis Maillot, *L'Introduction à l'Etude du Droit Musulman* (Paris, 1953) p. 180; Y. Linant de Bellefonds, *Traité de Droit Musulman* (The Hague, 1965) p. 43.
33 See Chapter 5, section 1.
34 Riḍā, *Al-khilāfah*, pp. 91–4.
35 Ibid. p. 91.
36 Ibid. pp. 94–5.
37 Ibid. pp. 13–15.
38 Ibid. pp. 61–2.
39 See, for instance, *al-Manār*, vol. XII, pp. 390–6; vol. XVI, pp. 774–6; vol. XXV, p. 761, etc.
40 Hourani, *Arabic Thought*, p. 231.
41 Kerr, *Islamic Reform,* p. 176.
42 Hourani, *Arabic Thought*, p. 234.
43 Riḍā, *Al-khilāfah*, pp. 124–5.
44 E. I. J. Rosenthal, 'Some Reflections on the Separation of Religion and Politics in Modern Islam' (hereafter cited as Rosenthal, 'Reflections') *Islamic Studies,* III (1964), p. 264.

45 Richard P. Mitchell, *The Society of Muslim Brothers* (London, 1969) (hereafter cited as Mitchell, *Brothers*) p. 4. See also Ra'ūf Shalabī, *Ash-Shaykh Ḥasan al-Bannā' wa madrasatuh 'Al-Ikhwān al-Muslimun'* (Cairo, 1978) pp. 133–9.
46 Zakariyyā Sulaymān Bayyūmī, *Al-ikhwān al-muslimūn* (Cairo, 1979) (hereafter cited as Bayyūmī, *Al-ikhwān*) p. 90.
47 Ibid. p. 90, footnote 2; also Mitchell, *Brothers*, p. 14.
48 Bayyūmī, *Al-ikhwān*, p. 91.
49 Ibid. p. 118.
50 Mitchell, *Brothers*, pp. 89, 99; also Anwar el-Sadat, *In Search of Identity* (London, 1978) pp. 22–4; for Sadat's less inhibited accounts of the Free Officers' relations with the Brothers, see his *Revolt on the Nile* (London, 1957) pp. 26 ff., 30, 43 ff., 61 ff.; also Ishaq Musa Husaini, *The Moslem Brethren* (Beirut, 1956) p. 118.
51 Mitchell, *Brothers*, pp. 151–62.
52 Editorials of the *Majallat' al-Azhar*, issues of February and October, vol. XL (1968).
53 Ibid., especially the October issue, articles entitled 'The Jewish Attitude towards Islam and the Muslims in the "Initial Era" [*al-'aṣr al-awwal*]', 'The Jewish Role in the Hostility against the Foundation of Islam', and *'Isrā 'īliyyāt* in Qur'ānic Commentaries and the *Ḥadīth*'.
54 Nadav Safran, *Egypt in Search of Political Community* (Cambridge, Mass., 1961) p. 234.
55 Muḥammad Ghazzālī, *Min hunā na'lam* (Cairo, 1948) (hereafter cited as Ghazzālī, *Min hunā*) p. 49 (English translation by Isma'il el-Faruqi entitled *Our Beginning in Wisdom* (New York, 1975) p. 21).
56 Mitchell, *Brothers*, pp. 234–5.
57 Raf'at as-Sa'īd, *Ḥasan al-Bannā* (Cairo, 1977) pp. 83 ff.
58 Ghazzālī, *Kifāḥ dīn*, 3rd ed. (Cairo, 1965) pp. 133–9.
59 Ghazzālī, *Min hunā*, p. 25.
60 Ibid. pp. 22–3.
61 Ibid. p. 55.
62 Ibid. p. 21.
63 Ibid. p. 30–1.
64 Hourani, *Arabic Thought*, pp. 164–7.
65 Rashīd Riḍā, *Nidā' ila'l-jins al-laṭīf*, 2nd ed. (Cairo, 1947); see also Ṣalāḥ ad-Dīn (ed.), *Fatāwā al-Imām Muḥammad Rashīd Riḍā* (Beirut, 1970); see especially his fatwās on the abuses of polygamy (vol. I, pp. 118–27), teaching literacy to women (pp. 66–7), equality between men and women in all matters except 'private and public guardianships' (*al-wilāyāt al-'āmmah wa'l-khāṣṣah*) (vol. III, pp. 933–4), the unveiling of women's faces (vol. II, pp. 679–83) and women's praying in mosques (vol. II, pp. 436–7).
66 Ghazzālī, *Min hunā*, pp. 182–4.
67 Ibid. pp. 199–205.
68 Ibid. p. 179.
69 Ibid. pp. 176–7.
70 Ibid. p. 207.
71 For a sympathetic account of their activities and programmes, see Riḍā Gul-surkhī, 'Fidā'īyān-i Islām, āghāz-gar-i junbish-i muṣallaḥānih dar Irān', *Iṭṭilā'āt*, no. 15843, Urdībihisht 10, 1358 (30 April 1979) (hereafter cited as Gul-surkhī, 'Fida'īyān-i Islām'), where there is also a reference to a book by

Navvāb Ṣafavī himself, entitled *Barnāmih-i ḥukūmat-i fidā'īyān-i Islām* (Tehran, 1329); also Muḥammad Riḍā Hakīmī, *Tafsīr-i āftāb* (Tehran, 1357/1977) (hereafter cited as Ḥakīmī, *Tafsīr-i āftāb*) pp. 231 ff.

72 Gul-surkhī, 'Fidā'īyān-i Islām', p. 4.

73 Ḥakīmī, *Tafsīr-i āftāb*, p. 234.

74 Faḍl Ibn Ḥasan Ṭabarsī, *Majma' al-Bayān* (Cairo, 1354/1935, vol. III, pp. 187–8.

75 Muḥammad Ḥusayn Ṭabāṭabā'ī, *Al-mīzān fī tafsīr al-Qur'ān* (Beirut, 1390/1970) (hereafter cited as Ṭabāṭabā'ī, *Al-mīzān*) vol V, pp. 328 ff.

76 Muḥammad Rashīd Riḍā, *Tafsīr al-Manār* (Cairo, n.d.) (hereafter cited as Riḍā, *Tafsīr*) vol. VI, pp. 365–6. Riḍā explains that the term 'fighting against God' (*ḥarb Allāh*) has been used four times in the Qur'ān: only in one of these it means usury, and in the rest the normal meaning of 'resorting to arms and highway robbery' (*ishhār aṣ-silāḥ wa qat' as-sabīl*) is intended (ibid. p. 356).

77 P. J. Vatikiotis, *The Modern History of Egypt* (London, 1969) pp. 194–5.

78 Riḍā, *Tafsīr*, vol. VI, p. 355.

79 Ṭabāṭabā'ī, *Al-mīzān*, vol. V, p. 326.

80 Riḍā, *Tafsīr*, p. 366.

81 *The Holy Quran with English Translation and Commentary* (published 'under the auspices of Hazrat Mirza Bashir-ud-Din Mahmud Ahmad') (Qadian, India, 1947) vol. I, pp. 622–3.

82 For personal appreciations of Maudūdī's life and ideas see *Islamic Perspectives: Studies in Honour of Sayyid Abul A'la Mawdudi*, edited by Khurshid Ahmad, Zafar Ishaq Ansari (Jeddah, 1979) especially pp. 265–89. For a critical review of the Jamā'at's activities see Kalim Bahaduri, 'The Jama'at-i-Islami of Pakistan: Ideology and Political Action' (hereafter cited as Bahaduri, 'Jama'at-i-Islāmī'), *International Studies*, XIV (New Delhi, 1975) pp. 69–84, where a comprehensive bibliography is also given.

83 Manzooruddin Ahmad, 'Sovereignty of God in the Constitution of Pakistan', *Islamic Studies*, IV (1965) pp. 201–33. Richard S. Wheeler, *The Politics of Pakistan* (Ithaca, N.Y., 1970) pp. 151 ff. Leonard Binder, *Religion and Politics in Pakistan* (Berkeley, 1961) (hereafter cited as Binder, *Pakistan*) pp. 315–44. Rosenthal, *Islam*, pp. 203 ff.

84 G. W. Choudhury, 'New Pakistan's Constitution', *The Middle East Journal*, XXVIII (Winter 1974) p. 12.

85 Ibid. p. 11.

86 Binder, *Pakistan,* p. 75.

87 Abu'l A'lā Maudūdī, *Mafāhīm Islāmiyyah ḥawl ad-dīn wa' d-dawlah* (Kuwait, 1394/1974) pp. 146–9. For Maudūdī's differences with the traditionalist 'Ulamā' see Binder, *Pakistan*, pp. 73 ff.

88 L. S. May, *The Evolution of Indo-Muslim Thought* (Lahore, 1970) (hereafter cited as May, *Indo-Muslim Thought*) p. 324.

89 K. K. Aziz, *The Making of Pakistan* (London, 1967) pp. 105–6.

90 May, *Indo-Muslim Thought*, pp. 324, 336–7.

91 Maudūdī, *The Process of Islamic Revolution* (Lahore, 1955) (hereafter cited as Maudūdī, *Islamic Revolution*) pp. 25–6.

92 Ibid. p. 4.

93 Ibid. p. 34.

94 Ibid. p. 4.

95 Ibid. pp. 37–55.

96 Ibid. p. 62.
97 Ibid. p. 35.
98 Ibid. p. 5.
99 Ibid. p. 22.
100 Ibid. pp. 8–10.
101 Ibid. pp. 7–8.
102 See his *Islamic Law*, edited by Khursid Ahmad (Karachi, 1955) p. 57; also *Islamic Law and Constitution* (Karachi, 1955); *Political Theory of Islam* (Lahore, address delivered in 1939) (hereafter cited as Maudūdī, *Political Theory of Islam*); Rosenthal, *Islam*, pp. 137–53.
103 May, *Indo-Muslim Thought*, pp. 336–7.
104 Maudūdī, *Mā hiya'l-Qādīyāniyyah* (Kuwait, 1967) p. 178.
105 Maudūdī, *Al-Islām fī muwājahat 'at-taḥadiyyat' al-mu 'aṣirah* (Kuwait, 1391/1971) pp. 229–40.
106 Ibid. p. 238.
107 Ibid. p. 240.
108 Maudūdī, *Al-Islām al-yawm* (Kuwait, 1973) p. 62, also pp. 49–52. See also his *Mas'alah milkiyyat'al-arḍ fi'l Islām* (Kuwait, 1389/1969) where he argues that it is illegal to take lands out of private hands in order to collectivise them (pp. 91–2).
109 Maudūdī, *Al-Islām fī muwājahah*, p. 234; see also his *Islamic Way of Life* (Lahore, 1955) p. 44.
110 Maudūdī, *Political Theory of Islam*, p. 62.
111 Ibid. p. 111.
112 Ibid. pp. 220–1.
113 Herbert Feldman, *From Crisis to Crisis* (Oxford, 1972) p. 73. See also Lawrence Ziring, *The Ayyub Khan Era* (Syracuse, 1971) pp. 46–7; and Bahaduri, 'Jamā'at-i-Islāmī', p. 74, where there is also a reference to an article in *Tarjumān al-Qur'ān* defending Mauduḍī's decision on canonical grounds.
114 See Muḥammad Asad's *The Principles of State and Government in Islam* (Berkeley, 1961) especially pp. 30 ff. The crucial feature of Asad's scheme of the Islamic state is that in identifying its principles, he relies solely on the 'clear textual ordinances' (*nuṣūṣ*) of the Qur'ān and the Tradition as constituting 'the real, eternal *sharī'ah* of Islam'. He thus excludes *fiqh* or jurisprudence, holding that "the far larger area of things and activities which the Law-Giver has left unspecified – neither enjoining nor forbidding them in *naṣṣ* [textually defined] terms – must be regarded as allowable (*mubāḥ*) from the *shar'ī* point of view" (ibid. p. 13). This obviously allows considerable scope for a libertarian interpretation of Islam.

Chapter 4

1 Rifā'ah Rāfi' aṭ-Ṭahṭāwī, *Manāhij al-albāb al-'aṣriyyah fī mabāhij al-ādāb al'aṣriyyah* (Cairo, 1912) p. 99. See also Albert Hourani, *Arabic Thought*, p. 99.
2 On 'Abd Allāh Nadīm's concept of *waṭan*, see Angelo Sammarco, *Histoire de l'Égypte Moderne* (Cairo, 1937) p. 318.
3 Shaykh Ḥusayn Marṣafī, *Al-kalim ath-thamān* (Cairo, 1298/1880–1) pp. 2–15.
4 Sylvia Haim, 'Islam and the Theory of Arab Nationalism', *Die Welt des Islams* (New Series), IV (1956) pp. 132–3.
5 Hisham Sharabi, *Arab Intellectuals and the West* (London, 1970) p. 119.

6 'Abd ar-Raḥmān al-Bazzāz, *Min waḥy al-'urūbah* (Cairo, n.d.) (hereafter cited as Bazzāz, *Min waḥy al-'urūbah*) p. 199.
7 Ibid. p. 200.
8 Ibid. p. 200–1.
9 Ibid. p. 206, see also Bazzāz's other book, *Hādhih qawmiyyatunā* (Cairo, 1964) p. 62.
10 Muḥammad Darwazah, *Al-waḥdat' al-'Arabiyyah* (Beirut, 1957) pp. 60 ff., also *Nash'at' al-ḥarakat' al-'Arabiyyat' al-ḥadīthah* (Beirut, 1949) pp. 10–14. Sāṭi' al-Ḥusrī, *Mā hīya' al-qawmiyyah*, 2nd ed. (1963) pp. 251–7. Bazzāz, *Hādhih qawmiyyatunā*, pp. 238–9, where similar views by such Christian writers as Qusṭantīn Zurayq are quoted.
11 For fundamentalist denunciations of nationalism, see Muḥammad Aḥmad Bāshmīl, *Al-qawmiyyah fī naẓar al-Islām* (Beirut, 1960).
12 Abdu'l 'Azīz ad-Dawrī, 'Al-juzūr at-tārīkhiyyah li'l-qawmiyyat' al-'Arabiyyah' in *Dirāsāt' al-qawmiyyah* (Beirut, 1960) p. 13. For Rashīd Riḍā's attacks on the Umayyads see his *Al-khilāfah aw' al-imāmat' al-uẓmā*, pp. 44–5, 130.
13 On the relationship between Arab nationalist and Islamic tendencies, see Aḥmad Ṭarabayn, *Al-waḥdat' al-'Arabiyyah fī tārīkh mashriq al-mu'āṣir, 1800–1958* (?Beirut, n.d.) pp. 326–42.
14 Marcel Colombe, *L'Évolution de l'Égypte* (Paris, 1951) pp. 171–2.
15 *Majallat' al-Azhar*, XXIV (1952) pp. 137–40.
16 Ibid. XXVII (1956) pp. 937–41, XXVIII (1956) pp. 337–44.
17 For a critical study of the ideology of Iranian nationalism in the nineteenth century see Firaydūn Ādamiyyat, *Andīshi-hā-yi Mīrzā Āqā Khān Kirmānī* (Tehran, 1346/1967) pp. 248–68, *Andīshi-hā-yi Mīrzā Fatḥ 'Alī Ākhūnd Zādih* (Tehran, 1349/1971) pp. 109–36, *Andīshi-yi taraqqī va ḥukūmat dar 'aṣr-i Sipahsālār* (Tehran, 1349/1971) pp. 160–2.
18 Shaykh ar-Ra'īs Qājār, *Ittiḥād-i Islām* (Bombay, 1894) pp. 74–5.
19 Murtaḍā Muṭahharī and S. H. Nasr, 'The Religious Sciences', in *The Cambridge History of Iran* (Cambridge, 1975) vol. IV, pp. 464–5.
20 Murtaḍā Muṭahharī, *Khidamāt-i mutaqābil-i Irān va Islām* (Tehran, 1348) pp. 40–8.
21 Ibid. p. 77.
22 Ibid. pp. 83, 122.
23 Ibid. pp. 114–16.
24 On Firdawsī's nationalism see Mujtabā Minuvī, *Firdawsī va shi'r-i ū* (Tehran, 1346) pp. 29–64.
25 Hannah Arendt, *On Revolution* (New York, 1963) (hereafter cited as Arendt, *Revolution*) p. 23.
26 [Khājah] Naṣīr Ṭūṣī, *Akhlāq-i Nāṣirī* (Lahore, 1952) p. 232.
27 Arendt, *Revolution*, p. 39.
28 Aquinas, *Selected Political Writings*, edited by A. P. D'Entrèves (Oxford, 1948) p. 113.
29 H. Kabir, *Science, Democracy and Islam* (London, 1955) pp. 7–10.
30 Ibid. p. 11.
31 Ibid. p. 15.
32 Ibid. p. 18.
33 Aḥmad Shawqī al-Fanjarī, *Al-ḥurriyyat' as-sīyāsiyyah fi'l Islām* (Kuwait, 1973) p. 31.
34 Ibid. p. 34.

35 Ibid. pp. 47–48.
36 Ibid. p. 49.
37 Ibid. pp. 51–2.
38 Ibid. pp. 42–3, 124–62.
39 Ibid. pp. 69–80.
40 Ibid. pp. 50, 63, 73.
41 Ibid. p. 51.
42 Ibid. pp. 81–2.
43 Nadav Safran, *Egypt in Search of Political Community* (Cambridge, Mass., 1961) p. 217.
44 Ibid. pp. 220–1.
45 Ibid. p. 217.
46 Abdul-Hadi Hairi, *Shī'īsm and Constitutionalism in Iran* (Leiden, 1977) p. 220. The author makes similarly critical remarks on Nā'īnī's ideas on equality (p. 234) and separation of powers (p. 220).
47 Steven Lukes, *Essays in Social History* (London, 1977) p. 34.
48 Ibid. p. 41.
49 See Muḥammad 'Abduh, *Al-a'māl āl-kāmilah*, edited by Muḥammad 'Amārah (Beirut, 1972), vol. III, p. 485. Also Sayyid Jamāl ad-Dīn al-Afghānī and Muḥammad 'Abduh, *Al-'Urwat' al-wuthqā* (Cairo, 1957) pp. 128–34.
50 Muḥammad Ḥusayn Ṭabāṭabā'ī, *Ravābiṭ-i ijtimā'ī dar Islām*, collected and translated from his *Tafsīr al-mīzān* by Muḥammad Javād Ḥujjatī Kirmānī (Tehran, 1348) pp. 21–42.
51 Ibid. pp. 65–7.
52 Ibid. p. 68.
53 Ibid. pp. 100–2.
54 Ibid. pp. 69, 74.
55 'Abd al-Aziz al-Badrī, *Ḥukm al-Islām fi'l-ishtirākiyyah* (Medina, 1966) pp. 122–5.
56 Ibid. pp. 142–4.
57 For studies on the crisis of liberalism in these countries see P. J. Vatikiotis, *Modern History of Egypt*, 2nd ed. (London, 1978) pp. 317–42; R. Cottam, *Nationalism in Iran* (Pittsburgh, 1964) pp. 33–50; C. H. Dodd, *Politics and Government in Turkey* (Manchester, 1969) pp. 107–80. For Pakistan see the notes to Chapter 3.
58 See M. H. Kerr, 'Emergence of a Socialist Ideology in Egypt', *Middle East Journal*, XVI (Spring 1962) pp. 127–45; S. Serafy, 'Economic Development by Revolution', ibid. XVII (Summer 1963) pp. 215–31; Fayez Sayegh, 'The Theoretical Structure of Nasser's Arab Socialism', *St Antony's Papers, Middle Eastern Affairs*, no. 4 (1965) (hereafter cited as Sayegh, 'Nasser's Socialism') pp. 9–56.
59 Sayegh, 'Nasser's Socialism', pp. 27, 35, 39–41.
60 On Nāṣir's attitude towards Islam as a political force, see this author's 'The Impact of the West on Arab Nationalism' (Ph.D. diss., London University, 1962) pp. 276 ff.
61 Gamal 'Abdul Nāṣir, *The Philosophy of Revolution* (Washington, 1955) pp. 88 ff.
62 For references, see this author's 'Islam and Socialism in Egypt', *Middle Eastern Studies,* IV (1967–8) pp. 141–72.
63 'Iṣmat Ṣayf ad-Dawlah, *Usus ishtirākiyyat' al-Islām* (Cairo, 1965) p. 5.

64 Ibid. p. 9.
65 Ibid. p. 412.
66 Kamāl Raf'at, 'Khaṣā'iṣ al-ishtirākiyyat' al-'Arabiyyah', in *al-Akhbār* (March 18, 1962).
67 Ṣalāh Mukhaymir and 'Abduh Mikhā'īl Rizq, *Fi'l ishtirākiyyat' al-'Arabiyyah* (Cairo, 1964) pp. 110–11.
68 Some examples of this critical approach will be given in Chapter 5, under 'Martyrdom'.
69 Ishaq Musa Husaini, *The Muslim Brethren* (Beirut, 1956) p. 78.
70 Patrick Seale, *The Struggle for Syria* (London, 1965) p. 180.
71 Muṣṭafā as-Sibā'ī, *Ishtirākiyyat' al-Islām* (Damascus, 1958) (hereafter cited as as-Sibā'ī, *Ishtirākiyyah*) pp. 13, 115 ff., 59 ff.
72 Ibid. p. 17.
73 Ibid. pp. 17–18.
74 Ibid. pp. 33–4.
75 Ḥamdī Hāfiẓ, *Al-ishtirākiyyah wa't-taṭbīq al-ishtirākī fi'l-jumhuriyyat 'al-'Arabiyyah* (Cairo, n.d.) p. 291 (quoting a speech by Naṣīr). See also Nazīh Muḥammad aṣ-Ṣādiq al-Mahdī, *Al-milkiyyah fi'n-niẓām al-ishtirākī* (thesis, Cairo, n.d.) p. 39; Ma'rūf ad-Dawālibī, *Naẓarāt Islāmīyyah fi'l ishtrākiyyat al-thawriyyah* (Beirut, 1955); Aḥmad Shalabī, *Al-ishtirakiyyah* (Cairo, 1966) pp. 74–83; Muḥammad Mukhtār Amīn Makram, *Ḥawl al-ishtirākiyyat' al-'Arabiyyah* (Cairo, 1966) pp. 35 ff.
76 Sibā'ī, *Ishtirākiyyah*, pp. 38, 89–100.
77 Ibid. pp. 43–65.
78 Ibid. pp. 69–85.
79 *Al-mu'tamar al-awwal li-majma' al-buḥūth al-Islāmī* [Report of the First Congress of the Association for Islamic Research] (al-Azhar, 1964) p. 331.
80 Ibid. pp. 135–251.
81 Ibid. p. 394.
82 *The Resolutions and Recommendations of the Second Congress of the Association for Islamic Research* (Cairo, 1965).
83 W. C. Smith, *Islam in Modern History*, p. 157.
84 Quṭb's two important works in this respect are: *Al-'adālat' al-ijtimā'iyyah fi'l-Islām*, 6th ed. (Cairo, 1964) (hereafter cited as Quṭb, *Al-'adālat*) and *Ma'ālim fi't-ṭarīq* (Cairo, n.d.) (hereafter cited as Quṭb, *Ma'ālim*). On the point at issue see his *Al-'adālah*, p. 97.
85 Quṭb, *Ma'ālim*, especially pp. 52 ff., 213.
86 Quṭb, *Al'adālah*, p. 292. The same theme has been developed in Muḥammad Quṭb's *Jāhiliyyat' al-qarn al-'ishrīn* (Cairo, 1964).
87 Qṭb, *Ma'ālim*, pp. 120–41.
88 Ibid. pp. 1, 147 ff.
89 Ibid. pp. 154, 160; Quṭb, *Al-'adālah*, pp. 36 ff.
90 Quṭb, *Ma'ālim*, pp. 145–6, 185–6, 192–4, 197.
91 Quṭb, *Al-'adālah*, p. 18.
92 *Tafsīr-i sūrah-i Anfāl*, Commentary on the verse 1 of the Sūrah 'Spoils of War' in the Qur'ān, clandestine publication, mimeographed (Tehran?, n.d.) p. 19, also pp. 6 and 15. This, of course, has been selected as an example from many others.
93 Ibid. p. 19.
94 Mazheruddin Siddiqi, 'General Characteristics of Muslim Modernism',

Islamic Studies, IX (1970) pp. 33–68. See also J. M. S. Baljon, *Modern Muslim Koran Interpretation* (Leiden, 1966), pp. 16 ff.

95 ʻAlī Sharīʻatī, *Dars-hā-yi Islām-shināsī*, duplicated by the Islamic Students. Association of Europe, the United States and Canada (n.d.) pp. 48–50 (see also *On the Sociology of Islam*, lectures by ʻAlī Sharīʻatī, translated by Hamid Algar (Berkeley, 1979) pp. 82 ff.

96 Ibid. p. 77.

97 Ibid. p. 78.

98 Ibid. p. 89. For Sharīʻatī's criticism of Marxism from a religious standpoint, see, *inter alia*, his *Insān, Islām va mak tab-hā-yi maghrib zamīn* (Therna, n.d.).

99 Sharīʻatī, *Dars-hā-yi Islām-shināsī*, p. 95.

100 Ibid. p. 87.

101 Sharīʻatī has replied to some of his traditionalist critics in *Mīz gird, pāsukh bi su'ālāt va intiqādāt*, published by Ḥusayniyyah-i Irshād (Tehran, 1354/1975).

Chapter 5

1 On modern Shīʻī views on *ijtihād* see Muḥammad Jawād Maghnīyah, *At-tafsīr al-kāshif* (Beirut, 1968) (hereafter cited as Maghnīyah, *At-tafsīr*) vol. I, pp. 259–60; Muḥammad Jawād Maghnīyah, *Min hunā wa hunāk*, pp. 261 ff. While earlier Sunnī writings in this century expressed reservations on *ijtihād* (*Nūr al-Islām*, II 3 (1931) pp. 170–3; III 4 (1932) pp. 280–8; *Liwā' al-Islām*, XV (1961) pp. 220–8, 293–6), later publications supported it (*Al-mu'tamar al-awwal li-majmaʻ al-buḥūth al-Islāmi* [Proceedings of the First Congress of the Association for Islamic Research] cited in note 79 to Chapter 4.

2 ʻAlī Dawānī, *Waḥīd Bihbihānī* (Qum, 1338/1959); Murtaḍā Muṭahharī, ʻIjtihād dar Islām', in *Marjaʻiyyat va ruḥāniyyat* (Tehran, 1341/1962) (hereafter cited as Muṭahharī, ʻIjtihād') pp. 35–68.

3 Muṭahharī, ʻIjtihād', p. 182.

4 Maḥmūd Ṭāliqānī, ʻTamarkuz va ʻadam-i tamarkuz dar marjaʻayyiat va fatvā', in *Marjaʻiyyat va ruḥāniyyat*, pp. 201–13.

5 For a daring criticism of the attitudes of the Iranian Shīʻī ʻUlamā' in the modern period by an ʻinsider' see Naṣīr ud-Dīn Amīr Ṣādiqī, *Ruḥāniyyat dar Shīʻah* (Tehran, 1349/1970) and the second volume of the same book, entitled *Hayāhū* (Iṣfahān, 1349/1970).

6 On the foundations of the ʻUlamā's' power in the nineteenth century see Hamid Algar, *Religion and State in Iran* (Berkeley, 1969) (hereafter cited as Algar, *Iran*) pp. 1–25. For a theoretical discussion on the sources of their authority in general see Joseph Eliash, ʻMisconceptions Regarding the Judicial Status of the Iranian Ulama', *International Journal of the Middle East*, X (1979) pp. 9–25; and the present author's article on the ʻUlamā' 's ideological contribution to the Constitutional Revolution in *Yād-nāmih-i Ustād Muṭahharī* (Tehran, forthcoming).

7 See, for instance, Aḥmad Kasravī, *Dīn va sīyāsat* (Tehran, 1348), p. 11.

8 Algar, *Iran*, p. 22.

9 Firaydūn Ādamiyyat, *Īdeologīe-yi nadhḍat-i mashrūṭih* (Tehran, 2535/1977) p. 228.

10 Ādamiyyat, *Andīshih-i taraqqī va ḥukūmat*, p. 159.

11 Ādamiyyat, *Amīr Kabīr va Irān*, 3rd ed. (Tehran, 1348/1959) pp. 417–28.

12 Niyazi Berkes, *The Development of Secularism in Turkey* (Montreal, 1964) pp. 367 ff.
13 Aḥmad Kasravī, *Tārīkh-i mashrūṭih-i Irān*, 6th ed. (Tehran, 1344/1965) (hereafter cited as Kasravī, *Tārīkh*) pp. 315–16.
14 Muḥammad Bāqir Khunsārī, *Rawḍāt' al-jannāt* (Tehran, 1306/1888) pp. 35–6.
15 Muṭahharī, 'Ijtihād', p. 45.
16 N. J. Coulson, *A History of Islamic Law* (Edinburgh, 1964) pp. 107–8.
17 Aḥmad Kasravī, *Bi-khānand va dāvarī kunand*, 3rd ed. (Tehran, 1336/1957) p. 105.
18 Abu'l Ḥasan Muḥammadī, *Mabānī-i istinbāṭ-i ḥuqūq-i Islāmī* (Tehran, 2535/1977) (hereafter cited as Muḥammadī, *Mabānī*) p. 154.
19 Muḥammad Ḥusayn Nā'īnī, *Tanbīh al-ummah wa tanzīh al-millah*, with introduction and footnotes by Sayyid Maḥmūd Ṭāliqānī, 5th ed. (Tehran, 1358/1979) (hereafter cited as Nā'īnī, *Tanbīh*) pp. 74–5.
20 Muḥammadī, *Mabānī*, pp. 164–70.
21 Kasravī, *Tārīkh*, pp. 371–2.
22 Shams Kāshmarī, *Kalimah Jāmi'ah* (Tehran, n.d.) pp. 22–3; Muḥammad Gulbun, 'Asnādī dar bārih-i-mashrūṭih-i-Irān', *Barrisī-hā-yi tārīkhī*, v 3 (1349/1960) p. 159; Abdul-Hadi Hairi, *Shi'ism and Constitutionalism in Iran*, p. 213.
23 Kulaynī, *Kāfī* vol. I, pp. 87–8.
24 See, for instance, Ḥajj Mīrzā Muḥammad Ḥasan Āshtīyānī, *Kitāb al-qaḍā* (Tehran, 1327/1948) p. 7.
25 Ruḥullāh Musavī Khumaynī, *Ṇāmih ī az Imām Kāshif al-Ghitā'* (Tehran, 1356/1977) pp. 116–18.
26 Nā'īnī, *Tanbīh*, pp. 80–5.
27 See note 11 to the Introduction.
28 *Kalimāt' al-muḥaqqiqīn*, a collection of thirty treatises on land-tax, of which five are known as *Kharājiyyāt* (Tehran, 1315/1897) pp. 95–7.
29 Muḥaqqiq Sabzavārī, *Rawḍat al-anwār-i 'Abbāsī* (Caro Minasian Collection, no. 47, Wadham College Library, Oxford) p. 9.
30 Nā'īnī, *Tanbīh*, p. 13.
31 Ibid. pp. 46, 57–8.
32 For classical Shī'ī treatment of *taqiyyah* see Fayḍ Kāshānī, *Kitāb al-wāfī* (Tehran, 1357/1938) vol. I, part 3, pp. 121–4; [Muḥammad Ibn al-Ḥasan] al-Ḥurr al-'Amilī, *Wasā'il ash-shī'ah* (Cairo, 1377/1957) vol. I, p. 108. E. Kohlberg, 'Some Imāmī-Shī'ī Views on Taqiyya', *Journal of American Oriental Society*, XCV (1975) pp. 395–402. See also notes 39 and 42 below.
33 H. Corbin, *En Islam Iranien* (Paris, 1971) vol. I, pp. 6, 30 ff., 117.
34 'Alī Tehrānī, *Taqiyyah dar Islām* (Tehran, 1352/1973) pp. 6–7, 45, 54–6, 80.
35 Ibid. pp. 26–8.
36 Ibid. p. 34.
37 Ibid. p. 30. See also Ibn Idrīs, *Kitāb as-sarā'ir* (Tehran, 1390/1970) p. 203.
38 Tehrānī, *Taqiyyah*, pp. 54–79; Magnīyah, *At-tafsīr*, vol. II, pp. 41–5, vol. IV, p. 556; 'Abd ar-Razzāq al-Ḥasanī, *Ta'rīf ash-Shī'ah* (Sidon, 1352/1933) pp. 53–4.
39 Ibn Idrīs, *Kitāb as-sarā'ir*, pp. 160–1.
40 Sayyid Aḥmad Ṭayyibī Shabistarī, *Taqiyyah, amr bi ma'rūf wa nahy az munkar* (Tehran, 1350/1971) pp. 79 ff., 170.
41 Ibid. pp. 100–134, 164–170.

42 Ibid. p. 101. See also Shaykh Muḥammad Ḥasan an-Najafī, *Jawāhir al-Kalām* (Tehran, 1392–8/1972–8) vol. XXI, pp. 352–410.
43 Murtaḍā Muṭahharī, *Dah guftār* (Tehran, ?1356/1977) pp. 65–6.
44 Muḥammad Mukrī, *Shāhnāmih-i ḥaqīqat*, quoted in Shāhrukh Miskūb's *Sūg-i Sīyāvush* (Tehran, 1351/1972) pp. 87–9. Also consult Sīmīn Dānishvar's novel *Sauwishūn* (Tehran, 1348/1969), where, at the end, the mourning for Ḥusayn merges with that for Siyāwush, pp. 275, 300.
45 R. Strothmann, 'ta'zīya' in *Encyclopedia of Islam*, 1st ed., p. 712.
46 A. J. Wensinck, *A Handbook of Early Muhammedan Tradition* (Leiden, 1960) p. 250.
47 ['Abū Ja'far Muḥammad Ibn 'Alī] Ibn Bābūyih, *'Uyūn akhbār ar-riḍā*, ed. S. M. Lājevardī (Qum, 1377/1957) pp. 299–300.
48 Mullā Muḥammad Mahdī Narāqī, *Muḥriq al-qulūb* (Tehran, 1247/19..) (hereafter cited as Narāqī, *Muḥriq*) p. 4. For Narāqī's life and work, see Sayyid Jalāl Ashtīyānī's introduction to *Qurrat' al-'uyūn* (Tehran, 1357) pp. 51–6.
49 Ṣadr ad-Dīn Vā'iẓ Qazvīnī, *Rīyāḍ al-quds*, 2nd ed. (Tehran, 1377) vol. II, pp. 113–14.
50 ['Abū Ja'far Muḥammad Ibn Ḥasan Ibn 'Alī] aṭ-Ṭūsī, *al-Amālī* (Najaf, 1384) vol. I, p. 6.
51 Narāqī, *Muḥriq*, p. 4 (a).
52 Jean Calmard, 'Le mécénat des représentations de ta'zieye', in *Le Monde Iranien et l'Islam* (1974) pp. 76, 119.
53 Abū Bakr Ibn al-'Arabī, *Al'awāṣim min al-qawāṣim* (Cairo, 1387/1967) pp. 231, 233) (hereafter cited as *'Awāṣim*).
54 Ibn Khaldūn, *The Muqaddima*, translated by F. Rosenthal (New York, 1958) vol. I, p. 443.
55 See Khaṭīb's footnotes, for instance, on pp. 32–4 of *'Awāṣim*.
56 *ar-Risālah*, IV 146 (1355/1936) pp. 613–15. There might have been other writers before Māzinī who discussed Ḥusayn's drama from a modernistic standpoint. In 1932, for instance, an issue of the periodical *al-Muqtaṭaf* (v 80, p. 627) carries a brief review of a book by 'Alī Jalāl al-Ḥusaynī Bey, entitled *Al-Ḥusayn 'alayhi' s-salām* published by the Salafiyyah Press, praising it as an impartial study, but the present author was unable to see this book.
57 'Abbās Maḥmūd al-'Aqqād, 'Ḥusayn abu'sh-shuhadā'' in *Islāmiyyāt* (Cairo, 1959) pp. 41–9, also pp. 10–11.
58 Ibid. p. 52.
59 Ibid. p. 79, also p. 71.
60 Ibid. pp. 80–1.
61 'Abd ar-Raḥmān ash-Sharqāwī, *al-Ḥusayn thā'iran, al-Ḥusayn shahīdan* (Cairo, 1969); on Ḥusayn's modest political aims see vol. I, p. 60; on the upsurge of popular feelings in his movement, see vol. I, p. 211; for his soliloquy, see pp. 66 ff.
62 Aḥmad 'Abbās Ṣāliḥ, 'Aṣ-ṣirā' bayn al-yamīn wa'l-yasār fi'l-Islām' in *al-Kātib*, IV (1965) pp. 49, 50, 52.
63 *al-Liwā' al-Islām*, x 6 (1956) pp. 364–8.
64 Ibid. XIX 10 (September 1965) pp. 645–58.
65 Khālid Muḥammad Khālid, *Abnā' ar-rasūl fī Karbalā'* (Cairo, 1968) p. 35.
66 Ibid. p. 34.
67 Ibid. pp. 196–200.

68 E. W. Lane, *An Account of the Manners and Customs of the Modern Egyptians* (London, 1871) vol. II, pp. 148–54. The author describes how the anniversary of Ḥusayn's martyrdom gives rise to joyous festivals in Cairo.

69 Niʿmatullāh Ṣāliḥī Najaf-ābādī, *Shahīd-i jāvīd* (Tehran, 1349/1970) (hereafter cited as Najaf-ābādī. *Shahīd-i jāvīd*) pp. 12, 89, 91, 93.

70 Ibid. p. 8.

71 Ibid. pp. 95–108.

72 Ibid. pp. 120–36.

73 Ibid. p. 108.

74 Ibid. p. 109.

75 Cf. Shaykh Ṣadūq, *Uyūn akhbār ar-Riḍā*, p. 226; Kulaynī, *kafī*, vol. I, pp. 322 ff.

76 Najaf-ābādī, *Shahīd-i jāvīd*, pp. 246–339.

77 Khumaynī, *Ṇāmih ī az Imām Kāshif al-Ghitā'*, pp. 181 ff.

78 See, *inter alia*, 'Abd aṣ-Ṣāḥib Sayyid Muḥammad Mahdī Murtaḍavi, *Javāb-i ū az kitāb-i ū, ya pāsukh-i shubahāt-i shahīd-i jāvīd* (Qum, 1350/1970); Sayyid Ḥasan Ḥujjat, *Valāyat va 'ilm-i Imām* (Tehran, 2535/1977); Muḥammad Mulīmī. *Valāyat az dīdgāh-i marja'iyyat-i Shī'ah* (Tehran, 2535/1977).

Index

Only the text has been indexed. In a few cases, entries stand for general concepts rather than for exact literal equivalents; e.g., 'ideology' refers not only to this word, but also to discussions on the intellectual efforts justifying political systems. Brief definitions have been given for most terms, but not for those indicating sects, schools and trends, which have sometimes been defined in the text. Contrary to the system adopted in the text, capital letters have been used *mainly* for proper nouns.